Transitions

Teaching Writing in Computer-Supported and Traditional Classrooms

New Directions in Computers & Composition Studies
Gail E. Hawisher and Cynthia L. Selfe, Series Editors

Computers and the Teaching of Writing in American Higher Education, 1979–1994: A History
Gail E. Hawisher, Paul LeBlanc, Charles Moran, and Cynthia L. Selfe, 1996

The Rhetoric of Electronic Communities
Tharon Howard, 1997

Nostalgic Angels: Rearticulating Hypertext Writing
Johndan Johnson-Eilola, 1997

The Computer and the Page: Publishing, Technology, and the Classroom
James Kalmbach, 1997

Transitions: Teaching Writing in Computer-Supported and Traditional Classrooms
Mike Palmquist, Kate Kiefer, James Hartvigsen and Barbara Goodlew, 1998

A Rhetorical Ethics and Internetworked Writing
James Porter, 1998

Opening Spaces: Critical Research Practices
Patricia Sullivan and James Porter, 1997

Transitions
Teaching Writing in Computer-Supported and Traditional Classrooms

by Mike Palmquist,
Kate Kiefer,
James Hartvigsen,
and Barbara Goodlew
Colorado State University

Ablex Publishing Corporation
Greenwich Connecticut
London, England

The photos in Figures 1.2 and 1.4 are used courtesy of Colorado State University Photo Archives. Copyright Colorado State University. The photo in Figure 1.3 is used courtesy of Cynthia L. Selfe. Copyright Cynthia L. Selfe. All other photos are used courtesy of author Mike Palmquist.

Printed in the United States of America

Library of Congress Cataloging-in-Publication Data

Transitions: teaching writing in computer-supported and traditional classrooms/ by Michael Palmquist . . . [et al.].

p. cm.—(New directions in computers and composition studies)

Includes bibliographical references and index.

ISBN 1-56750-352-7.—ISBN 1-56750-353-5 (pbk.)

1. English language—Rhetoric—Study and teaching. 2. English language—Rhetoric—Study and teaching—Technological innovation. 3. Report writing—Study and teaching—Technological innovations. 4. English language—Computer-assisted instruction. 5. Report writing—Computer-assisted instruction. 6. Report writing—Study and teaching. 7. Information technology. I. Palmquist, Michael. II. Series.

PE1404.T74 1998

808'042'07—dc21 97-23867

CIP

Ablex Publishing Corporation
55 Old Post Road #2
P.O. Box 5297
Greenwich, CT 06830

Published in the U.K. and Europe by:
JAI Press Ltd.
38 Tavistock Street
Covent Garden
London WC2E 7PB
England

For Our Families

Contents

Acknowledgments

The arguments we make in this book extend and refine work that we and others have conducted over more than 15 years. Key events that shaped our decision to collaborate on this project took place long before three of the four authors even entered the field. At the Conference for College Composition and Communication in 1981, Kate Kiefer lunched with Valerie Arms, Hugh Burns, Audrey Roth, and Helen Schwartz. By the end of lunch Kate had volunteered to coordinate a Special Interest Group meeting at the next CCCC. At the 1982 CCCC meeting, Kate met with Bill Wresch and the other contributing authors to his vital, early practitioners' text, *The Computer in Composition Instruction: A Writer's Tool.* The burgeoning interest in computers and composition evidenced by this group and the SIG meeting convinced Cindy Selfe and Kate to found and co-edit *Computers and Composition*, which subsequently emerged as the leading scholarly journal in computers and writing studies. This early work and the work of Gail Hawisher, who took over as co-editor in 1988, spurred the efforts of a growing number of scholars who recognized the importance of computers in writing and writing instruction. We are profoundly grateful to Cindy and Gail for their contributions to the field of computers and writing. Likewise, we are indebted to all the early explorers of computers and writing who helped create such a tightly knit community.

When Mike Palmquist began his graduate work in rhetoric at Carnegie Mellon in 1986, he found a rapidly maturing field that caught his immediate interest and a mentor who became a friend and co-author on several research reports. Chris Neuwirth, then a first-year assistant professor who had already established herself as a leader in the computers and writing community, involved Mike in her research and helped focus his interest on computers and writing. One of those research projects—a collaborative effort between Chris Neuwirth, Karen Hartman, Lee Sproull, and Sarah Kiesler—provided the foundation for the study on which we partially base this book.

In addition to Chris Neuwirth, several of the faculty and graduate students in the English Department at Carnegie Mellon, among them David Kaufer, Dick Hayes, Chris Haas, Cindy Cochran, and Tom Hajduk, contributed to the growing body of scholarship on computers and writing. In addition, several important scholars in the computers and writing community, among them Trent Batson,

Nancy Kaplan, Bob Kozma, Helen Schwartz, and John Thiesmeyer, each spent a year as visiting scholars at Carnegie Mellon during Mike's graduate study. Their willingness to share their insights about computers and composition—and to welcome a newcomer to the field—contributed in important ways to this book.

We are indebted to our colleague, Dawn Rodrigues, who played a significant role in obtaining funding for our study and who collaborated with Kate on an earlier, qualitative study of basic-writing students in computer-supported writing classes. Our discussions with Dawn have helped shape the arguments we make in this book. For that and for her support as we worked on the Transitions Study, we are deeply grateful.

Thanks to our careful and helpful readers. Anne Gogela, who at the time was making her own transition from the traditional to the computer classroom, provided us with detailed and perceptive comments on early chapters of the book. Janet Bacon gave us valuable insights as she applied arguments developed in an early draft of this book to teacher training at Arizona State University. Will Hochman, clearly one of the most dedicated and caring teachers we have come to know, helped us refine our arguments as we worked on the final draft of the book. Mark Bruce and Kathy Northcut, valued colleagues who have been an important part of our teacher training program for the past two years, commented on a late draft of the book from a teaching and teacher-training perspective. We are also indebted to the anonymous reviewers who offered constructive comments on our overall argument.

We wish to acknowledge as well the financial support we received for this project. The research we report would not have been possible without support from the Colorado Commission on Higher Education and Colorado State University.

Most important, we thank all the students and teachers—especially those in the Transitions Study and the New Teachers Study—who let us watch them in the classroom, who shared their insights and their teaching techniques with us, who helped us understand the reasons for their successes and failures, and who finally just cared so much about quality teaching that working with them has been continually inspiring.

Foreword

We title this book *Transitions* for two reasons. First, as part of a discipline, we are making a technological transition. Our growing access to computers and computer networks changes the way we think about what it means to write and to be a writer. We see signs of this trend in both the popular press, which focuses so much attention on information technology, and in scholarly journals and books, which raise new challenges to traditional notions of text, reader, and writer. This ongoing discussion, as well as the move by many educational institutions to equip some of their writing classrooms with computers and computer networks, has led many of us to re-examine our roles as writing teachers.

This process does not, of course, drive us in a single direction. While some teachers explore how computers can "de-center" the classroom, in effect giving students greater control over class activities and writing, other teachers look to technologies that allow them to increase their control of the classroom and their students. For examples of the former, we might turn to computer-supported writing classrooms in which students work relatively independently, working on their assignments during class sessions and choosing when to discuss their writing with classmates and the teacher. For examples of the latter, we might consider programs that allow teachers to view and even to control what appears on their students' screens. Or we might consider commenting programs that require students to complete particular exercises (e.g., a review of comma usage) before seeing the rest of the teacher's commentary on a text.

Regardless of the directions in which new technologies lead individual teachers, as a discipline we are clearly moving toward new conceptions of writing and writing instruction. As we make that transition, we can benefit by reflecting on where we have been as teachers and where we seem to be heading. This book provides an opportunity for us as writers and, we hope, for you as readers to consider how to make that transition more beneficial for our students and ourselves.

Transitions is also an appropriate title for this book because it reflects the transitions that we make when we move from one classroom setting to another. Our experience suggests that traditional and computer-supported classrooms challenge teachers in different ways, leading teachers to develop specialized techniques to reach the same curricular goals. As teachers find themselves moving from one setting to another, and particularly when they move back and forth between settings in the same term, they may consider whether one setting has advantages over the other and whether techniques that they have used in one setting might prove useful in the other.

In this book, we argue that the lessons we learn as teachers in one setting shape our teaching in the other. We do not argue that one setting is necessarily a better overall teaching environment than the other as much as we argue that each encourages different kinds of teaching strategies. As we make this argument, we concentrate on what our teaching experiences and observations of other teachers suggest about the ways each setting supports the teaching and learning of writing. We know that those of us who have invested our professional energies in creating effective writing curricula and teaching strategies for traditional classrooms will be reluctant to set those aside when teaching in computer-supported classrooms. We realize, as well, that those of us who have developed writing curricula and teaching strategies for computer-supported classrooms are equally reluctant to set those aside when we teach in traditional classrooms.

The transitions we focus on in this book are occurring on both individual and disciplinary levels. As individual teachers explore the potentials and limitations of computer and network technologies and share their insights with colleagues, the field is moving toward a fuller understanding of the advantages and disadvantages of those technologies. In this book, we add our voices to the discussion of where we are heading as a field and what it means to be a writing teacher who makes the transition from one classroom setting to another.

Our overall goal in this book—to explore the contextual interactions between technology and writing instruction—leads us in two directions:

- to examine how computers and computer networks shape writing and writing instruction, and
- to reflect on how specific types of writing instruction shape the ways teachers and students use technology.

Our exploration of the impact of technology on instruction begins by recognizing that writing is inherently technological. As Walter Ong notes, the alphabet is itself a technology, as are the techniques for inscribing and preserving texts. Since the Sumerians began keeping records on clay tablets nearly five millennia ago, writers have searched for more convenient, efficient, and permanent ways to record texts. Similarly, as new technologies have arisen, displacing in turn clay tablets, quill pens and, most recently, typewriters, teachers have explored and adapted to them. Apparent disagreements between Donald Murray and Quintilian about the care one should take when inscribing a text, for instance, may have as much to do with differences between paper, parchment, and magnetic media as they do with theories of invention.

Not all new technologies, of course, have lived up to expectations. Although it is tempting to believe that technology by itself will change, even enhance, instruction, we need only reflect on research conducted in the 1930s and 1940s on the effects of typewriters on the quality of student writing to realize that technology alone does not make students better writers. Like many other scholars in the field of computers and writing, we believe that we must avoid the kind of "techno-centrism" that puts technology before teachers and students as the most important agents of change in a classroom. In this book, we argue that it is not access to a particular technology that matters—be it electronic mail, electronic bulletin boards, real-time online discussion, Web browsers, or word processing—but rather how that technology is used to meet curricular goals.

Given our interests in technology, however, we are also concerned that it not be dismissed out of hand. Many criticisms of computer-supported writing instruction stem from a conception of computer as glorified typewriter. If, in fact, computers are used as typewriters—as simply a way to prepare a completed draft for submission—we should expect little from them. But if we think about them creatively and critically, we are likely to find, as did the teachers we profile in this book, that computers and computer networks can help teachers and students change the context of the classroom. As we occasionally remind our students, if we had continued to think about the telephone in the same limited way that some people think about computers, we might still be using it as a glorified telegraph, writing down messages and delivering them by hand from central offices.

As our brief sketch of technology issues suggests, we have chosen to place *instruction*, rather than technology, at the center of our discussion. It is not particular software that interests us so much as the ways in which teachers and students put that software to use. This decision did not, of course, emerge from a vacuum. Our experiences as teachers, as students, and as researchers shaped the decisions we made as we wrote this book and as we designed and conducted the studies we discuss in it.

As teachers and students, we bring a variety of experiences to this project. Mike and Kate have each taught in computer-supported writing classrooms for more than a decade, while James Hartvigsen taught introductory composition as a graduate teaching assistant before beginning work on the study that forms the basis for much of our discussion in this book. Barbara Goodlew, who recently completed her undergraduate degree in English, was enrolled in several undergraduate writing courses taught by faculty in our department immediately before and during the study. These differing experiences have shaped the arguments we make in this book. In fact, long before we even considered writing this book, we found ourselves in wide-ranging discussions of the issues we explore here.

Those discussions helped us, individually and as a group, to articulate more clearly our fundamental beliefs about writing instruction and the supporting role technology should play in the writing program at our institution. Our beliefs start with an understanding that writing competency develops not through accretion of small chunks of knowledge, but rather through immersion in the experience of inquiring, reflecting, and writing about issues and ideas. In our collective experience, learning about writing happens when writers compose meaningful texts and receive feedback from careful readers. In our view, the writing program at our institution succeeds because it clearly articulates and consistently monitors its progress toward the following goals:

- focus on academic writing;
- focus on the writing process, not exclusively on product;
- focus on audiences and purposes;
- focus on identifying students' strengths and weaknesses as writers and supporting students at their level of development as they move toward writing more effective academic prose;
- maintain connections between reading, writing, and thinking; and
- work toward a long-term goal of helping students see writing as a fundamental act of critical thinking and learning.

In other words, although we identify certain writing subskills that we ask students to practice—for example, adding specific detail—we do not focus on activities that distance the writer from the act of writing. For instance, our writing program does not include drill-and-practice—on paper or on computer—in parts of speech or sentence identification. Instead, we focus on exploring the personal and rhetorical aspects of writing within a curriculum that moves from personal essays to academic argument to rhetorical analysis of the discourse conventions in our students' major areas of study.

When we consider the use of particular technologies in our writing classrooms, we focus on whether they can help our teachers and students move toward our program's goals. Because drill-and-practice software designed to teach students parts of speech does not support any of those goals, we do not ask students to use such software in our writing program. And although we find that some students want to learn the details of a sophisticated word-processing program, presentation software package, or graphics tool, we do not use them in our writing program unless students use them *as writers.*

Some teachers might argue that our approach is too conservative and that students learn about writing simply by exploring new technologies. Because our institution requires students to take only one semester-long writing course, however, we believe that we must concentrate on using technology in ways that most directly support writing instruction.

Our experiences in the classroom have made perhaps the most important contribution to this book. Without those experiences, we might never have become interested in computers and writing. And even if we had become interested and set out to study the area, we wouldn't have known what questions to ask or how to ask them. Having asked those questions, however, we turned to our experiences as researchers to find out how to answer them.

As researchers, we bring similarly diverse experiences to this project. Mike's interests in computers and writing date to the early 1980s when, after typing four drafts of a novel, he bought his first computer hoping to escape forever the Sysiphian task of typing, retyping, and retyping. He subsequently built up a successful freelance writing business, complete with a business card that proudly proclaimed, "Word Processing Capabilities." When his wife, Jessica, decided to pursue a master's degree in professional writing at Carnegie Mellon in the fall of 1986, Mike enrolled in the doctoral program in rhetoric.

As a graduate student, Mike worked on several projects sponsored by Carnegie Mellon's Center for Educational Computing in English. Those studies explored the impact of computer-mediated communication in classroom settings and on the composing processes of individual writers. One study in particular played a major role in this book (reports of this study can be found in Hartman et al., 1991, and Neuwirth et al., 1993; see the list of related readings at the end of the book for complete citations). It involved a semester-long study of the teachers and students in two traditional and two computer-supported writing classrooms. Although the study did not control for teacher effect, it raised a number of issues about the impact of computer technologies on writing instruction. Among those issues were the impact of network-communication technologies on students of different abilities and on face-to-face interaction inside and outside the classroom. The Transitions Study, which we focus on in this book, essentially replicates that study with added control for teacher effect, added emphasis on interaction and student attitudes about writing, and more extensive analysis of teacher attitudes and behaviors.

In addition to work on funded research projects at Carnegie Mellon, Mike also conducted a study of two computer-supported writing classrooms, each taught by the same teacher (see Palmquist, 1990, and Palmquist, 1993, in the list of related readings). This study, the basis for his dissertation, explored student interaction, student attitudes about writing, and student learning within the context of each classroom. The study drew on information from classroom observation, teacher and student interviews, student texts, network communication, and various measures of student attitudes and knowledge about writing. For this book, the study contributed to our understanding of classroom context in using computer technologies, in particular network-communication technologies, and to our understanding of network communication and student writing performance. The study also provided techniques for tracking and analyzing interactions among students and between teachers and students.

Unlike Mike, who benefited greatly from the work of scholars who came before him, Kate is a "first-generation" computer and writing scholar. She completed her doctorate at Ohio State and then joined the faculty at Colorado State University in 1979. In the early 1980s, she became interested in the potential connections between computers and writing and began working with Charles Smith. Together they established, in 1981, what may have been the first computer lab dedicated to writing instruction. Shortly afterward, Kate and Charles entered into an agreement with Bell Labs to develop and assess the Collegiate Version of Writers' Workbench, an early style-checking program. Kate subsequently teamed with Cindy Selfe to found *Computers and Composition*, now the leading journal in computers and writing studies.

In 1989, with Dawn Rodrigues, Kate conducted a semester-long observational study of three basic writing classrooms in which an observer recorded class activities, interactions between students and teachers, interactions among students, and uses of computer technologies. In addition, Kate interviewed teachers and collected and analyzed curricular materials and student texts. Although results of the study were not submitted for publication, they led to changes in the way computer-supported writing classes were taught at CSU. They also shaped our understanding of the role computer technology can play in writing instruction, and as a result have contributed to our writing of this book. Kate also conducted an informal study of teachers adapting to the computer classroom in 1992. Details from those interviews also substantiate our findings in the Transitions Study and appear at several points in this text.

Although Jake and Barb brought no formal research experiences to the Transitions Study, their lack of "insider status" in the computers and writing community proved extremely beneficial, particularly when we found ourselves trying to understand results that we simply hadn't anticipated. Their fresher perspectives—in particular, their more recent experiences as students and their relative lack of expectations for specific findings of the Transitions Study—allowed us to explore the information we gathered for this project in ways that Mike and Kate might have failed to consider.

Our overview of our experiences as teachers, students, and researchers foregrounds the role collaborative work has played in the development of our thinking about computer-supported writing instruction. This reflects the collaborative nature of scholarship in the computers and writing community in general. Whether at a conference, on the Internet, or walking down the hall between classes, members of the computers and writing community tend to share—sometimes with astounding speed—new developments in technology and teaching strategies.

We also tend to debate—sometimes at astounding length, but almost always to good purpose—issues of teaching and learning. Those of us who have been in the community for more than a few years know that some topics will surface again and again in discussions on listservs such as Megabyte University or ACW-L (the Alliance for Computers and Writing listserv). The Mac versus PC debate and the grammar debates re-emerge, it seems, on a semi-annual basis.

One of the most important topics of continuing discussion is differences between traditional and computer-supported writing classrooms. Too often, discussions addressing this topic tend to focus on which setting is "better." We argue that answers to questions about which setting is "better" depend on the goals of particular teachers and students. With that said, however, we must note that most of the evidence about differences between traditional and computer-supported writing classrooms is anecdotal. Of the research studies that directly addressed differences between classroom settings, few controlled for teacher effect—the single most important influence on what and how students learn. Moreover, many studies of learning in computer-supported writing classrooms focused largely on a single issue—for instance, the use of a particular technology, such as electronic mail, word processing, bulletin boards, or chat programs. Still others used a limited number of observational techniques to study the classroom—for instance, surveys or participant interviews. (For a list of studies of teaching and learning in computer-supported writing classrooms, please see the list of related readings at the end of the book.)

Not surprisingly, many questions remain unanswered about teaching and learning in computer-supported writing classrooms. In part, this stems from the relative youth of our field. Perhaps more to the point, the issues that we address have changed radically as new technologies have emerged and been adapted for writing classrooms. When the field of computers and writing emerged in the early 1980s, the primary interests of scholars included word processing, computer-aided instruction, and the potential uses of grammar and style checkers. The dream of many teachers and researchers at that time was that computers might remove the drudgery associated with responding to student writing, that teachers might at last deal with the central issues of writing, such as audience, purpose, development, and organization, and no longer need to spend time on punctuation, grammar, and spelling.

As a field, we quickly learned that the technology that might liberate us from composition drudgery remains in the future. In the meantime we have turned our attention to newer technologies, including electronic mail, electronic bulletin boards, and real-time chat programs such as those studied in Trent Batson's ENFI project. Most recently, we've turned our attention to hypertext, multimedia, the Internet (and in particular the World Wide Web), MOOs, MUDs and MUSHs, video-conferencing, and work-group technologies that promise to make our work with computers even more effective and intriguing.

Through all these changes, we have struggled as a community first to define the issues we face, understanding that those issues shift quickly, and then to understand their implications for teaching and learning. Essentially, scholars in the field of computers and writing are aiming at a moving target. As we gain an understanding of the impact of one set of technologies on writing instruction, another comes along to capture our attention and to change the nature of the classrooms we want to study.

The shifting context of computer-supported writing instruction has led us, as a result, to focus on instruction rather than on specific technologies. This focus has allowed us to address issues of teaching and learning in computer-supported classrooms in ways that will help writing teachers successfully adapt new technologies in the future. Readers looking for discussions of specific software programs will not find them in our discussion. What you will find here are discussions of interactions among classroom context, curricular goals, student expectations, and technology. Our discussions of technology will focus, however, on the effects of general classes of technology (word processing, electronic mail, chat programs, and Web browsers, for instance) rather than on the features of specific programs. Readers interested in exploring the specifics of particular programs would do well to consult some of the related readings we list at the end of the book or to seek information on those programs from the numerous Web sites that are springing up to provide information about particular software packages.

This book contains ten chapters. In the first chapter, "Framing the Issues: Setting Context and Narrowing the Focus," we explore the larger contexts for our studies and develop in detail our rationale for focusing on certain issues within the writing classroom context.

In Chapter Two, "Exploring the Issues: Studies of Teaching and Learning About Writing in Computer Classrooms," we provide a detailed overview of the studies that serve as the foundation for this book. We discuss those studies, the Transitions Study and the New Teachers Study, in light of their central research questions, the methods we used to collect information to help us answer those questions, and the methods we used to analyze that information.

In Chapter Three, "Contrasts: Teaching and Learning About Writing in Traditional and Computer Classrooms," we review key results of the Transitions Study. Our discussion here is meant as a synthesis and preview of the issues we explore in greater detail in the next four chapters: (a) classroom dynamics and issues of authority in teacher-centered and student-centered classrooms, including interaction patterns inside and outside the classroom; (b) impacts of each classroom setting on student writing; (c) curriculum design and class planning; and (d) the translation of teaching practices from setting to setting.

Chapter Four, "Classroom Dynamics," explores how the teaching styles of the four teachers in the Transitions Study shifted according to the setting in which they were teaching. Our discussion of those shifts draws on our interviews with the teachers and their students, the teachers' reflections on those shifts in their teaching logs, and our observations of their classrooms. Our discussion also draws on our findings concerning student interaction, both inside and outside the classroom, in the two settings.

In Chapter Five, "Writing in the Classroom: Student and Teacher Perspectives," we explore differences in student attitudes toward writing in class. Our study indicates that students in the traditional classes viewed in-class writing as intrusive and unnatural, while students in the computer-supported classes saw it as both natural and nonintrusive. Students in the two classroom settings also exhibited different writing behaviors, with students in the computer-supported classes engaging in more extensive revision than their peers in the traditional classes. In this chapter, we explore those differences through the lenses of student and teacher interviews, focusing in particular on their implications for teaching techniques in each setting.

Chapter Six, "Building on Our Strengths: Adapting Teaching Strategies," looks closely at the daily plans used by each teacher in the two settings. Our discussion focuses on: (a) the tendency of teachers to orchestrate activities in the traditional setting, while letting things develop with less teacher-intervention in the computer classroom; (b) the greater reliance on student writing as a central part of the class plan in the computer classroom; (c) the greater reliance on full-class discussion in the traditional classroom; and (d) the greater frequency of student/teacher mini-conferences in the computer classroom.

In Chapter Seven, "Curriculum Design: Doing More with Less," we focus on teaching techniques in computer-supported writing classrooms. We focus, in particular, on general principles that guide the overall development of course curricula and on using specific technologies to support writing instruction.

Chapter Eight, "Technological Complexities: Dealing with the Complications of Computers and Computer Networks," explores the challenges that teachers face in computer-supported classrooms. In this chapter, we consider strategies that teachers use to deal with problems such as the failure of individual computers, network applications, and the network itself.

Chapter Nine, "Training Other Teachers: Creating Teacher-Training Programs for Technology-Based Instruction," draws on our discussion in the previous chapters. In this chapter, we consider the implications of our findings for teacher-training programs.

In our final chapter, "Pondering the Future of Computer-Supported Writing Instruction," we explore several issues that bear on our discussions in the book. These include the resources needed to support computer-based writing instruction, the growing technological sophistication of our students, and looming changes in computer and network technologies.

Readers less interested in research design and results may want to skip Chapters Two and Three, which concentrate primarily on the two studies. Key results from the studies appear throughout the book, however, even as we shift our main focus to their implications for teaching.

Because we discuss some of those results in Chapter One, we provide a brief overview of each study here. The Transitions Study, conducted in 1993–1994, followed four teachers as they taught what was essentially the same composition course in both a traditional and a computer-supported classroom. To observe the teachers and students who participated in the study, we used a number of quantitative and qualitative data gathering techniques. The New Teachers Study, begun 18 months later and ongoing as this book goes to press, follows three teachers, none of whom had taught writing before, as they learned to teach writing in computer classrooms. To follow the teachers in the study, we used a more limited array of observational techniques, primarily interviews, teacher self-reports, classroom observation, and analysis of class materials.

As a final note, we call your attention to two elements of the book. We considered carefully the role that scholarly citation should play in our discussion. The already vast—and growing—body of scholarship that addresses computer-support for writing instruction tempted us to cite heavily through in-text citation. Ultimately, however, we choose to minimize our references to the work of other teachers and researchers in favor of a more straightforward discussion of the issues. Following Chapter Ten, we include lists of related readings that address the issues we raise throughout the book.

Second, note the sidebars, beginning in Chapter Four and continuing through Chapter Nine, that address specific teaching strategies relevant to the discussions in each chapter. The "Teaching Strategies" sidebars highlight immediately practical advice for teachers who are new to computer classrooms and willing to adapt computer classroom techniques for the traditional classroom. Each contains brief descriptions of a teaching strategy and, where appropriate, commentary on the strategy by the teacher or teachers who use it.

This practical element captures for others some of what we learned in our personal transitions between traditional and computer-supported classrooms. If, through this text, we contribute to the discipline's transition toward a thoughtful integration of computer technologies and teaching, then we will indeed have reached our goals.

1

Framing the Issues: Setting Context and Narrowing the Focus

Like any snapshot, our look at classrooms, teachers, and students in *Transitions* focuses the reader's eye. As we move from chapter to chapter, we call your attention to various aspects of our snapshot, sometimes asking you to explore specific elements within its borders and sometimes asking you to focus on distinctions between foreground and background issues. As we begin our discussion, we ask you to consider that, although the borders of the snapshot define a particular set of concerns, those concerns do not exist in a vacuum. Beyond the borders of our snapshot, the context of our studies extends well beyond what we can treat in detail in this book. In this chapter, we briefly explore the contextual elements that remain outside—and yet nonetheless strongly shape—the issues we focus on in the book as a whole. We also call your attention to key aspects of the background that set our focal points in relief. Finally, we outline the issues that we believe constitute the most important elements of our inquiry.

COMPUTERS IN THE SOCIAL CONTEXT

Throughout this book, we focus on teachers and students in different classroom contexts. We cannot forget, however, that the largest context for our study is a maelstrom of technological change, not just in education but in society at large. For example, when we designed the study, few of our teachers used the World Wide Web for classroom work; as we drafted initial chapters of this book, teachers were incorporating more and more Web work into classes; as we complete work on the final revision of this book, teachers in our program now assume that most students already know how to negotiate the Web, at least superficially, even before they arrive in first-year composition. The pace of technological change is a blessing and a curse to educators and researchers. As more tools become more accessible to students entering the university, teachers can reasonably expect some students to have more knowledge of and comfort with emerging technologies. Yet teachers must also be aware that other students will enter their classrooms lacking experience with computers. As a result, teachers must constantly adapt not only to a changing environment in their computer-supported classrooms but also to a changing student audience.

We cannot shut our eyes to this crucial context for our study, but neither can we focus on it. Rather, we present details from our study to show how teachers and students adapt to change. By focusing on adaptive strategies, we may not touch on the hardware and software most in favor at a given moment, but we can, we think, help teachers see ways to move between traditional and computer-supported classrooms and from the computer-supported classrooms of the mid-1990s to the higher tech classrooms of the next century.

Not only are hardware and software changing rapidly. Public acceptance—and use—of computer technologies is burgeoning, and with this rapid acceptance of computer technologies into our daily lives come new expectations about how computers fit into educational institutions. There will be more, rather than less, public demand for skillful and efficient uses of computers in education. There will be more, rather than less, demand for equitable access to computers, not only for word processing but also for Internet searching, electronic communications,

and collaborative work. As computers become more tightly woven into the fabric of the workplace, home, and school, inequities will become glaring holes in that fabric. Schools and other public institutions will take on greater and greater burdens for helping all students learn an increasing number of "fundamental" computer skills.

Our educational uses of computers will also certainly be shaped by the larger social discourse on and about computers. As more and more computer users drop into Internet chat rooms, will students find it harder or easier to take seriously our academic exercises based on chat programs? As more and more computer users adopt electronic mail for business and social interchanges, will we see e-mail evolve into a distinctive genre (see the extended discussion by Spooner & Yancey, 1996; Holdstein, 1996; Miller, 1996; Sosnoski, 1996), or will it explode into multifaceted discourses for business, school, and home? No doubt the larger context of social discourse will affect educational practices in ways we cannot now foresee.

Our point here is that we cannot confidently predict the future of computers in society, and yet we must continue to adapt to social change as it affects our institutions, our classrooms, our teachers, and our students. Looking at multiple perspectives on teachers and students in transition gives us, we believe, the most effective way to highlight positive strategies for adapting.

INSTITUTIONAL AND PROGRAM CONTEXT

Another contextual extension of our snapshots is the institution and program in which we work. Colorado State University is a medium-sized land-grant university with a long history emphasizing scientific and technical expertise. Not surprisingly, early efforts to bring computers into the English Department received whole-hearted support from administrators. Perhaps surprisingly, those efforts also received whole-hearted support from faculty members within the English Department. Each successive effort—to expand computers labs, to offer word processing services not only to students registered in English classes but also to others writing substantial papers across campus, to convert traditional classrooms to computer-supported classrooms, to bring Writing Center services on line—has met with enthusiastic support inside and outside the Department.

Moreover, we enjoy strong support for the composition program itself, both from our colleagues in the English department and from institutional administrators. This support has allowed us to assemble a strong composition faculty and to obtain the technical support and training resources necessary to keep our computer-supported classrooms and the composition program as a whole running smoothly.

We also know just how lucky we are. We know how isolated a single composition specialist can feel in a department dominated by literature faculty. We know how isolated a computers-and-composition specialist can feel in a program

dominated by non-computer (or even anti-computer) composition faculty. We know how difficult it can be to incorporate computers into a composition program that has no stated goals. We know how exhausting it is to install and service computers and networks, to run all the training programs, and to provide all the links from the composition program to the rest of the university.

Finally, we know that teachers cannot ignore their institutional and programmatic context when they consider how to incorporate computers into their writing classes. Many of the decisions teachers would like to make for themselves are seemingly cast in stone by the institution and program. Budgets (which we may not be able to influence) constrain flexibility. Hiring policies and exigencies affect not only the expertise we'd like to draw upon from colleagues but also the continuity of small changes we might make. Even the curricula of the courses we teach can be imposed from above, particularly if students must meet "exit" requirements at the end of the course or program.

In subsequent chapters, we do not directly address our institutional and programmatic context. We are aware, however, that the support we enjoy as a result of this context makes possible our discussion in those chapters.

BACKGROUND: WHAT TEACHERS BRING WITH THEM TO THE CLASSROOM

Another important aspect of context framing our discussion is teachers' background and expectations. Like everyone else, the teachers we train and those we

observed in our studies share in the social trends that value and devalue certain elements of computer technology. Teachers of writing, fortunately, are more likely than most to be aware of how language and computers interact. They are also, of course, much more sensitive to issues of writing theory and pedagogy, particularly how computers might support and subvert pedagogy.

Teachers cannot help bringing into the writing classroom their deep-rooted assumptions about education in general and teaching roles in particular. As part of the background in our snapshot, we need to consider how the mental models of good writing and teaching affect what teachers can and cannot easily change in their day-to-day teaching practices. Moreover, teachers bring with them not only the social context and the mindset of a teacher, but also specific critical questions and concerns. Some of these critical questions focus on the efficacy of computers in the classroom; others focus on technology versus rhetoric. We take up each of these background points—mental models, efficacy of computers, and what to teach—in turn.

Mental Models of Good Teaching and Good Writing

Without a doubt, some elements of our models of good teaching come from teachers who have influenced us, as well as from early experiences from collaborative work with peers and perhaps from tutoring. For some teachers, coaching or training experience in some other discipline (music, karate, business) forms part of the background for this mental model. Interactions with siblings and parents probably also form parts of the model. Teacher education or training programs (either coursework or orientation/training programs) also color the picture of an ideal teacher.

Although we cannot trace with certainty all the influences on our model of an ideal teacher, that model clearly shapes what we expect of ourselves when we step into a classroom. If our model is narrowly patterned on one particular teacher or specific pedagogy, then the model might interfere with our ability to adapt to new teaching contexts.

For example, one of the teachers in the Transitions Study received her early schooling and training in Britain. Even though all her graduate work and teaching occurred in a typical American setting, the teaching model this teacher brought to our computer classroom emphasized certain kinds of behavior. Although Jen[1] admits that she is uncomfortable with elements of the teaching model from her youth, she clearly found it difficult to change her mental model when she first began teaching in our computer classroom. In interesting ways, this model seems to have limited her flexibility in adapting to the computer classroom. For instance, most teachers quickly discover that lectures are difficult to deliver and to listen to in the computer classroom. Most teachers work hard to discover and develop other ways to pass along information that students might otherwise get in presentational mode. Jen, however, persisted through an entire year in our computer classroom with "mini-lectures" of 10 to 30 minutes in each class session. In Jen's mental model, a teacher usually assumes center stage, and she found that position harder to relinquish than most of the other teachers with whom we've worked.

Similarly, we cannot trace all the influences on our models of "good writing." We are undoubtedly affected both by all that we read and all that teachers and respected readers have told us about our writing through the years. We are shaped by the successes and failures we have had as writers in various contexts, academic and non-academic. No matter the source of the influences, though, our mental models of good writing shape what and how we teach. Most teachers probably develop a preliminary "theory" about writing and writing instruction based on their experiences as writers and writing students. As they study writing more closely, however, many teachers discover that they must actively examine underlying and generally unarticulated principles they hold dear. The transition between classroom settings often triggers such a pointed analysis of assumptions about good writing.

Nonetheless, teachers may need specific reminders of the background they bring to the classroom. They may, in fact, need considerable self-awareness to take advantage of training programs designed to orient them to non-traditional classrooms. Teachers who clearly see how their mental models match with the teaching environment generally have a better chance of exploiting their teaching strengths in a computer classroom.

Critical Question: Do Computers Add Value in the Classroom?

Since computers were first discussed as tools for teaching writing in the early 1980s, teachers and administrators (not to mention students and taxpayers) have asked for evidence that computers help students become better writers. The evidence has been slow in coming. Studies conducted to date have presented only bits and pieces of an answer. In the meantime, many teachers have given up waiting for a definitive answer. We feel an obligation, however, as trainers of teachers who work in computer classrooms, to address the issue of whether computer-supported writing classrooms offer students real benefits.

A number of researchers have noted a significant affective response that consistently shows up in studies of students using word processing in writing classes. (For teachers interested in the articles reporting this research, please see the titles listed under Related Readings.) Students surveyed in this research feel more positive about their writing instruction when they have access to word processing, either inside or outside the classroom. Moreover, those students who take a writing course in a computer classroom typically report little apprehension about using computers—not a surprising finding since most studies have involved students who had a choice about whether to enroll in a course taught in a computer classroom. However, these students also typically feel more positive about their learning experience and less apprehensive about writing generally than students who complete writing courses in traditional classrooms. As Caitlin,[2] one of the teachers in our year-long Transitions Study, told us:

> [O]n my final, I asked my computer classroom students what they thought about having the class in a computer classroom. [I]f they could take it over, would they take it in a computer classroom? And they all said, "You betcha," and that they would recommend for other people to take it in the computer classroom.

Some writing teachers and researchers argue that this affective response is short-lived and will fade as students become more and more accustomed to using word processing on their own. Others argue that any factor that improves students' attitudes toward writing provides a positive element in the writing classroom and may have a positive effect, ultimately, on how much students learn in writing classes or, perhaps, on how much they are willing to continue writing after the class ends. Still others maintain that affective responses are much less important than evidence of real improvement in writing skill.

To answer the last group, researchers have labored long. To date, the research is still ambiguous. Most researchers have found that students writing with word processors (either inside the classroom or in a lab setting) *produce more writing* than students in a traditional classroom with no computer lab. Whether that writing is of higher quality is still hotly debated. Researchers looking specifically at revisions produced with and without computers have not shown consistent and significant improvements in writing in all cases. Ultimately, our ability to measure real improvement in writing depends so much on how we define the variables and on so many intangibles that large-scale quantitative research has so far failed to document significant improvement in student writing among students who use computers. To quote Jen, "A lazy devil may not transform him[self] into a gung-ho student just because he's hunched over a computer." Individual motivation may account for more of the inconsistent results than any other factor.

Given the lack of quantitative evidence to support the benefits of using computers in writing instruction, teachers must carefully consider the potential advantages and disadvantages of moving to a computer classroom. Will they find clear benefits or will they simply be giving their students an opportunity to explore new gadgets? Will they find, as Caitlin did, that computer classrooms don't support teaching techniques that are successful in traditional classrooms:

> I think group work, the traditional kind of "get into groups with a task, work through that task, and then share with the large group, which grows into a large-group discussion," works much better in the traditional classroom for me than it does in the computer classroom. I just have not been real successful in making group work work very well in the computer classroom.

Should teachers give up their time-tested techniques and risk losing valuable teaching techniques in a new environment? Do computers add enough value to offset these potential losses in the writing classroom? We must answer *no* if we put computers at the center of our concern, that is, if we ask questions such as these:

- Can the computer by itself help students improve their writing?
- Can the presence of a computer motivate students to generate more writing?
- Can computer activities unrelated to significant writing experiences help students improve their writing?

But we see benefits for writers using computers if we ask these questions instead:

- Can writing teachers see more of their students' writing when they write in a computer classroom?
- Can teachers intervene helpfully in students' writing process when they write in a computer classroom?
- Can teachers plan classroom activities and class plans to motivate students to write more in class and thus build toward their out-of-class writing experiences?

In other words, we must question the efficacy of computers in the writing classroom, but we must ask the right questions and look at the entire classroom context—institutional context, student involvement, teacher preparation and philosophy, and electronic support for writing. In Chapters Four through Eight, we take up these aspects of classroom context in much more detail.

Critical Question: Just How Much Technology Must Teachers Know?

Like all teachers, writing teachers need to feel confident about the material they teach when they enter a classroom. And in a traditional classroom setting, writing teachers do feel confident. When we ask writing teachers to consider teaching in a computer setting, however, we find that many fear that technical knowledge will become more important than rhetorical knowledge.

One of the most common concerns teachers express is that they will not know how to help students with computer glitches. For example, some are initially afraid that the printer will malfunction and they won't know how to make it stop spewing out blank paper, or that students will lose work and they will not be able to help retrieve it. Even though we provide technical assistance at all class hours, teachers still cite their concerns about "losing face" in front of students. The teachers want to do their own trouble-shooting in the computer classroom but realize that they simply don't have enough technical background to handle all the problems that might—and sometimes do—occur during class time.

Furthermore, in our experience, teachers seldom assign a computer exercise or ask students to use some feature of a word processor or network communications programs without having mastered these features themselves. Learning the technology well enough, not just to use it, but to imagine useful teaching options for it, requires time and confidence. As Candace, a teacher in the Transitions Study, told us:

> I guess my thing was also not letting the technology at any point get in the way of what we're doing, and until I feel really comfortable with that so that I'm not fumbling for 20 minutes during class I'm probably not going to do it. So the onus is going to be on me to get comfortable with it first.

Perhaps even more of a concern for novice teachers in a computer setting is how to avoid turning the class into an exploration of technology rather than an exploration of writing. Every teacher fears that students will need so much information about word processing and the computer network that the first weeks of class will not include instruction in writing. Even with specific guidance about how to incorporate instruction in word-processing features into writing tasks, teachers in our computer classroom still point out that

> [The technology] really slowed me down and we didn't get much done for about two weeks while we were trying to figure it out. And now I've sort of had to find a balance between using it and not using it (Candace).

> [F]rom a perspective of "What are the goals in my classroom?" you're thinking, "Why am I spending all this time teaching computer technology?" (Caitlin)

and

> [I]t's like I said in the meeting. It's not that I resist the technology. It's just that I feel there's so much to get through that I really don't have the time sometimes to devote to it. (Jen)

Even experienced teachers discover, when they move into this new instructional setting, that they must question the balance of technology and rhetoric. Again, because technical expertise, or lack of it, is a key element teachers bring with them to the classroom, we return to this critical question in coming chapters.

BACKGROUND: WHAT STUDENTS BRING WITH THEM TO THE CLASSROOM

As Jen explains pointedly in describing the lazy versus "gung-ho" student, and as writing teachers are all too aware, students bring with them attitudes about writing that may or may not lead to productive behaviors in a writing classroom. Moreover, just as we cannot detail all the influences leading to a teacher's mental model of good writing, we cannot detail students' mental models either. It's clear, however, that students bring with them not only a mental model of good writing

but also a personal assessment of how their writing typically fits that model. As writing teachers, we have long realized that we simply have to cope with the helpful and harmful models of writing that students bring with them to our classes and with the positive and negative attitudes about writing that emerge from those models.

More and more, students will also surely bring attitudes about computers to the writing classroom. Often, these models are based on the ubiquity of computers in business settings. It's impossible to ignore computers in medical and insurance offices, billing agencies, personnel offices, drivers' license bureaus, retail stores, auto repair shops, and so on. Students know that most jobs they will get after high school or college will require some computer familiarity. The computer classroom, then, brings out their attitudes and preconceptions about computers and writing. Some students choose computer-supported classes because they have had positive experiences with computer-supported writing in the past and feel comfortable with it. Other students choose computer-supported classes because they have never touched computers before and figure now is a good time to learn. Still other students, we suspect, fear computers but recognize that they will be hard to avoid in most business settings (computers have invaded even McDonald's, after all). And so teachers in computer-supported classrooms must consider yet another layer of complexity.

We should also note briefly that some of our colleagues are increasingly distressed by students' general attitudes about college. If students expect to do little work, then the computer-supported classroom might look more attractive because students get to work on their assignments during class and avoid some tedious out-of-class work. Students are also savvy enough to know that teachers in computer-supported classrooms are probably more likely to accept Internet sources in addition to library texts for research papers. Because Internet searching can be much less time-consuming than library searching, some students might choose a computer-supported classroom to cut corners in the research process.

Finally, in our experience, students also bring good will with them to the classroom. They recognize their teachers' enthusiasm for writing and, in computer-supported classrooms, for using computer technology to improve writing. Although we must negotiate myriad attitudes and expectations, we count on students' good will as a positive element in the classroom context.

FOCAL POINTS OF THE PICTURE

What we finally focus on in this book can be viewed from two quite different perspectives. The *teacher perspective* prompts us to ask: What do we learn about ourselves as teachers when we move back and forth between computer and traditional classrooms? The *student perspective* prompts us to ask: What do students learn as writers in each setting? Although these questions are general, they sug-

gest that we must place ourselves and what we know of our teaching styles and approaches, our strengths and weaknesses, into the picture. But we must also bring all that we know about our students because students at different levels of development or motivation change the classroom environment much more than computers do.

Teacher Perspective: What Do We Learn About Ourselves as Teachers?

Over the many years that we've trained teachers to teach in computer classrooms, we've consistently remarked that those who know little about their own teaching styles and preferences are unlikely to feel comfortable moving into a non-traditional teaching environment. A teacher who chooses to teach in a new environment obviously feels ready for a challenge, a change in more than just the setting. The successful teachers we've worked with over the years embrace the pedagogical changes that the computer room opens up for them.

What we've all learned, however, is that teaching techniques are not the only things that change. Teachers, too, change with the new environment. And because the environment calls for certain kinds of change, teachers who know less about themselves may be unprepared for the changes they must make in their teaching styles.

Teachers, typically, are accustomed to self-evaluation as well as evaluation by others, and thus many keep logs or more informal notes of "class plans" and "what worked" (or didn't work). Kate, for instance, revises class plans immediately after class so that the next repetition of a course won't have the same flaws.

Similarly, Mike keeps a running list of changes in a file called "next time." For the most part, this kind of self-evaluation usually focuses on specific activities rather than larger strengths and weaknesses in teaching skill.

Moving into a computer classroom or moving back into a traditional classroom, however, requires a shift in self-evaluation from the local to the global level. In other words, looking only at specific activities in the context of a given day's plan is not likely to result in the kind of large-scale changes in approach and strategy that might be needed for an effective transition from a traditional to a computer classroom or vice versa. This kind of self-examination is harder for teachers to carry out, both because it takes a great deal of time and because it requires persistent adjustment and re-examination to change our approaches to teaching.

For example, when Kate first began teaching in the computer classroom almost 10 years ago, she quickly realized that her students' attitudes about writing during class differed from those of her students in traditional classrooms. Whereas many students in her traditional classrooms refused to take seriously time set aside to write about assigned readings, students in the computer classroom appeared much more willing to write. When she asked her computer-classroom students to write about their reading assignments, she found that classroom discussions improved. Eventually, writing about the assigned readings became a fixture in Kate's class activities. So far, so good—Kate used the computer effectively to help students think more carefully about connections between reading and writing.

Yet when an outside observer visited her class, he commented that Kate didn't consistently allow adequate time for full discussion of the readings. Now Kate faced a dilemma—should she continue to let students write extensively about their readings or should she shift more time to large-group discussion? This question was complicated by Kate's assessment of her teaching strengths. She had never felt completely confident in her role as a discussion leader and, as a result, had typically devoted class time to other activities, even in her traditional classrooms. Kate wondered whether, because of her concerns about how effectively she could guide discussion, she had allowed one element of the computer room to dominate her daily plans. Yet she didn't want to sacrifice the personal interaction with readings that the computer classroom had allowed her to foster.

How to balance the two? Teachers with different strengths and weaknesses consistently discover that the computer classroom allows them both to avoid weaknesses and exploit strengths. Reflective teachers use the classroom environment to learn new ways to improve rather than simply avoid their weaknesses (Kate continues to use the writing-about-reading prompts in every class, but she now also uses a variety of activities to encourage students to share and test their perceptions and insights. Leading large-group discussion as advocated by her observer is still not her most comfortable role in the classroom, so she uses a mix of small-group discussion activities, electronic mail exchanges, and occasional large-group discussions to bring students into dialogue about their reading and writing.)

A major factor in developing new strengths in the computer classroom is time. Every teacher we've talked with about making the transition from traditional to computer classrooms has pointed out that time for adapting is crucial. In the first semester, so many changes occur that teachers often feel overwhelmed. But as several semesters go on, teachers note that the environment begins to feel natural and that they can be more self-reflective about their teaching styles and personal adaptations to the computer classroom. Teachers at the end of their first year of teaching in the computer classroom often say, "Yes, I've made the adjustment; I've learned what I need to know about myself and the classroom to teach effectively in the computer classroom." Later in their careers, however, the same teachers tell us that, although the first year may have had the greatest changes, changes continued to occur for three, four, or more years. One of the teachers we worked with over several years told us that she used evolution as a metaphor for her development as a teacher. She observed that, following an explosion of change in the first semester she taught in a computer classroom, she went through several semesters in which she slowly adapted and refined elements of her teaching. In total, these changes resulted in radical shifts in her teaching, yet the pace of change was anything but steady.

In Chapters Four through Eight, we explore what teachers learn about teaching as a result of moving back and forth between traditional and computer classrooms. Throughout our discussion, we focus on the need—no matter where we teach—to consider carefully how and when we interact with students, how the environment encourages or discourages composing during class, and how teaching strategies change not only because of our strengths as teachers but because of features of the classroom itself.

Student Perspective: What Do Students Learn as Writers?

As we mentioned above, students' goals and expectations, as well as their anxieties and motivation levels, can make or break a writing class. Adding computers simply complicates an already complex teaching/learning dynamic. As we review our anecdotal experience and multiple classroom observations from over 10 years of supervising teachers and combine that information with data collected during our Transitions and New Teachers Studies, three key issues emerge that focus our attention in our view from the students' perspective:

- the ability of peer reviewers and teachers to *intervene* effectively in the writing process,
- the ability of writers to engage in substantial *revision* of work in progress, and
- the ability of students to *interact* with each other as well as with the teacher.

Before moving on to Chapter Two, we look at each of these key issues briefly.

Intervention

Educators at all levels recognize the need to observe students and then to intervene at the point where teacher guidance is most likely to help students learn. Some educators, however, clearly have advantages over others. A swimming coach, for instance, sees that a learner sinks rather than swims—and, more important, sees *why* someone heads to the bottom of the pool. Writing teachers, in contrast, seldom see writers at work because students do most of their writing outside of regular classrooms. The writing teacher, then, cannot see how the student is doing until the paper comes in for the teacher's comments. Bob Zoellner, in a classic argument for behaviorism, argued in 1969 that teachers should observe the behavior of students *as they write* so that immediate feedback could be provided on successful and unsuccessful behaviors. Although we would dispute the premises of behavioral psychology, the computer classroom now provides the environment that Zoellner argued for so strongly 25 years ago.

In the computer classroom, teachers see students work through their writing. On assigned tasks and on freewriting or drafting, students' writing-in-progress is generally public and available for the teacher to review. A student with writer's block is much easier to identify in a computer classroom because the teacher can see from across the room that a student's screen is blank and that the student is not typing. In response, the teacher can ask why the student is not writing; if appropriate, the teacher can talk through the problem with the student and possibly suggest remedies for the block. Similarly, students who misunderstand an assignment can ask the teacher or a classmate to look at a few sentences on the screen and give feedback about whether or not the writing is on track. Students writing only general statements and ignoring detail can get immediate guidance—again from peers or teacher—about how to become more specific. As Anita, a teacher in the Transitions Study, so aptly describes, the computer classroom allows early and frequent opportunities to help students overcome the myriad writing problems they encounter as they work through complex writing tasks:

> One of the great things about a computer classroom [is that] you can walk around and say, "Oh, this paragraph is effectively written," or "Try this," or whatever. And I was just so concerned about making sure that they were even in the ballpark with the assignment. You can facilitate on assignment concerns in the regular classroom because they can bring in stuff and you can go around and say, "Okay. Where are you at? What are you having troubles with?" But you get to really see more writing in the computer classroom and intervene in the writing, the actual composing of the words and how they work in terms of reader and audience.

Students clearly appreciated the flexibility of the computer classroom because it gave them constant access to teachers' comments:

> You're writing in class and you're getting critiqued in class. And you can ask her right there. You know, what do I need to work on? And you can see the paper on screen and if she tells you to delete something you can just delete it or add this. It's all right there.
>
> I just rolled over in my chair and said, "Will you read this and comment on this?" She said, "Sure.". . . I've asked her questions on lots of stuff. Just, "How should I put this? Is this okay to put in a formal paper?" You know, certain things like that. "Is this okay?" Just roll over and ask her. Yeah. It's really easy to get feedback from her like that.

Students also remarked that interventions needn't always be individual to be helpful:

> And she does a lot of individual help, and she does a lot of group help. If she sees everyone making the same type of mistake, she'll get up and do a short discussion on it. And then she'll do individual help, just answering questions about anything. How to document the periodical that you used from "does this sound right?" "Can I put this in?" "Am I being opinionated?" I mean she just will answer anything. Very, very helpful. She's a good resource.

With these resources available to them in the computer classroom, students learn not only about their writing but also that intervention in writing need not be disruptive. Students and teachers who can see writing-in-progress come to understand the supportive function of teacher feedback throughout the writing process.

Revision

The debate about whether students revise more substantially with word processors still goes on. Most teachers agree, however, that students are more *likely* to revise if revising is mechanically easy to do. As Anita's comments suggest, teachers in the Transitions Study felt strongly that students better understand the importance of revision when class time is consistently set aside for revising work-in-progress:

> If you have time, composing and revising in class is just so valuable because you send a message that the real—you can use all the theory you want to but you have to practice. And that's basically it. In the traditional classroom, you give them all the theory and they go out and you hope they practice.[3]

From the students' perspective, the message in the computer classroom is loud and clear: we care so much about the quality of your papers that we encourage you to take class time to revise and to consult with readers so that you can revise still more effectively. The students in the Transitions Study clearly seemed to get this message. As one student pointed out:

> With the computer it's a lot easier to make changes so I'm more apt to make more changes. I can just bring it up, you know, retrieve it, and then look at it. If you write it, then you have to re-type the whole thing. . . . With computers you can keep changing it, and it's a lot quicker and easier. So you can spend a lot more time with revision than with re-writing it, which is good.

The teachers in the Transitions Study noted repeatedly that students revised throughout the writing process and that the printed drafts of their papers did not capture all the revisions they made on screen. As Caitlin explained:

> And those students [from the computer class], I thought, had tons and tons and tons more interim submissions . . . in the second round of portfolio revisions. I had lots more conferences outside of class in my office with them. I had tons more contacts with them in the classroom with them coming to me and asking me these questions about this or about that. And they just plain worked harder. There was much less screwing around going on and they took advantage of the time they were given to work on portfolio revisions.

As we continue to fill in the snapshot from the students' perspective, the ease of revision becomes a crucial factor that contributes to student attitudes, interactions, and overall satisfaction with their first-year composition experience.

Interactions

Just as students have more control over their time and activities in a computer classroom, so too do they have more control over who they talk to and who they share their writing with. In the Transitions Study, we discovered that students talked to each other more often in the computer classroom than in the traditional classroom. Of course, we were concerned that perhaps these student-student interactions were off-task (about a football game or an upcoming chemistry test). In our classroom observations, however, we found that students were no more likely to exchange comments about non-class items in the computer classroom; on the contrary, students in the *traditional* classroom were more likely to discuss off-task topics. Students in the computer classroom typically talked to each other about their writing, asking for impromptu peer review or advice as problems developed. As Caitlin told us:

> I think there's more unstructured exchange of ideas about papers in the computer classroom than there is in the traditional classroom. There's more just saying, "I just wrote this introduction. Will you look at it?"

A student described this process in more detail:

> There was two girls who sat next to me. We would help each other. I'd have them read the paper, and they'd give me their opinion, or if they understood my point. We

> helped each other a lot. And if I needed information that could help her on her idea or subject, then I would tell her about it. So I did work with two other girls in the class quite a bit on helping each other. [Interviewer: At what point in the drafting did you help one another out? Or was it throughout the drafting?] It was probably just throughout. I mean we would sit on the computer when we would have time in class to work. And we would just turn and, I don't know, "What's a word? Give me another word for a thing or . . ." because she told me that I couldn't use it because it's too vague. So we'd sit there and just help each other like that. And toward the end of our drafts we would exchange papers when we thought we were almost done. Just to see what they thought. It was kind of nice.

Teachers also commented that students in the computer classroom seemed less territorial and more willing to move around the classroom to work with more members of the class, that they viewed the classroom as a less formal but serious work site, and that they seemed to know each other better. As Caitlin told us:

> It would be very interesting for me to see the compiled data from the contact sheets because it seems to me that my students in the computer classroom were talking to each other tons more than my students in the traditional classroom. And talking to a [greater] variety of people.

Our classroom observations, as well as data collected from contact sheets (which we describe in the next chapter), confirm these impressions that students had more frequent and more meaningful contacts with peers in the computer classroom. The data also confirmed that students had more frequent contacts with teachers as well. As Anita pointed out, interactions with teachers seem to flow naturally from a classroom context that encourages both individual work and teachers' ability to track that work in progress:

> I still think that giving them time to draft and allowing me time to go one-on-one around the room and answer individual questions is the best. It just seems like the writers are individuals themselves or have individual questions. And being in the computer room . . . it seems to be better because the rest of them are still working. But I can still address individual needs. . . . I tend to get to know the students better in the computer classroom than in the regular classroom. It has nothing to do with my attitude. It just has to do with contact.

FRAMING THE ISSUES

Having briefly sketched the context for our snapshots, we turn now to the studies that give us the details of our snapshots of teachers and students in traditional and computer-supported writing classrooms.

2

Exploring the Issues: Studies of Teaching and Learning About Writing in Computer Classrooms

As we first envisioned it, this book would report the results of the Transitions Study with appropriate digressions into issues of teaching and training. That vision gave way fairly quickly, however, to one focusing primarily on teaching and training and, in particular, on the challenges teachers face as they move between traditional and computer-supported writing classrooms. This shift has entailed expanding the range of evidence we use to support our arguments. Aside from the fact that a single research study cannot supply us with everything we need to make our arguments, our experiences as teachers and researchers go far beyond them. As a result, we draw on those experiences—both research- and classroom-based—throughout this text.

Our decision to draw on a fuller range of experiences to support our arguments does not mean, however, that the Transitions Study and a follow-up study that we refer to as the New Teachers Study no longer contribute significantly to our discussion. Much of the support for our arguments in subsequent chapters comes from these studies, as do most of the illustrative quotations from teachers and students. Because we draw so heavily on their results in subsequent chapters, we describe in detail the methods we used to conduct them.

THE TRANSITIONS STUDY

We conducted the Transitions Study during the 1993–1994 academic year. We observed two teachers during each semester as they taught the same introductory college composition course in two different settings, one a traditional classroom and the other a networked, computer-supported classroom. Each teacher designed a syllabus to meet the stated goals of the course:

- to introduce students to college composition by completing five major papers over the course of the semester,
- to follow a process-oriented approach to writing, and
- to focus on both personal and academic writing.

Each teacher used the same texts and gave the same assignments in the two classroom settings, but teachers had latitude to explore the best strategies for working in each setting. In the study as a whole, we focused in particular on teachers' perceptions of the strategies they adapted for each setting and on students' interactions with teachers and classmates in each setting.

The study took place at Colorado State University, a land-grant institution that draws most of its 22,000 students from Colorado and surrounding states. Colorado State University has invested heavily in its campus-wide computer network during the past decade. Its fiber-optic network supports communication across the University and, through gateways, to the Internet. The computer-supported classroom links to the campus network through one of the University's 50-odd Banyan VINES servers. The VINES network allows computer users to log into their accounts from any computer connected to a VINES server, regardless of their home server. In practical terms, this means that students and teachers who participated in the study had access to their network accounts from hundreds of computers in offices and public labs across the campus.

In 1993–1994, the computer-supported classroom used in our study had 24 IBM PC-compatible computers running Microsoft Windows 3.1. The computers in the classroom were in their second year of use. In 1993–1994, approximately 500 students took courses in the computer-supported writing classroom. Students had access to word processing programs, electronic mail, electronic bulletin boards, the CARL online library system, and a real-time chat utility. Students had access to the classroom during the evenings. In addition, they could drop into a 45-station open-access word processing and Internet lab, which is also housed in the English Department, from 8:00 a.m. to 11:00 p.m. on weekdays and for shorter periods on weekends. Since the study was conducted, a second computer-supported writing classroom has been created, doubling the number of students taking courses in computer-supported writing classrooms.

The software in the computer-classrooms has been adapted to support writing instruction through customized button bars, macros (sequences of program commands initiated via command keys or, as in our computer-classrooms and labs, mouse clicks), and other options built into our programs. One feature used extensively by the teachers in the study is DAILY, a function that allows students to begin work on their assignments even before the teacher arrives in class. When they click on the DAILY button in the word processor's toolbar, students access the day's assignment. Typically, teachers ask students to engage in write-to-learn activities at the beginning of class. Those activities provide a basis for subsequent discussions and activities during the rest of the class period.

As we note in the Foreword, the Transitions Study emerged in part from a long-standing interest in computer-supported writing instruction at Colorado State University. In 1981, the first computer-supported writing lab was established at the University. In 1987, the first computer-supported writing classroom was created with support from AT&T Bell Labs. In 1994, a second classroom was created. Since 1988, teacher training for the computer classrooms has been an ongoing activity. New teachers are not allowed to teach in the classroom unless they attend mandatory instruction sessions; experienced teachers are strongly encouraged to attend, both to hone their teaching skills and to help build a supportive network among teachers who use the classrooms.

Participants

Four teachers and 173 students participated in the study. The students chose a section knowing whether the class was taught in a computer or a traditional classroom. Of the students who enrolled in the eight sections, only one student declined to participate in the study. The students, as a group, ranged in age from 18 to 40, with the average falling between 19 and 20. Males comprised 55 percent of the group, and females comprised 45 percent. They were predominantly European-American (81.5%), with the remainder a mix of African-American, Asian-American, Hispanic, and Native-American students. Their high school class ranks ranged from 25th percentile to 99th percentile, with an average of 74.3 percent.

We selected the four teachers because of their proven strengths as teachers. Each teacher had consistently received high ratings on student evaluations, particularly in our required first-year composition course. We had also observed each of these teachers on several occasions before the study and knew that they had proven teaching skills. To compensate for the extra time involved in keeping a record of their teaching and participating in interviews, each teacher received $500 to participate in the study. The four teachers brought a variety of teaching experiences to the study:

- "Anita" joined the study in her twelfth year of teaching, with both high school and university teaching experience. She has taught writing with computers since 1984.
- "Caitlin" participated in the study during her fifth year of teaching. She, too, has both high school and university teaching experience. During the study, she taught her third section in the computer classroom.

- "Candace" was in her fifth year of teaching writing (composition and creative writing) at the university level. She has no high school teaching experience. She was the least experienced teacher in the computer classroom, teaching just her second class in that setting during the study.
- "Jen" completed her fourth year as a teacher during the study. Her experience includes university and community college composition classes. At the time of the study, she completed her second semester in our computer classroom and her fourth semester as a computer classroom teacher.

Data Collection

Our design allowed us to collect a great deal of information. We collected demographic information about each student who participated in the study. We surveyed students concerning their attitudes about writing, about computers, and about specific classroom practices at the beginning and the end of each semester. We observed each classroom and interviewed, at the beginning and the end of each semester, 36 of the 173 students who participated in the study. We interviewed each teacher at the beginning, middle, and end of each semester. Each week, we asked students to report their interactions with their teacher and classmates. We copied electronic exchanges between teachers and students. And we collected intermediate and final drafts of each student's papers. We also asked each teacher to keep a detailed teaching log, in which they recorded their observations about their daily teaching activities and in which they collected their teaching materials. In the next sections, we discuss each of these activities in greater detail.

Student information

Demographic information on students included sex, ethnicity, standardized test scores, composition placement examination score, high school grade point average and high school class rank, CSU grade point average, accumulated course credits, credits taken during the semester in which they participated in the study, major college and department, and minor college and department. This information was entered into a data set and used in subsequent analyses.

Student surveys

Student surveys, conducted at the beginning and end of the semester, consisted largely of Likert-scale questions that addressed attitudes toward writing and computers, previous writing instruction, reading and writing practices, and perceived helpfulness of comments received from classmates and teachers. The survey items typically asked students to indicate their agreement or disagreement with the item. The survey at the beginning of the semester included items about previous writing instruction not included in the second survey. The second survey included items concerning helpfulness of the feedback they received from classmates and teachers. The completed surveys were coded and the responses analyzed statistically. Typically, coding involved combining the scores on several related items into a single measure. For instance, the scores from four items combined for a single score for writing anxiety while the scores from 11 other items combined for a single score for computer anxiety. The materials section at the end of the text includes the two questionnaires.

To gauge student attitudes about writing, we included items from previous studies on our survey. The measures of student writing confidence were drawn from a study conducted by Mike Palmquist and Richard Young that explored the connections between student attitudes about writing and notions of giftedness. The writing anxiety scale used in this study was a subset of the Daly and Miller writing anxiety scale that predicted the overall scale.

We used the following items to measure writing confidence:

- I am able to express myself clearly in my writing.
- I am no good at writing.
- Compared to other students, I am a good writer.
- Teachers who have read my writing think I am a good writer.
- Other students who have read my writing think I am a good writer.
- My writing is easy to understand.

We used the following items to measure writing anxiety:

- I avoid writing.
- Writing is a lot of fun.
- I enjoy writing.
- Discussing my writing with others is an enjoyable experience.

We also assessed student anxiety about using computers. We drew our questions from several computer anxiety instruments and adapted them as needed to reflect the situation students encountered in our computer classroom. We used the following items to measure computer anxiety:

- The challenge of learning about computers is exciting.
- I am confident that I can learn computer skills.
- Anyone can learn to use a computer if they are patient and motivated.
- Learning to operate computers is like learning any new skill—the more you practice, the better you become.
- I feel apprehensive about working with computers.
- I have difficulty in understanding the technical aspects of computers.
- It scares me to think that I could cause the computer to destroy a large amount of information by hitting the wrong key.

- You have to be a genius to understand all the special commands used by most computer programs.
- If given the opportunity, I would like to learn about and use computers.
- I have avoided computers because they are unfamiliar and somewhat intimidating to me.
- I feel computers are necessary tools in both educational and work settings.

To assess students' previous writing instruction, we included items on the first survey that asked about the activities and feedback they experienced in previous writing classes. We broke these items into two groups, one focusing on grammar-oriented instruction and the other on process-oriented instruction. We used the following items to measure grammar-oriented instruction:

- I've taken some courses that focused primarily on spelling, grammar, and punctuation.
- Some of my former writing teachers were more interested in my ideas than in my spelling, punctuation, and grammar.
- Some of my former teachers acted as though the most important part of writing was spelling, punctuation, and grammar.

We used the following items to assess process-oriented instruction:

- On some of my past writing assignments, I have been required to submit rough drafts of my papers.
- In previous writing classes, I've had to revise my papers.
- In some of my former writing classes, I've commented on other students' papers.
- In some of my former writing classes, I've spent a lot of time working in groups.

To assess student attitudes about the helpfulness of the comments they received on their writing from classmates and teachers during the semester and about collaboration during and outside of class, we included several additional items on the second survey. To assess teachers' comments, we asked students to indicate how helpful each of these types of feedback had been:

- Hand-written comments on my papers from my teacher.
- Spoken comments on my papers from my teacher.
- Face-to-face discussions about my writing outside of class with my teacher.
- Computer-based comments (e.g., WordPerfect, Electronic Mail) on my papers from my teacher.[4]

These items asked students to assess the helpfulness of comments received from classmates:

- Hand-written comments on my papers from my classmates.
- Spoken comments on my papers from my classmates.
- Face-to-face discussions about my writing outside of class with my classmates.
- Informal discussions immediately before and after class as a means of talking with my classmates.
- Computer-based comments (e.g., WordPerfect, Electronic Mail) on my papers from my classmates.[5]

To assess student attitudes about peer review sessions during class, we used the following items:

- Workshops in this course helped improve my writing.
- I would have preferred to work on my writing assignments without having to sit through in-class writing workshops.
- I found that comments from my classmates resulted in significant changes to my papers.

To assess students' willingness to talk with their teachers about their writing, we used the following items:

- I found it easy to talk with my instructor about my writing for this class.
- I asked my instructor questions during class (during discussions, during workshops, or as I was working on a paper) several times this semester.

We also asked students about the kinds of writing and reading activities that they typically engaged in. To assess the amount and kinds of writing that students did, we asked them how frequently they engaged in the following activities:

- Write in your journal
- Write poetry on your own
- Write letters to friends or family
- Write fiction
- Write papers for class
- Write for publication

To assess the amount and kinds of reading that students did, we asked them how frequently they engaged in the following activities:

- Read the newspaper
- Read fiction for pleasure
- Read magazines
- Read for class

Classroom observations

We observed each class three or four times during the semester. Our observations focused on content of the class, interactions between students and the teacher, and interactions among students. In each case, we observed corresponding lessons in each classroom setting. Occasionally this meant observing the two classrooms on different days. If a particular lesson (e.g., the introduction of a new assignment) was taught on Monday in the traditional classroom, but difficulties with the computer network meant that the computer classroom had fallen behind and the assignment was introduced on Wednesday in the computer classroom, we observed the traditional classroom on Monday and the computer classroom on Wednesday.

Observers recorded their notes on an observation worksheet (see the materials appendix at the end of the book for a copy of the worksheet). Because three members of the project team observed the classrooms (Mike, Kate, and Jake), we had to reconcile numbers of interactions observed by different people. One observer, for instance, might count something as an interaction that another might not, or an observer might count an intermittent conversation between two students as a single interaction or as several interactions. We assumed, however, that a given observer would remain fairly consistent within the context of a given observation session. Our response to this challenge was to calculate ratios between the two classroom settings for each observer and to average those ratios across the three observers.

Student interviews

Jake interviewed 36 students from the four classes at the beginning and end of the semester. The interviews were audiotaped and transcribed. Each student who completed the two interviews received $25. Each interview lasted between 30 and 60 minutes. We planned to interview five students from each class. In three classes, however, we recruited only four students who met our selection criteria and who arrived for their initial interview. In the fourth class, one student interviewed at the beginning of the semester subsequently dropped the class. We selected students on the basis of their placement scores, their sex, their representativeness of the various ethnic groups in our student population, and their willingness to participate in the interviews.

At the beginning of the semester, we asked students questions about their writing skills and processes, their attitudes about collaborative work, the way they interacted with classmates and teachers, and their use of computers for writing. At the end of the semester, we asked students about changes in their writing processes, who they worked with during the semester and how they got in touch with those people, their use of computers for writing, and their perceptions of the class they had just completed. The interview questions for students appear in the materials appendix at the end of the book.

Teacher interviews

Jake interviewed the four teachers at the beginning, middle, and end of the semester. The interviews were audiotaped and transcribed. At the beginning of the semester, we asked teachers questions about their approaches to writing, their approaches to teaching, and their use of technology to support writing instruction. In the middle and at the end of the semester, we asked them about differences between the two classroom settings, their transitions between settings, their teaching in each setting, and their use of technology. Jake asked follow-up questions and adapted the standard questions as he saw fit during the interview. See the materials appendix at the end of the book for teacher interview questions.

Weekly interaction reports

Each week, we asked students to record their contacts with classmates, their teacher, or Writing Center tutors. To make it easier for students to respond, we provided them with a contact sheet that listed each classmate's name, their teacher's name, and the generic "writing tutor." Students noted if the contact occurred in or out of class and also whether the contact was face-to-face, via telephone, electronic mail, or some other medium that students could specify. (Students could, of course, write notes by hand or use our electronic bulletin board or chat programs.) At the end of the semester, we tallied all reported contacts for each student and included their average contacts with classmates and teacher inside and outside of class in a data set. The materials appendix at the end of the book includes a sample contact sheet (with teacher and student names removed).

Electronic exchanges

Teachers saved all the electronic mail correspondence with students. For privacy reasons, however, we did not collect electronic mail exchanged between students. We could not record the transcripts of exchanges conducted through the chat program used during the study (Banyan VINES Chat) because the program does not generate and save transcripts. In addition, although Usenet bulletin boards were established for each computer class, none of the teachers used bulletin boards for class activities.

Student texts

We collected student texts from all students. We photocopied drafts submitted on paper and archived drafts submitted electronically.

Teacher logs

We designed the teacher logs to capture as much information as possible about the planning and execution of classes, contacts with students, and teachers' perceptions of students' progress. At the beginning of the semester, we gave teachers a list of prompts to complete their teacher logs. (The prompts appear in the materials appendix at the end of the book.) Key information that emerged from the teacher logs included contacts with students, changes made during class sessions in response to differences between settings, and successes and difficulties teachers encountered in each classroom. Initially, we asked teachers to indicate the students they talked to during each class. We dropped this prompt, however, after discussions with the teachers indicated that they had difficulty recalling who they did and did not talk with during each class.

Data Analysis

We conducted analyses of the collected information to answer specific questions about teaching writing and learning to write in the two classroom settings. Our interest lies especially in the differences teachers perceived between the two classroom settings, the transitions teachers made between the two settings, and the performance and behavior of students in the two settings. In particular, we looked at differences in interaction, in writing performance, and in attitudes toward writing. To address these issues, we used both statistical analysis of the quantitative data collected during the study and holistic/interpretive analysis of the classroom observations, student and teacher interviews, student texts, and teacher logs. We discuss the key findings in the next chapter.

THE NEW TEACHERS STUDY

The New Teachers Study began in the fall of 1995, when we asked three teachers who had no experience teaching writing to teach in one of our computer-supported writing classrooms. Until this time, we asked only experienced teachers to teach in computer-supported classrooms. Our experience with the Transition Study and with training teachers to teach in the computer-supported classrooms provided us with a good understanding of the challenges teachers faced when they began teaching in our computer-supported classrooms, but we had questions about how new teachers would react. We suspected that new teachers might enter the computer classroom with fewer preconceptions about the environment, but we worried that they might feel overwhelmed by the demands of teaching both for the first time and with computers.

Asking new teachers to take on the challenge of teaching with computers presented us with an ethical dilemma. What would we do if our worst fears were confirmed: that new teachers could not adapt to the computer-supported writing classroom? Would it be fair to the teachers to force them to adapt? Would it be fair to students to ask them to take composition in an environment for which their teachers were unprepared? What would we do if it appeared that students were receiving inferior instruction?

We ultimately decided to carefully monitor the teachers and students involved in this study and to move them to a traditional classroom if the situation overwhelmed them. We also decided to create a special audit section in the same computer classroom in which they taught.[6] Like our new graduate teaching assistants observing an experienced teacher in a traditional classroom, our new graduate teaching assistants teaching in the computer classroom observed an experienced teacher in the same setting. Mike taught the audit section that the new teachers observed, and he met with them regularly during the semester to provide support for their teaching.

To follow the progress of the new teachers, we interviewed them at the beginning and end of the first semester they taught and observed them as part of our regular training program. We subsequently interviewed each teacher at the end of each semester in which they taught. They completed teacher logs in which they reflected on their teaching during the first semester of teaching and provided us with the course materials they prepared. One teacher completed her graduate study at the end of the second semester of teaching, while two others continued into a second year.

The three teachers, Amy, Ellen, and Linda, were all enrolled in the Master's program in English. Amy and Ellen were new students, while Linda was in her second year of study when she began teaching. Amy and Ellen, both in their late twenties, had left academe for several years before pursuing graduate study. Linda, who received her undergraduate degree in the 1970s, had returned to the University for a second B.A. in natural resources and was concurrently pursuing her M.A. in English.

The students enrolled in Amy's, Ellen's, and Linda's classes did not participate in the study and we collected no information from them. Our primary goal was to better understand the challenges faced by new teachers as they learned to teach in a computer-supported writing classroom.

CONCLUDING REMARKS

Because of the multiple data collection techniques used in both studies, we cannot begin to share the volumes of data we collected. We hope, however, that seeing the details of the research design helps you create a context for the results we discuss in following chapters.

3

Contrasts: Teaching and Learning About Writing in Traditional and Computer Classrooms

In Chapter One, we sketched the context of our studies of traditional and computer-supported writing classrooms. In Chapter Two, we sharpened the focus somewhat as we detailed the two studies that constitute the research focus of this text. In this chapter, we highlight the results of both the Transitions Study and the New Teachers Study and break out key issues that deserve fuller treatment in a text designed to help teachers accept the challenge of crossing the boundaries between traditional and computer-supported writing classrooms.

When we planned the two studies, our research questions focused directly on the concerns of teachers and students. We assumed that the goals of teachers would not change as they moved from one setting to another, but that teachers would use different teaching strategies to achieve them. We expected that differences between the two settings might lead students to act differently, and perhaps even to learn different things about writing. We also believed that the core of what they learned—about considering audience and purpose, about developing and supporting ideas, about planning, drafting and revising, about collaborating with each other—would be similar. Moreover, we assumed that differences in the two classroom settings might lead students to develop different attitudes about writing and possibly even different behaviors as writers and collaborators. In sum, we expected that the central goals of a writing course would be met in both settings, but with differences in the teaching and learning in traditional and computer classrooms.

With these thoughts in mind, we set out to explore in as much detail as possible the kinds of teaching and learning that occurred in the traditional and computer-supported writing classrooms in our institution. We chose not to focus on specific technologies, reasoning that the technologies would change long before the results of our studies could be shared with others. Instead, we explored how teachers made the transitions between the two settings, how students and teachers interacted with each other in the two settings, and how students and teachers thought about and engaged in writing in the two settings.

As you'll see, this book is less about the impact of particular technologies on teaching and learning than it is about the impact of shifting the context for teaching and learning. Whether teachers find themselves in classrooms that rely heavily on network-supported real-time interaction or in classrooms with stand-alone computers that are used primarily for word processing, we hope that teachers will recognize and transfer results of our studies to their contexts. We do not aim to set up a model with universal application to all computer-supported writing classrooms or to define all the challenges faced by teachers moving between traditional and computer-supported writing classrooms. Instead, we provide a detailed discussion of the contexts we observed so that teachers can apply our findings to their teaching.

The questions we asked as we designed our studies focus on:

- teaching strategies and class preparation;
- teacher attitudes about teaching in the two classroom settings;
- interactions among students and between teachers and students;
- student attitudes about writing, and
- student writing performance.

In the rest of this chapter, we sketch broad outlines of our findings. In subsequent chapters, we take up in greater detail the issues raised here.

CHARACTERIZING DIFFERENCES BETWEEN TRADITIONAL AND COMPUTER-SUPPORTED WRITING CLASSROOMS

The Transitions Study and the New Teachers Study provide us with a great deal of information about teaching and learning in traditional and computer-supported writing classrooms. Our exploration of that information reveals several themes:

- Differences between classroom settings had a clear impact on daily planning, both in the kinds and the number of activities that teachers asked students to carry out.

- Teachers adopted different roles in the two classroom settings. Teachers reported that they felt the need to take charge in the traditional classrooms, leading them to conduct more front-of-the-classroom activities (large-group discussions, lectures) in the traditional classrooms than in the computer classrooms. In contrast, they indicated that they expected students to take more responsibility for their learning in the computer classrooms. They described their role in the computer classrooms as facilitator rather than leader and typically asked their students to work in small groups or to write during class rather than to engage in large-group discussions or listen to lectures.
- Students in the computer classrooms talked with their classmates and with their teachers much more frequently during class than did students in the traditional classrooms. Moreover, conversations among students in the computer classrooms tended to focus on writing, while those in the traditional classrooms tended to focus on issues unrelated to the class.
- The computer classroom functioned primarily as a work site, where students and teachers talked about writing in progress. In their interviews, teachers and students called attention to the benefits of talking about student writing as it was being written, among them the impact on revising and student improvement during the course. In contrast, teachers remarked—and students confirmed in their interviews—that students resisted writing in the traditional classrooms.
- As the semester progressed, teachers transferred successful activities from the computer classroom into the traditional classroom. In particular, they asked their students in the traditional classrooms to engage in more writing during class, and they explored ways to foster more interaction during class sessions.
- Teachers and students addressed the need to introduce new technologies to students early in the course and to link technology clearly to the goals and content of the course. However, the teachers that we observed tended to resist adopting technologies with which they were unfamiliar even when they believed the technology could help their students become better writers.
- Students in the two classroom settings differed in their attitudes about writing and in the relationships among attitudes about writing, writing performance, previous writing instruction, and interaction with classmates and teachers. Among other findings, students in the computer classrooms ended the course with higher levels of confidence in their writing ability and showed greater enthusiasm about writing than students in the traditional classrooms. Previous writing instruction also correlated with student writing performance in the computer classrooms. Students who reported that their writing instruction had focused heavily on grammar and mechanics tended to receive lower grades on their writing assignments.

In the rest of this chapter, we take up each of these themes in greater detail. Before we turn to those discussions, however, we address an issue critical to any study based on comparison—the similarities and differences between the two groups of students we studied.

Differences Between Students at the Beginning of the Study

We based our study largely on comparison. In general, we looked for differences between classroom settings and changes in student behaviors and attitudes over time. To make valid comparisons, we needed to ensure—before we analyzed the data—that the groups of students we compared were similar.

To accomplish this goal, we compared scores on standardized tests and on our University's composition placement examination, and on our measures of writing anxiety, writing confidence, computer anxiety, and experience in previous writing classes. We based our comparisons on information drawn from students' academic records and from surveys administered at the beginning of the semester.

We did not find significant differences in students' test results on the English portion of the ACT or in the verbal scores on the SAT. We also found no significant differences in students' grade-point average earned in high school or in their CSU composition placement exam scores. For those students who had accumulated credits at CSU prior to taking first-year composition in our study, there were no significant differences between groups in grade point average earned at CSU or in the number of credits passed at CSU.

We saw no significant differences between the two groups of students on our measures of writing anxiety or confidence in their writing ability. We did, however, find differences in their reported levels of anxiety about using computers. In their responses to our survey at the beginning of the semester, students in the computer classrooms reported significantly lower levels of anxiety about using computers than did students in the traditional classrooms. On a one-to-five scale, with one indicating the lowest level of anxiety and five indicating the highest, students in the computer-supported classrooms had an average score of 1.76, while their peers in traditional classrooms had an average score of 1.99.

When we asked students about their experiences in previous writing courses, we found no significant differences between classroom settings in students' responses about grammar instruction. However, we found significant differences between students in the computer and traditional classrooms on our measure of process-based writing instruction. Students in the traditional classrooms indicated that they engaged in activities such as composing multiple-draft assignments and participating in peer-review workshops more frequently than did their peers in the computer classrooms. Previous process-based writing instruction was measured on a one-to-five scale, with one indicating little such instruction and five indicating high levels of process-based instruction. Students in the traditional classrooms reported an average score of 4.02 in process-based instruction, while students in the computer classrooms reported an average score of 3.74.

In general, the key differences between students in the two classroom settings were computer anxiety and process-oriented instruction in previous writing courses. The latter difference surprised us, but not the former. We believe that the difference in computer anxiety reflects students' decisions to enroll in a computer-supported or traditional class. In a traditional experimental study, students are randomly assigned to teacher and classroom setting. However, our study was conducted using a "quasi-experimental" design, that is, one in which "naturally occurring" classrooms were studied. In our case, students knew whether the course was taught in a computer-supported or a traditional classroom because a note to that effect appeared in the course catalog. The lower level of computer anxiety among students in the computer-supported classrooms may reflect a conscious decision on the part of some students to avoid the computer-supported sections or, alternatively, to seek them out. The students indicated that they "agreed" or "strongly agreed" that they weren't particularly anxious about using computers.

The difference between classroom settings in reported process-oriented instruction is more difficult to explain. We initially thought that the difference might reflect students' decision to choose a computer or traditional classroom setting, but we found only a minimal correlation (–.060) between computer-anxiety and reported process-oriented instruction. Similarly, we saw no significant correlations between reported process-oriented instruction and standardized test scores, high school or university grade-point averages, or scores on the composition placement exam. We suspect that attempting to explain this difference would result in little more than speculation, so we leave you with the straightforward observation that a difference existed which we find difficult to explain.

We turn now to the seven themes that we identified above:

- curricular issues;
- teacher roles;
- interaction among classmates and between students and teachers;
- the classroom context;
- transfer of activities from the computer to the traditional classrooms;
- the introduction and use of technology in the computer classrooms, and;
- student attitudes and writing performance.

Curricular Issues: Relationships Between Classroom Context and Class Plans

When we asked about planning, the four teachers in the Transitions Study called attention to three key differences between the classroom settings: students seemed much more interested in writing during class in the computer classrooms, the presence of computers in the computer classroom greatly expanded the range of activities that could be carried out, and the complications of using computers reduced time for activities. When students in the computer classrooms began writing, they wanted to continue writing, regardless of whether they were working on a draft of a major assignment or on an in-class exercise. Recognizing this, the teachers searched for other ways technology could support student writing—for instance, using the Internet to locate sources for writing assignments or using electronic mail to comment on drafts. As Candace told us:

> I can't see one [teaching technique] at this point, that I can't do in my computer classroom that I could do in a traditional classroom, and there's a million things that I can do in the computer classr‑ om that I can't do in the traditional classroom.

Perhaps because in-class drafting and revising took up a significant part of class sessions in their computer-supported classrooms, the teachers told us that they felt greater flexibility in scheduling activities in the traditional classrooms. Reflecting on her experiences teaching in computer and traditional classrooms over a period of nearly 10 years, Anita observed:

> In the regular classroom, there's more room for activities. I hesitate to plan tons of activities for the computer classroom because we have these wonderful tools that help the students write. And you know, you like to put them on the machines. You like to get them writing. I think in the regular classroom, I'm more apt to group them up and make them talk about a study question and so on.

In addition to concerns about the activities they wanted to use in each classroom, the four teachers told us that they struggled with questions of how similar they wanted their daily plans to be. Although their goals as teachers remained the same regardless of classroom setting, they discovered that techniques which worked successfully in one classroom did not work as well—or even at all—in the other. Caitlin learned, for instance, that whole-class discussion—a technique at which she was adept in the traditional classroom—did not succeed in the computer classroom:

> When I was trying to do the same lesson plan in the traditional classroom and the computer classroom, whole-class discussion was just not working in the computer classroom. My students weren't focused in on it, they weren't getting the main points that I wanted them to get out of the discussion. They weren't thinking. I knew they could think that way and they just weren't doing it. And so, you know, I'd come back and think, "My gosh! My morning class, they came up with this and this and this and this." And so, I stopped and thought, "Am I doing something wrong because I'm in the computer classroom? Do I need to structure this differently?" And so, I moved away from whole-class discussion and we don't have very much. . . . I try to make everything tie back very directly with what the students are writing. But even more specifically, that seems to need to happen in the computer classroom and I wasn't doing that as well as I should have in the beginning.

Caitlin adds that she initially thought the problem with full-class discussions stemmed from her students. "When I started thinking about the differences, my thought process was 'What are the differences between my traditional classroom and my computer classroom? Well, my traditional classroom is going well. My computer classroom, my students are just dumb.'" When she stepped back from that line of thought, she says, she began to consider seriously the differences in classroom contexts, which led to class plans containing different mixes of front-of-the-classroom instruction, group work, and in-class drafting.

Adapting Teaching Roles to Classroom Context

In addition to differences in the kinds and number of activities that the teachers used in each setting, they called attention to differences in the roles that they adopted in each classroom. Each of the four teachers in the Transitions Study commented that they differed in the way they related to their students and in what they expected from their students. In general, the four teachers believed in a student-centered approach to teaching composition. Yet they found themselves relying on activities that were more teacher-centered in the traditional classroom, such as lecture and whole-class discussion, and on activities that were more student-centered in the computer classroom, such as in-class drafting and mini-conferences. At least in part, these differences stemmed from what they expected from students in each classroom. Caitlin indicated that she expected students in the computer classroom to take more responsibility for their own learning:

> I would say I do a better job of making my students more personally responsible for figuring things out on their own in the computer classroom . . . I give them a chance to write, to discuss a little bit, with their peers around them and then I ask, "Do you have any questions? Is there anything you feel like we need to talk about?" And then we'll move on. And so they're more responsible, I would say, for saying, "This is a problem, I don't understand this." Or "I don't know what's going on." Where, because I think I have whole-class discussion in the traditional classroom, I feed them more information."

Similarly, Anita said that she expected more from the students in her computer classrooms:

> Teaching in the regular classroom, I feel the need to orchestrate much more. "Okay, we're going to do this, this, this, and this. Students, okay get prepared to do this, blah, blah, blah. Okay, now we're going to do this." In the computer classroom, we always have a mission. . . . I literally could go in there and say, "Okay, pre-write." And they would know how to do it . . . I could say, "Okay, read this story and write a paragraph on whatever." And that would be perfectly okay. It wouldn't seem lazy; it wouldn't seem like I wasn't doing my job.

These differences in expectations affected the degree to which the teachers saw themselves as leaders or facilitators and the extent to which they adopted a formal or informal stance in the classroom. For Anita, this meant that she took on different teaching roles in each classroom:

> I'm more of an organizer in the regular classroom. I'm more of a facilitator in the computer classroom . . . When I facilitate, I'll let the student determine how they need me. In the regular classroom, I have to pre-determine how the students need me and then I have to make that work. In the computer classroom, I let them determine what they need from me more so. If you're a good instructor, you'll make sure you're moving the thought processes toward the end goal—more effective writing. But I find it much more unstructured in the computer classroom.

The other teachers echoed Anita's comments, describing the different roles they adopted in terms of formality, teacher-centered versus student-centered teaching, and coaching metaphors. In each case, the teachers felt that they adopted the role of leader in the traditional classroom and of supporter in the computer classroom.

Interaction Among Classmates and Between Students and Teachers

One of the most striking differences between the two classroom settings was interaction during class sessions. Our observations of the classrooms, along with student and teacher reports of their interactions, indicate that students in the computer classrooms had significantly higher numbers of contacts with classmates and teachers than did students in the traditional classrooms. Moreover, our observations and our interviews with students suggest that the interactions among students in the computer classrooms focused on writing, rather than social issues, while the opposite was true of interactions among students in the traditional classrooms. Commenting on the differences in her interactions with students in the two classrooms, Jen observed:

> I think it's different just because you get to walk around while they're drafting, and you can interact with them very much during the drafting phase . . . I try to do that in the traditional classroom when they're in workshop, but I think it's harder because they do less up-front drafting and revising in the classroom.

The other teachers echoed Jen's observation that the workshop atmosphere of the computer classroom contributed to their higher level of interaction with students. In addition, they noted that the majority of their interactions with students in the computer classroom were initiated by students and focused directly on their writing. Caitlin explained:

> The contact that I have with students is more closely related to the writing project that they're working on. And a lot of it is more student solicited.

> They're the ones that determine when they want me to help them with their writing, rather than me saying in the traditional classroom, "Okay, on Tuesday and Wednesday, we're going to have conferences." I have conferences with my students continuously in the computer classroom.

In contrast, noted Caitlin, the traditional classroom typically fostered different kinds of interactions between teachers and students:

> I think that a student in the traditional classroom has access to me the whole 50 minutes that we're in that classroom too, but so often things are large-group oriented that a student has to break out of that large group and ask an independent question that might be related very specifically to something on his or her draft and may not feel as free to do that as in the computer classroom where people are working very independently with input all of the time from the people around them. [In the computer classroom,] it's not such a break maybe in the flow of the class for an individual student to say, "Hey, Caitlin. Come over here and look at this."

In only one category of interaction—student contact with teachers outside of class—did the traditional classrooms have higher levels of contact than the computer classrooms. Yet this may stem less from reluctance on the part of students in the computer classrooms to seek out their teachers outside of class than from the sense that they didn't need to do so. A student in Anita's class said during an interview at the end of the semester:

> She leaves herself very open to just going up to her and ask her if she thought this was a good person to interview or if this resource would help or questions like that. I never went and made an appointment with her to discuss a paper outside of class, but that was mainly because during class I usually got a lot of her attention, and she would come around and make sure that she answered everyone's questions. Or did her best to. And she was very helpful. Very, very helpful.

A further factor that complicates direct comparison of out-of-class contacts is electronic interaction. If we include out-of-class interactions via electronic mail between teachers and students in our measure of out-of-class contact, then the computer classroom has a higher average level of student-teacher contact outside the classroom. Yet we must ask ourselves whether an electronic mail message is equivalent to a face-to-face meeting between a student and teacher. Counting electronic mail as a replacement for face-to-face contact is probably appropriate if the subject of the message is something that can be dealt with quickly and without the need for subsequent elaboration, as might be the case when a student asks about a homework assignment. When the subject of an electronic mail message concerns something as complex as the overall direction of a revision plan or a student's behavior during class, however, we suspect that teachers might prefer to discuss the issue with a student face-to-face.

Keeping these complications in mind, our analysis of the interaction data suggests that significantly more discussions of student writing occurred among classmates and between students and teachers in the computer classroom. In Chapter Four, we discuss in greater detail the types of interaction and the conditions that appear to have fostered them in the computer classroom.

The Classroom Context: Workshop Atmosphere Versus Traditional Atmosphere

A major reason for the higher levels of interaction in the computer classroom is a difference in the kind of work that took place in each classroom. We can describe the traditional classroom as a place where *writing was discussed*—during, for instance, lecture, whole-class discussion, group activities, or peer-review sessions. In contrast, we can describe the computer classroom as a place where *writing was done*—either during writing activities designed to prepare students for major writing assignments or during drafting or revising sessions for those major assignments. Each of the four teachers remarked on the extent to which the computer classroom immersed students in their writing and on the extent to which it fostered a workshop atmosphere with ongoing dialogue about students' writing. As Anita remarked:

> The computer classroom is much more writing oriented. You can say, "We're going to draft today." And you can't do that in a regular classroom. That time is so wonderful because students don't just sit and draft. They talk to their neighbor about their draft. They ask you questions. You filter around the room. It becomes a giant workshop. And yet, students are producing, so it's a workshop with some production going on. It's really pretty marvelous.

In contrast, the teachers felt that their students in the traditional classrooms resisted writing during class. In some cases, students felt that the writing they were asked to do in class was a waste of time, since they simply retyped it when they worked on their computers or word processors outside of class. In other cases, students apparently resisted because the notion of writing in a writing class was outside their experience and expectations. As Candace said:

> It's almost impossible to get people to draft with a pen and piece of paper in the traditional classroom . . . If I have students sitting around in a circle doing freewriting by hand, I find that they're resistant. They're lethargic. They roll their eyes. They often don't want to do it.

One of the students in a traditional classroom clearly voiced his resistance to writing during class. When asked how the class might be improved, he responded:

> I would say like don't have too much free time in class where you expect the students to write, you know . . . I didn't find it as helpful for me to try to write in class there . . . It was just difficult to try to write in that setting.

In Chapter Five, we discuss the issue of writing and revising during class in greater detail. In our discussion, we also address the impact of the classroom context on student improvement as writers, on student enthusiasm and confidence, and on student empowerment.

Transferring Activities from the Computer Classroom to the Traditional Classroom

As the semester progressed, the teachers commented in their interviews and teaching logs that they were beginning to transfer teaching strategies and classroom activities from the computer to the traditional classrooms. They attempted to create a workshop atmosphere in the traditional classrooms by requiring more in-class drafting, by encouraging more interaction during class, and occasionally by moving class sessions out of the classroom. They attempted to shift the focus of class sessions from the teacher to the students. And they attempted to adapt technology-based activities for use in the traditional classroom. Although these attempts met with varying degrees of success, they clearly indicate that the transfer of teaching skills between traditional and computer classrooms moves in both directions.

The attempt to create a workshop atmosphere in the traditional classroom was a clear response to what the teachers valued in their teaching in the computer classrooms. The teachers indicated in their interviews and teaching logs that they were optimistic about transferring to the traditional classroom some of the energy and enthusiasm exhibited by their students in the computer classroom. All the teachers indicated that they asked their traditional students to write more during class. Caitlin pointed out that she began to ask students in her traditional classrooms to use the DAILY activity that was used extensively in the computer classrooms. Adapting DAILY for the traditional classroom was fairly simple, according to Caitlin:

> I start a lot of my classes with "write-to-learn" type of activity. In the traditional classroom, it's just on the board and they begin class by coming in and sitting down and writing. In the computer classroom, it's in the DAILY. They come in and they access the DAILY and they get going. And so, I see that's something I didn't do as much in the traditional classroom before I taught in the computer classroom and that's something I think I've carried over.

In addition to incorporating more writing into their traditional classroom sessions, the teachers also made an effort to encourage more interaction in their traditional classrooms. Jen, the only one of the four teachers who consistently arranged the desks in her traditional classroom in rows rather than a circle, explained that she had initially viewed the rows as a barrier between her and her students. As the semester progressed, she worked to break down that barrier:

> I mean, I'm not scared of the rows. I used to be terrified of them, but now it doesn't make much difference. I'll walk down. I'll sit with students. I'll mingle because I think that's how I teach best, and I think that's how they learn best. They get lots of one on one help, and . . . a lot of that carries over from the computer room . . . Working in a computer lab may have helped me get to that point where I'm not scared to go into the middle of them and say "hey" and sit with them.

Caitlin adopted a different technique to encourage interaction between herself and her students. Taking a cue from the willingness of students in her computer classroom to discuss their writing with her, she actively encouraged her students in her traditional classroom to seek her out:

> What I ended up doing, kind of I think as an adjustment . . . I would write notes to them on their paper about things that were going on. But then, I would also say, "Why don't you come up and talk to me about this during class?" Then I could reinforce what I had written on their paper with some verbal conversation about it too. Because I saw how effective that was in the computer classroom.

A third strategy that the teachers used to make the traditional classroom more like a workshop was to change the location of class. Some class sessions were held in the library, where students worked one-on-one with their teacher while they looked for sources. Sometimes class sessions were canceled so that students could meet for extended conferences with their teachers. On still other occasions, classes were held in a location, such as an art gallery, where students wrote about what they saw around them.

In addition to creating a workshop atmosphere in the traditional classroom, the teachers also shifted the focus of the traditional classroom from the teacher to the students. Their desire to create a more student-centered environment in the traditional classroom may have resulted from the different levels of enthusiasm they saw among the two groups of students. It may have resulted from a desire to make students in the traditional classrooms more responsible for their own learning. Or it may have resulted from a strong belief that a student-centered approach to teaching writing is more effective than a teacher-centered approach. In their interviews, the teachers touched on one or more of these reasons. Caitlin realized that she wanted to move away from her initial training as a front-of-the-classroom teacher:

> I was trained by an education department to be a teacher. And what that means for many education departments is that you are THE teacher. And you do THE teaching. And it's taken me time to be able to give up that power in a sense . . . I knew I

> wanted to go in that direction with my teaching, but it was expedited by the computer classroom. Because it doesn't work to be the center of attention and to be ring leader in the computer classroom. There are a lot more interesting things in there—computers—than the teacher . . . So when I returned, then, to the traditional classroom, I didn't feel the need to be in that position again.

Teachers also adapted activities that relied on various technologies, such as commenting on a series of messages on a class bulletin board, for use in the traditional classroom. The DAILY exercises exemplify this transfer, but the teachers also explored how activities designed for electronic mail and electronic bulletin boards might fit into traditional classrooms. In her interview at the middle of the semester, Caitlin talked about her plans to adapt one of these activities:

> I thought about what I wanted my students to do in the computer classroom as far as discussion of e-mail and responding to each other's e-mail messages and things. So then I thought, "How can I have the same kind of discussion in the traditional classroom," so, I'm going to try and do it on paper. They each have a piece of paper and they write some ideas or thoughts or opinions and we kind of do the round robin thing where they pass it around the room and try to figure out, you know, in the end it'll come back to them. And hopefully then they'll be doing some responding to the responses that people put on their paper.

In Chapters Six and Seven, we discuss in greater detail the efforts teachers made to transfer teaching techniques and activities from one classroom setting to the other.

Introducing and Using Technologies

One of the most important questions we addressed in the Transitions and New Teachers Studies concerned the use and introduction of technologies in the computer classrooms. In interviews, teachers and students addressed the need to introduce new technologies to students early in the course and to link that introduction clearly to the goals and content of the course. However, the teachers resisted adopting technologies with which they were unfamiliar even when they believed the technology could help their students become better writers.

In the Transitions Study, the teachers were particularly interested in how they might more effectively introduce students to the technology available in the computer classrooms, particularly word processing, electronic mail, and Internet tools. The techniques they discussed ranged from providing detailed handouts to students to demonstrating the programs using LCD displays to providing almost no guidance and allowing the students to figure it out on their own. In all cases, the teachers indicated that computer use should begin on the first day and should directly support writing activities. One key concern the teachers voiced was the danger of separating the technology from the goals of the class. Ellen, who participated in the New Teachers Study, reflected on the changes she had made from her first semester in the computer classroom to the second:

> This semester I was much better in implementing the technology into the actual goals of what I wanted for the class. And of having the technology become part of that instead of thinking of the technology as something separate that I had to teach. I basically taught the technology in terms of what I thought was important for the writing class.

Like Ellen, Jen was concerned about the dangers of separating the technology from the course goals. In her final interview, she called attention to the downfall of using the technology simply because it was there, rather than because it met a specific course goal:

> I think it might be easy to be lulled into feeling that the technology is just so great, but you could end up taking up class time that they really need for all the things that we're trying to teach them. [Interviewer: So you can get lost in the technology?] Yeah, waste a lot of time setting up stuff for them to do which really—what did it teach them? It might have been fun. It might have been novel, but did it really help them become better writers?

As we worked with the teachers in both studies, we noted that all of them resisted using some technologies even when they felt that effective use of the technologies would benefit their students. The common thread running through the teachers' resistance to using certain technologies was a concern that, if the teachers did not feel confident using a particular program, then it couldn't be used effectively. For some teachers, this resistance was based on experience in the classroom. Candace explained in her mid-semester interview:

> There is a point where it really slowed me down and we didn't get much done or about two weeks while we were trying to figure [electronic mail] out. And now I've sort of had to find a balance between using it and not using it. I'm using it a lot more than I was last semester, but probably not as much as Mike would like to see me using it. I've had to find a workable balance, because we were spending so much time figuring it out. It really started to get in the way, and that's the point where I just pulled back and said, "OK, we're gonna use this and this," but, for example, we haven't used attachments very much. I'd like to use it again at least once more and they do send each other mail. And I encourage them to send me mail.

One of the teachers simply refused to move beyond her comfort zone in the computer classroom. By the middle of the semester, Anita, who had the most experience teaching in computer classrooms of all the teachers in the two studies, used the computers in an extremely limited fashion:

> I've gone back, even though I have WordPerfect with Windows and SharkMail and all of that, I've really gone back to using the computer the way I did before, as a real helpful tool for word processing.

In Chapter Eight, we explore strategies to deal with the complexities of using technology to support writing instruction. We revisit, as well, the ways in which the teachers introduced new technologies to their students.

STUDENT ATTITUDES ABOUT WRITING, STUDENT WRITING PERFORMANCE, AND RELATIONSHIPS AMONG ATTITUDES, PERFORMANCE, AND INTERACTION WITH CLASSMATES AND TEACHERS

In this section, we provide additional results of the transition study. The issues we cover in these sections have important implications for understanding the context of the two classroom settings. As topics in and of themselves, however, they do not lend themselves to detailed discussions. Because we want you to have access to as much information about the study as possible, however, we provide summaries of key findings in six areas:

1. computer anxiety;
2. writing confidence;
3. student perceptions of the helpfulness of feedback from teachers;
4. students' willingness to talk with their teachers;
5. student writing performance; and
6. the relationships between writing performance, attitudes about writing, and interaction with classmates and teachers.

Computer anxiety

We used surveys to track differences in student attitudes about writing and computers. As it did at the beginning of the semester, our end-of-the-semester survey indicated significant differences in computer anxiety between students in the traditional and computer-supported classrooms. On a one-to-five scale, with one indicating the lowest level of anxiety and five indicating the highest, students in the computer-supported classrooms averaged a score of 1.68 while students in the traditional classrooms averaged a score of 1.88. These scores decreased in both settings from the beginning of the semester.

Writing confidence

At the end of the semester, students in the computer classrooms reported higher levels of writing confidence than did their peers in the traditional classrooms. Writing confidence was measured on a one-to-five scale, with one indicating low confidence in writing ability and five indicating high confidence. At the end of the semester, students in the computer classrooms had an average score on the writing confidence scale of 3.54, while students in the traditional classrooms had a mean score of 3.33. Students in the computer classrooms also showed a significant increase in writing confidence over the course of the semester, with the average score rising from 3.43 at the beginning of the semester to 3.54 at the end. Students in the traditional classrooms showed no parallel increase.

The actual difference between the two classrooms, although statistically significant, is not large in a practical sense. We can't say, for instance, that students in the computer classrooms completed the semester feeling twice as confident as students in the traditional classrooms. However, the pattern is one that we believe is important. Not only was there a significant difference at the end of the semester, but there was a significant increase (when each student's scores at the beginning and end of the semester are compared) over the course of the semester in the computer classrooms but not in the traditional classroom. Students left the computer classrooms with more confidence in their writing ability than they had when they started the semester and were, on average, more confident in their writing ability at the end of the semester than were students in the traditional classrooms.

Student perceptions of the helpfulness of feedback from teachers and of their willingness to talk with teachers

Students in the traditional classrooms reported significantly higher perceptions of the helpfulness of comments received from teachers and willingness to talk to teachers about their writing than did students in the computer classrooms (see Figure 3.1). We rated each of the measures on one-to-five scales, with a score of one indicating low levels of perceived helpfulness or willingness to talk with teachers and a score of five indicating high levels of perceived helpfulness or willingness to talk with teachers. Students in the traditional classrooms averaged 4.35 for helpfulness of teacher comments, while students in the computer classroom averaged 3.90. Students in the traditional classrooms also averaged 4.31 on willingness to talk with teachers, while students in the computer classrooms averaged 4.03.

These differences in perceived helpfulness of teacher comments and reported willingness to talk with teachers surprised us. We had assumed that the higher overall levels of interaction between teachers and students in the computer classrooms that we observed and that students reported in their weekly interaction reports would translate into higher levels of perceived willingness to talk with teachers and perceived helpfulness of teacher comments. (We discuss interactions between teachers and students in Chapter Four.)

We suspect that these perceived differences might reflect the kinds of comments that students in the two classrooms received from their teachers. The

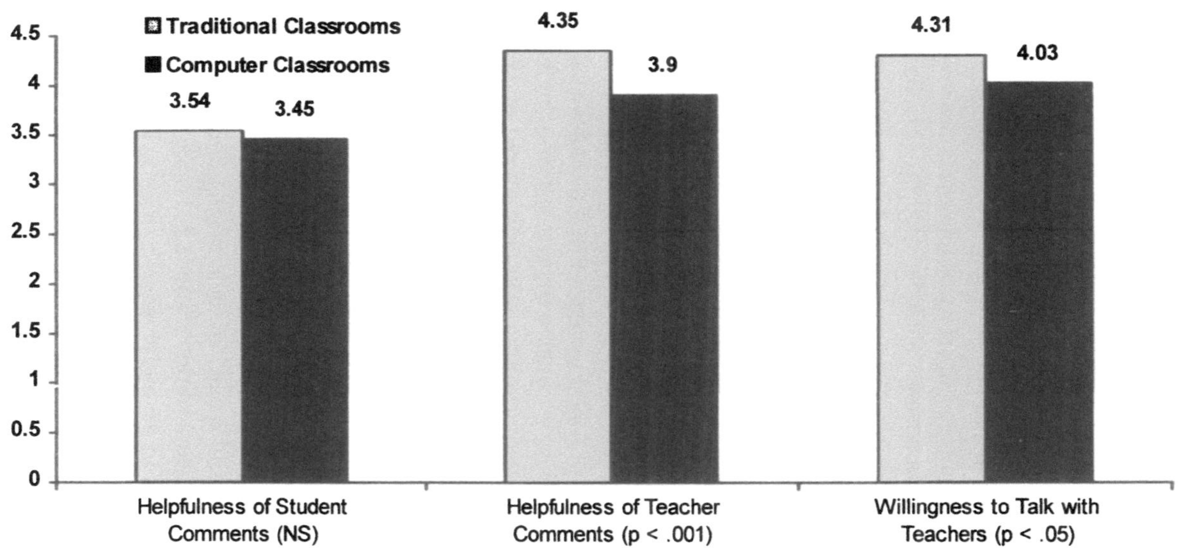

FIGURE 3.1. Perceived helpfulness of student and teacher comments and willingness to talk with teachers (from end-of-semester survey)

majority of feedback that students in the traditional classrooms received came in the form of written responses to graded assignments. In the computer classrooms, however, students received a great deal of additional feedback on their writing, not only after they had turned it in for a grade but also *as they were writing*. It seems possible that the atmosphere in the computer classroom, in which interactions between students and teachers were fairly casual and relatively frequent (compared to those in the traditional classrooms), contributed to students seeing their teacher's feedback on their papers as simply one more voice offering suggestions. In both classroom settings, students rated their teachers' comments as more helpful than their classmates' comments. But the rating for perceived helpfulness of teachers' comments was significantly higher in the traditional classrooms than in the computer classrooms. The average difference in perceived helpfulness was twice as large, in fact, in the traditional classrooms as it was in the computer classrooms.

Perhaps students in the computer classroom became more comfortable with feedback from their teachers than did students in the traditional classroom. In the computer classrooms, feedback from teachers became commonplace while, in the traditional classrooms, feedback was something out of the ordinary. In making this argument, we do not want to suggest that it's simply a case of familiarity breeding contempt so much as we want to suggest that frequent feedback on writing afforded by the computer classroom may have altered students' perceptions of the overall value of that feedback. It may be, of course, that the teachers were doing a better job of providing feedback to their traditional classroom students, but our classroom observations and our analysis of the written feedback that students received do not support this explanation.

Student writing performance

We did not find any differences in student writing performance between the two settings. Students received comparable grades on their written assignments and had comparable levels of quality in their writing. Students in the computer classrooms, however, both wrote more and appeared more willing to write during class than were their peers in the traditional classrooms. They also revised more frequently than did their peers in the traditional classrooms. We discuss these differences in greater detail in Chapter Five.

Relationships among writing performance, attitudes about writing, and interaction with classmates and teachers

We observed a number of differences between classroom settings in the relationships between writing performance, attitudes about writing, and interaction with classmates and teachers. Those differences include relationships between writing anxiety and interaction, student confidence in their writing ability and interaction, grades and interaction, and grades and previous writing instruction.

We found, in the computer classrooms but not in the traditional classrooms, that students with higher levels of writing anxiety were less likely to talk with their teachers before or after class and less likely to indicate a willingness to seek out their teachers or classmates outside of class. These students, however, were more likely than their classmates to communicate with their teachers by electronic mail (see Table 3.1). In the future, we hope to pursue questions about students' writing anxiety and out-of-class contact with teachers because these preliminary findings suggest that computer technologies may provide a specific benefit for these students.

We also saw, in the traditional classrooms but not the computer classrooms, that students with higher levels of confidence in their writing ability were less likely to interact with classmates outside of the classroom—and, conversely, that students with lower levels of confidence in their writing ability were more likely to interact with classmates outside of class (see Table 3.1). Again, we hope to follow up on the research reported here with additional study. We are particularly interested in identifying teaching strategies that encourage increased interaction during and outside of class.

Our third key finding concerning interaction applied to the traditional classrooms but not to the computer classrooms. In the traditional classrooms, grades for the course and for the second portfolio were negatively correlated with student/teacher contact outside of class and immediately before and after class (see Table 3.1). Similarly, in the traditional classrooms but not in the computer classrooms, scores on standardized tests (the ACT English score) were negatively correlated with frequency of out-of-class contact between students and teachers (see Table 3.1). We understand why students who feel more successful in class feel less need to seek out teachers, but the difference between the level of contact and setting surprised us. We look at these data in much more detail in Chapter Four when we examine specific levels of contact and grades.

Finally, in the computer classrooms but not in the traditional classrooms, students who reported higher levels of prior instruction that focused on grammar and mechanics had lower grades for the first portfolio, the second portfolio, and the course (see Table 3.1). Recall that at the beginning of the semester, we found no significant overall difference between classroom settings in the amount of prior instruction focusing on grammar. This suggests to us that the dynamic of the computer classroom builds on skills that receive less attention in courses that focus heavily on grammar and mechanics. We suspect that the difference between the two groups reflects the greater emphasis on a workshop environment in the computer classrooms (see our discussion of this difference in Chapter Five). Students who reported higher levels of previous writing instruction that focused on grammar and mechanics may have entered the computer classrooms at a disadvantage. Because their prior instruction focused more heavily on the product of writing, they may have been unprepared for a classroom environment that emphasized the process of writing. Clearly, writing teachers should consider

TABLE 3.1.
Selected Correlations Across Classroom Settings

Measure 1	Measure 2	Traditional classrooms			Computer classrooms		
		r	*n*	*p*	*r*	*n*	*p*
Writing Anxiety (beginning of semester)	Contacts Reported by Teachers that Occurred Immediately Before and After Class	.052	86	.634	–.231	78	.042
Writing Anxiety (end of semester)	Reported Willingness to Seek Feedback from Teachers or Classmates Outside of Class	–.194	84	.076	–.334	77	.003
Writing Anxiety (end of semester)	Total e-mail Between Student and Teacher	—	—	—	.263	77	.021
Confidence in Writing Ability (beginning of semester)	Reported Out-of-Class Contacts with Classmates	–.353	85	.001	.005	78	.963
Confidence in Writing Ability (end of semester)	Reported Out-of-Class Contacts with Classmates	–.245	84	.024	.050	78	.665
Grade for Course	Student Reported Contact with Teachers Outside of Class	–.232	90	.027	.070	83	.530
Grade for Course	Teacher Reported Contact with Students Immediately Before or After Class, Total	–.257	90	.014	.072	83	.517
Grade for Course	Teacher Reported Contact with Students Immediately Before or After Class, Teacher Initiated	–.271	90	.001	–.082	83	.460
Grade on Second Portfolio	Student Reported Contact with Teachers Outside of Class	–.261	90	.013	.266	83	.015
Grade on First Portfolio	Previous Writing Instruction that Focused on Grammar	–.037	64	.771	–.257	59	.049
Grade on Second Portfolio	Previous Writing Instructions that Focused on Grammar	–.013	85	.905	–.258	79	.022
Grade for Course	Previous Writing Instruction that Focused on Grammar	–.068	85	.535	–.260	79	.021
ACT English Score	Student Reported Contact with Teachers Outside of Class	–.301	66	.014	.033	63	.797
ACT English Score	Teacher Reported Contact with Students Outside of Class	–.402	66	.001	–.175	63	.171

this issue should they choose to teach in a computer-supported writing classroom. Teachers may find it helpful to determine if some of the students in their classes need additional help adapting to a classroom in which writing, revising, and interaction are so strongly emphasized.

CONTRASTS OR CONTINUUM

This chapter has focused on contrasts between the students in our traditional and computer classrooms, but we hesitate to conclude this chapter on that note. Although we pursue the differences between classroom settings in the next several chapters, remember that these differences represent a *continuum of change*. The differences are not black and white; the teachers in our studies do not throw out everything they know about teaching just because they move from one setting to the other. Rather, as they move between settings they adapt—to the setting and to their students. We look specifically at the interface between setting and group dynamics in the next chapter.

4

Classroom Dynamics: Interaction and Classroom Design

Writing instruction is, at its core, an act of sharing—a sharing of experience, knowledge, and motivation. In most writing classrooms, that sharing takes place through dialogue. This dialogue varies greatly from classroom to classroom and from teacher to teacher. In some classrooms, typically those based on a more presentational model, a teacher may dominate the discussion to the near exclusion of student voices. In others, student voices may play a dominant role. Although we believe that these differences stem primarily from the educational goals and philosophies of the teachers who design the curricula for specific courses, we also believe that the physical setting of a classroom affects the discourse that takes place within it.

Given our interests in the contrasts between traditional and computer classrooms, we are particularly intrigued by the potential impact of computers on classroom discourse. In addition, we are intrigued by the potential of network-communication tools, such as electronic mail, chat, and electronic bulletin boards, to extend that discourse beyond the classroom. Finally, although we did not address this question in the Transitions or New Teachers Studies, we question how the physical layout of computers in a classroom—for instance, in rows, in a circle, or in pods—shapes classroom discourse.

The Transitions Study allowed us to hold constant the most important factor in any educational study—the influence of the teachers participating in the study. Having the same teacher teach in both settings allowed us to look closely at the impact of computers on interaction inside and outside the classroom. The New Teachers Study gives us additional insight into teachers' understanding of how the technology in their computer classrooms shaped interaction with and among their students. Taken together, the two studies suggest that striking differences exist in the interactions taking place in the traditional and the computer classrooms. Our classroom observations and the reports of students and teachers clearly indicate that:

- the computer classrooms had significantly higher levels of contact among classmates and between students and teachers,
- conversations among students in the computer classrooms were more likely to address issues related to student writing than social issues, and
- students in the computer classrooms used electronic mail to communicate with their teachers outside of class for a variety of purposes, both social and academic.

Our analysis of the two studies suggests that at least two key factors contribute to the increased levels of interaction in the computer classrooms:

- the student-centered pedagogies that teachers adopted in the computer classrooms and
- the focus on in-class writing throughout the course.

In this chapter, we explore interaction in detail, focusing on face-to-face and electronic contacts inside and outside the classroom. We conclude the chapter with a discussion of how the physical layout of classrooms shapes the interactions that take place within them. In Chapter Five, we focus on in-class writing in the two classroom settings.

INTERACTION IN TRADITIONAL AND COMPUTER CLASSROOMS

As we noted in Chapter Two, we tracked interaction among students and between teachers and students in the Transitions Study in four ways. Every week, students reported interactions they had inside and outside of the classroom with classmates, teachers, and writing center tutors. On a class-by-class basis, teachers recorded their interactions with students immediately before and after class as well as outside of class. At several points during the semester, we observed the classrooms and noted the frequency and kinds of interactions immediately before, during, and immediately after class. Finally, we kept copies of electronic mail sent between students and teachers. In the New Teachers Study, we used a narrower range of information sources—interviews with teachers and classroom observation—to help us understand the interactions taking place in the classrooms.

The information we collected indicates striking differences in the amount and kinds of interactions that took place in the two classroom settings:

- Students in the computer classrooms talked during class with teachers and classmates more frequently than did students in the traditional classrooms.
- Student conversations in the computer classrooms tended to focus more on writing than on social issues while those in the traditional classrooms tended to focus more on social issues than on writing.
- Students in the traditional classrooms tended to meet face-to-face with teachers more frequently outside the classroom than did students in the computer classrooms. When we added interactions taking place via electronic mail, however, we saw that students from the computer classrooms had higher overall levels of interactions with teachers outside the classroom as well.

Some of the most intriguing findings of the Transitions Study concern not simply how often teachers interacted with students but with whom they interacted. For instance, teachers in the computer classrooms, tended to interact most often during class with students who were not doing well in the course (i.e., earning a grade of *D* or *F*). In contrast, in the traditional classrooms, teachers tended to interact least often during class with students who were not doing well in the course. Instead, the teachers tended to interact either immediately before or after class or outside of class with those students who earned lower course grades. In the next few sections of this chapter, we focus on how interaction inside and outside the classroom shaped the classroom dynamics of the traditional and computer classrooms.

Interactions Between Students and Teachers

Interactions during class

One of the most important differences between the traditional and computer classrooms is the amount and type of interactions that take place between students and teachers. Our interviews with teachers and students provide some insights into this difference. A student in a traditional classroom described a typical class session, beginning with a characterization of his teacher:

> She's got a pretty good personality, you know. She's always up. Sometimes she'll just come into class and she'll just start talking about her weekend. So we've kind of—in the first few minutes, we kind of waste them because we're always talking about other stuff. And then she'll say, "Okay guys. Let's get to work. Here's what we're going to do today." But I mean once we start say working on a revision, we're pretty quiet. And we work pretty diligently, I think. And then toward the last five minutes of class, you start hearing bags zipping up, and people start talking again.

> But I think for the most part in the mean time we are pretty—we work, and I mean there's not people back in the back corner talking. I mean it's a small classroom. It's almost like—it reminds me of when we were back in high school. Smaller classes. So we have to kind of stay on task, and she's pretty much in control with most of the class period.

In contrast, a student from the same teacher's computer classroom observed that a DAILY writing assignment at the beginning of class helped set the tone for the rest of the class meeting:

> I think the DAILIES are really good because you go in and you have a set thing that you need to get done before class starts. And you end up talking about your DAILY and talking about how it relates to whatever paper you're doing. A lot of times when we just finished a paper we'd go in the next day and brainstorm ideas for the next topic, and then that would help because you get to figure out what you want to talk about and if you're going to be able to talk about it or not.

This focus on student writing in the computer classroom appears to have had a strong impact on the interactions that took place between students and teachers. Typically, teachers circulated during class sessions in the computer classroom, responding to student questions and initiating discussions when it appeared that students were having difficulties with their writing.

Caitlin, who taught the two students just quoted, described differences consistent with her students' observations. In her interview at the middle of the semester, she observed:

> In the traditional classroom, I see myself in a more formal role in my interactions with students. Before class begins, we talk and we maybe discuss, "So how was your weekend Ms. M.?" That kind of stuff. But within the midst of class, I don't have as many individual contacts with the students. I'll wander up and down the rows as much as I can, but just physically, it's more difficult for me to have just one-on-one conversations with my students. I do that as much as I can, but it's just tougher. And my students in the morning, in the traditional classroom, chat much less than my afternoon class. I think they know each other less well than my afternoon computer classroom students.

As Caitlin explained, circulating among the students was easier in the computer classroom, and it resulted in getting to know those students better. Anita came to the same conclusion:

> I tend to get to know the students better in the computer classroom than in the regular classroom. It has nothing to do with my attitude. It just has to do with contact.

A key finding that emerges from the Transitions Study is that students in the computer classrooms reported significantly higher levels of interaction with their teachers during class than did students in the traditional classrooms (see Figure 4.1). Although the reported contacts appear low to us based on our classroom observations and the number of contacts reported by teachers in their interviews and teacher logs, the overall pattern is important. Students in the computer classrooms had more contact with their teachers than did students in the traditional classrooms.

Data from interviews and our classroom observations confirm this finding. In their interviews, as the previous quotation from Anita illustrates, teachers indicated that they interacted with their students much more frequently in the computer classrooms. When we examined the contacts recorded during our classroom observations, we saw that the higher level of contact in the computer classroom did not reflect an unwillingness of teachers to talk with students in the traditional classroom (see Figure 4.2). Rather, we found that the number of teacher-initiated contacts with students was roughly equal in the two settings. There was a clear difference, however, in the number of student-initiated contacts with the teacher, as demonstrated by Figure 4.2.

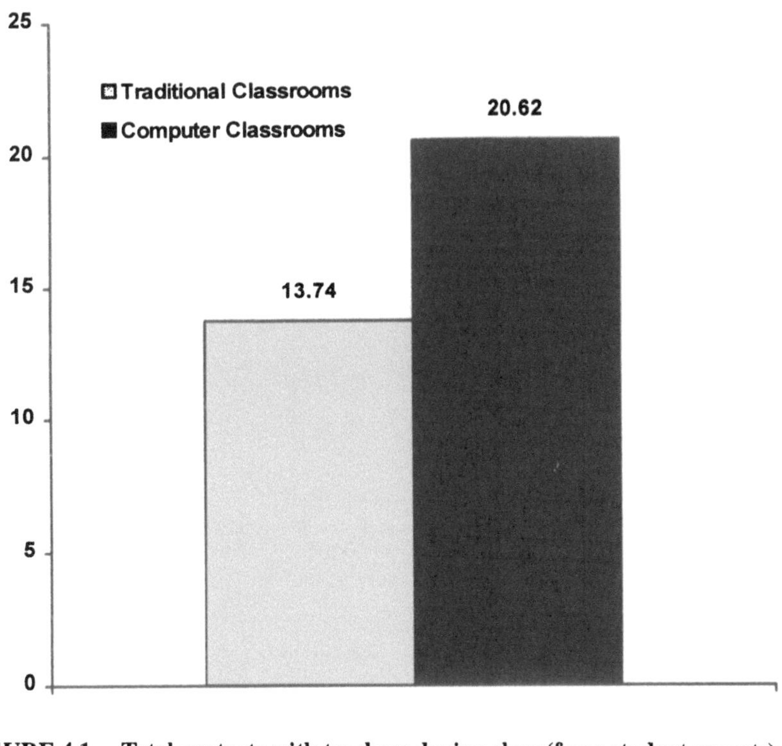

FIGURE 4.1. Total contacts with teachers during class (from student reports)

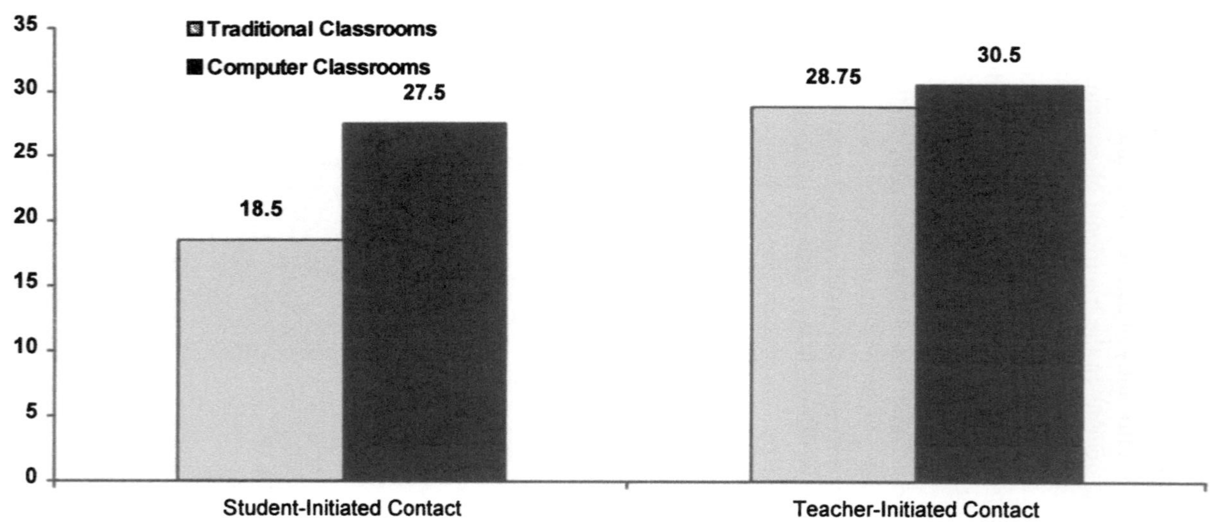

FIGURE 4.2. Average per-class student/teacher interactions noted in classroom observations

We are particularly intrigued by differences in the numbers of student/teacher interactions in students' weekly contact sheets and in our classroom observations. The high numbers of interactions that we observed, coupled with our experience as teachers, suggests that students under-reported the number of interactions they had with their teachers and classmates. Our classroom observations suggested, for example, that students in the computer classrooms talked with their teachers two to three times each class meeting. Yet their interaction reports indicated that they talked with the teacher only once or twice a week. We suspect that this discrepancy arises from students not recalling all their interactions with teachers, or possibly considering brief discussions as not worth reporting to us.

Besides differences in the interactions between students and teachers during class and in the willingness of students to initiate those interactions, teachers seemed to interact with different groups of students. In the traditional classrooms, most interactions between students and teachers during class occurred with students who were performing well in the class (see Figure 4.3). In contrast, although the overall level of interaction was higher across the board in the computer classrooms, teachers tended to spend more time with students who were earning lower grades. This was particularly true of students who earned a *D* in the course. In the traditional classroom, these students interacted with teachers less frequently than all other students. In the computer classrooms, these students interacted more frequently than all other students. (Those students who earned *Fs*

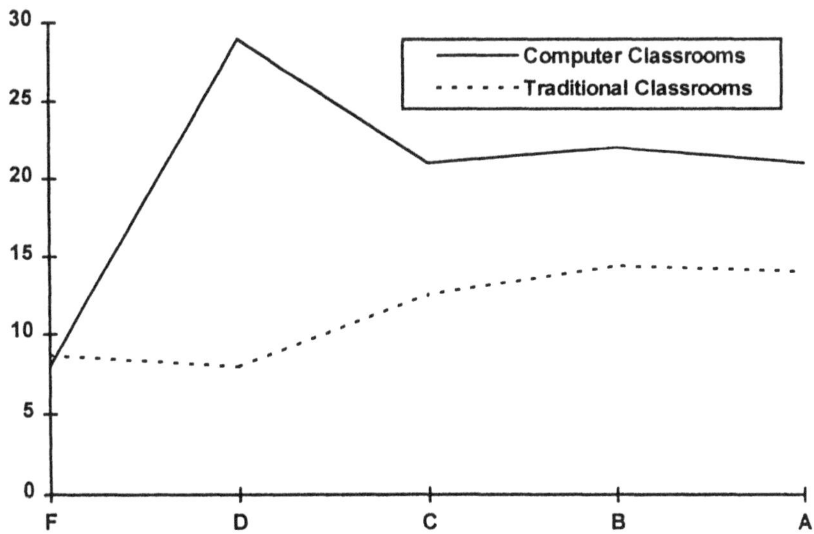

FIGURE 4.3. In-class interaction with students by course grade (from student reports)

in both courses typically missed several classes, which reduced their overall number of contacts with teachers.)

Interaction immediately before and after class

Students commonly interact with teachers immediately before or after class. We obtained information about these interactions from the teachers in the Transitions Study, who recorded these meetings in their teaching logs. Although we saw no differences between the two classrooms in this measure of interaction, we did find intriguing differences in the pattern of interaction (see Figures 4.4 and 4.5). In these interactions, we saw that, in the traditional classrooms, students earning lower grades tended to interact with their teachers much more frequently than their classmates who earned higher grades. In contrast, students from the computer classrooms interacted with teachers at the same level regardless of the grade. Moreover, students and teachers in computer classrooms had slightly higher overall levels of interaction than students and teachers in the traditional classrooms.

Interaction outside the classroom

Although teachers and students reported far different numbers of out-of-class contacts, we suspect that the difference stems from the definition of "out-of-class" contacts. Students may have classified contacts made immediately before or after class sessions as out-of-class contacts, while teachers differentiated between these and office-hour contacts. Whatever the cause of the difference, the

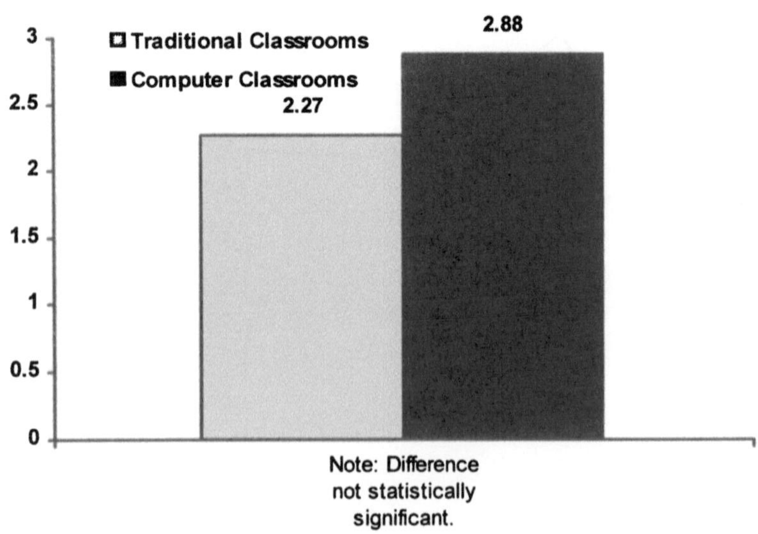

FIGURE 4.4. Average student/teacher contacts immediately before and after class (from teacher logs)

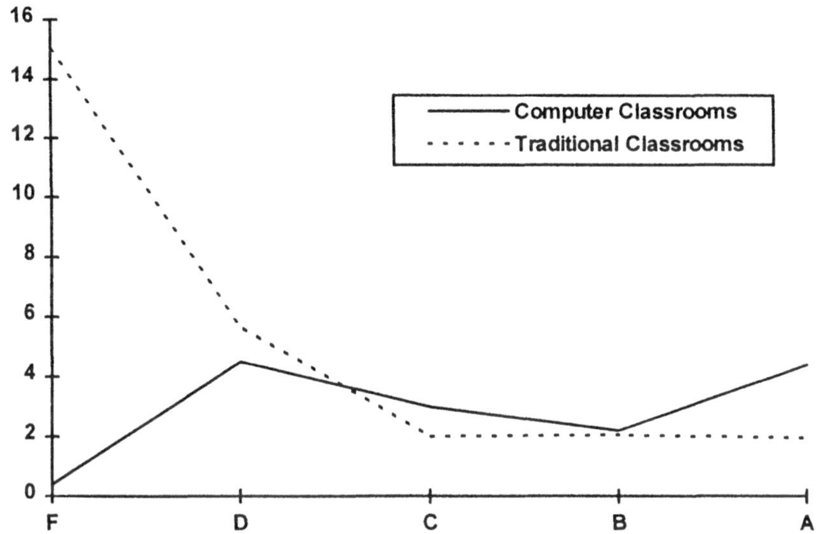

FIGURE 4.5. Average student/teacher contacts immediately before and after class by course grade (from teacher logs)

overall pattern is similar in both measures of out-of-class contact. Students in the traditional classrooms had a significantly higher level of face-to-face contact with their teachers outside of the classroom (see Figure 4.6). These contacts typically took place during office hours and involved discussions of student essays or of missed class sessions. In addition, as we show in Figure 4.7, the distribution of contacts by course grade parallels that seen for contacts immediately before and after class sessions. Students earning lower grades in the traditional classroom tended to meet more often with the teacher outside of class than their classmates earning higher grades, while the overall level of interaction among students in the computer classrooms was relatively similar across grade levels.

Two factors appear to have contributed to the higher overall level of out-of-class contact between students and teachers from the traditional classrooms. First, the teachers indicated that they sometimes canceled their traditional classes—in one case, for two weeks of class—to hold conferences with their students while continuing to meet in the computer classroom. Second, students in the computer classrooms indicated that they usually obtained the answers they needed about their writing during or immediately before class sessions. In their end-of-semester interviews, students from each of the computer classrooms discussed some of the reasons that they did not seek out-of-class advice from their teachers:

> I never went to her office just because . . . it was always outside of class that I was either working on the paper trying to use those comments or working on something

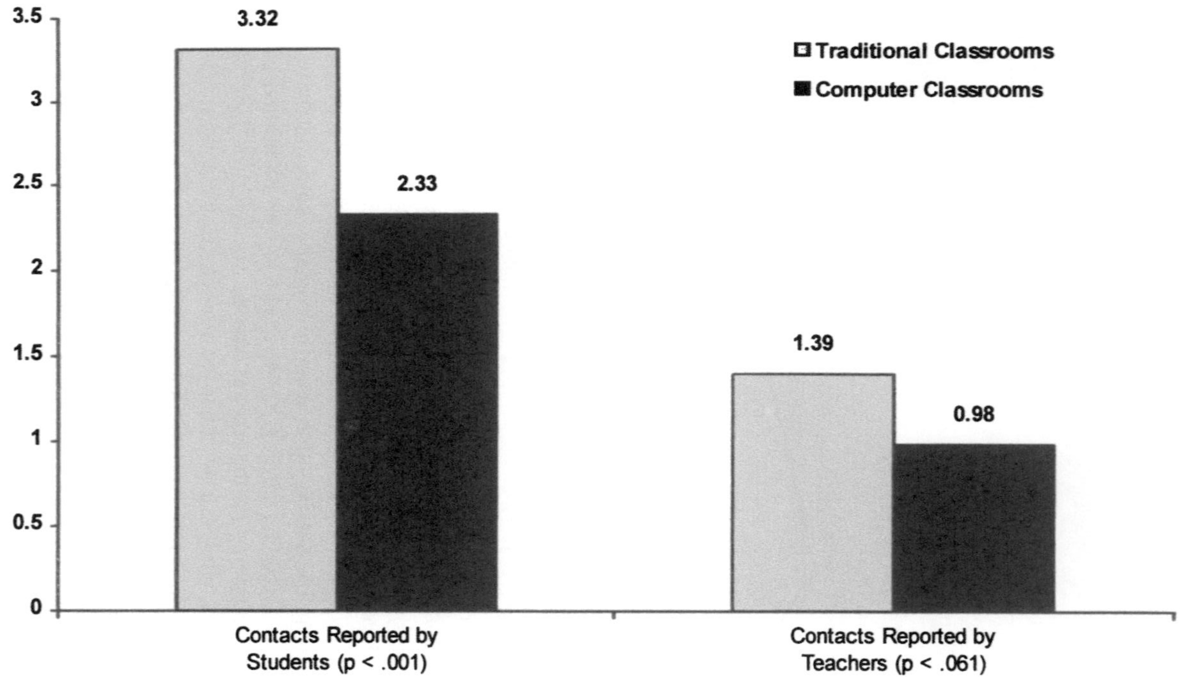

FIGURE 4.6. Average face-to-face student/teacher contacts outside of class

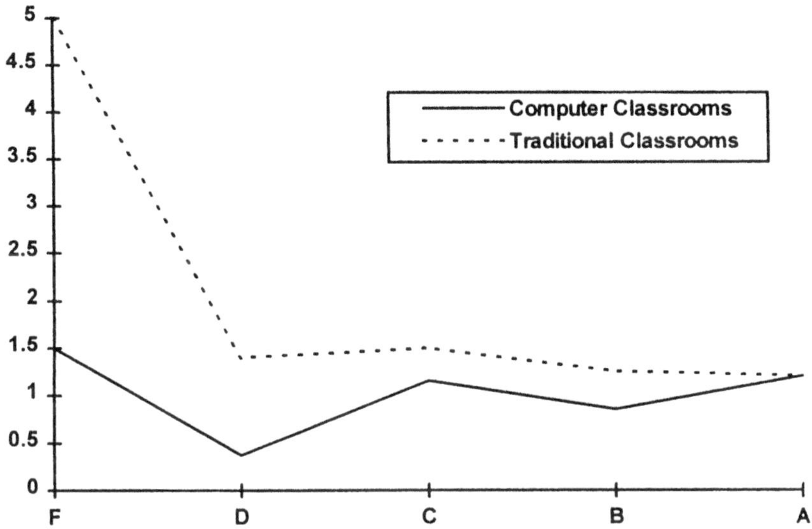

FIGURE 4.7. Average student/teacher contacts outside of class by course grade (from teacher logs)

> else. I have a, somewhat, busy schedule. So, I would talk to her in class . . . I sat down with her, basically, for about half an hour during class and said, "What can I do to this that will fit your criteria?" . . . Really, it was, as far as talking to her, it really helped. She used to come around the class and ask how we were all doing. If I had questions, I'd ask her. I never really went in for a special meeting or anything with her. But she was very approachable, definitely.

> Class starts at nine and the computer classroom opens at eight and I'd come in at 8:15 or 8:30 and sit there. And she's always there ready to help.

Interaction via electronic mail

Although students in the computer classrooms met with their teachers less frequently outside the classroom, they used electronic mail to communicate with their teachers. The use of electronic mail varied widely between classrooms and across students, but students clearly used electronic mail to supplement their face-to-face contacts with their teachers (see Figure 4.8). Students in the computer classrooms used electronic mail to communicate with their teachers about grades, to ask questions about assignments, to ask for feedback on writing assignments, to explain absences from class, and to socialize. Although all students on campus have access to electronic mail via accounts on the university's mini-computers (at the time of the study, more than 13,000 student accounts had been established), only one student in the traditional classrooms used electronic mail to communicate with a teacher—and that occurred only once.

On average, students in the computer classrooms exchanged 2.9 electronic mail messages with their teachers during the semester. The majority of students sent only one or two messages to their teacher, but roughly 20 percent of the students sent six or more messages to their teachers during the semester. Roughly half of the messages were social, with the remaining messages discussing issues related to the class.

We are particularly intrigued by the pattern of electronic mail exchanges in the computer classroom (see Figure 4.9). Students who earned lower grades for the course sent more electronic mail to their teachers, suggesting that this mode of communication may offer a means to enhance communication between teachers and students who are less likely to succeed in writing classes.

One of the students who received a lower grade for the course, a *C*, reflected on why she sent electronic mail to her teacher instead of setting up a face-to-face meeting:

> Sometimes where it was hard for me to talk to Ms. R. about, I would e-mail her a message and she'd write me back. I felt it was a little easier to talk to her that way. Kind of leaving a note and finding it and writing you one back. Kind of like going around it.

Candace, her teacher, indicated that more than one student used electronic mail to express concerns about grades that they might not want to raise in a face-to-face meeting:

> *[Interviewer: What sort of e-mail messages did they send you?]* Mostly about their grades, when they were concerned. And I think that maybe here's another thing. That probably allowed them to be more honest about what was really bothering them. In both cases, I got e-mail from the students and set up appointments with them afterward, but the initial contact was through e-mail . . . maybe having that

Our Teachers Disagree About When to Send E-Mail Their Classes:

- One teacher sends it all the time, especially for reminders about assignments.
- One teacher notes that sending e-mail to students varies with class.
- Another teacher only sends e-mail when students initiate it.
- Another teacher only sends e-mail to remind students that they have too many absences or a behavior problem that they might want to talk about in conference soon.
- Another teacher tells us, "As I get older and realize how unreliable my memory is, I send e-mail to students whenever I think of topics or sources that might help them with papers I know they're working on."

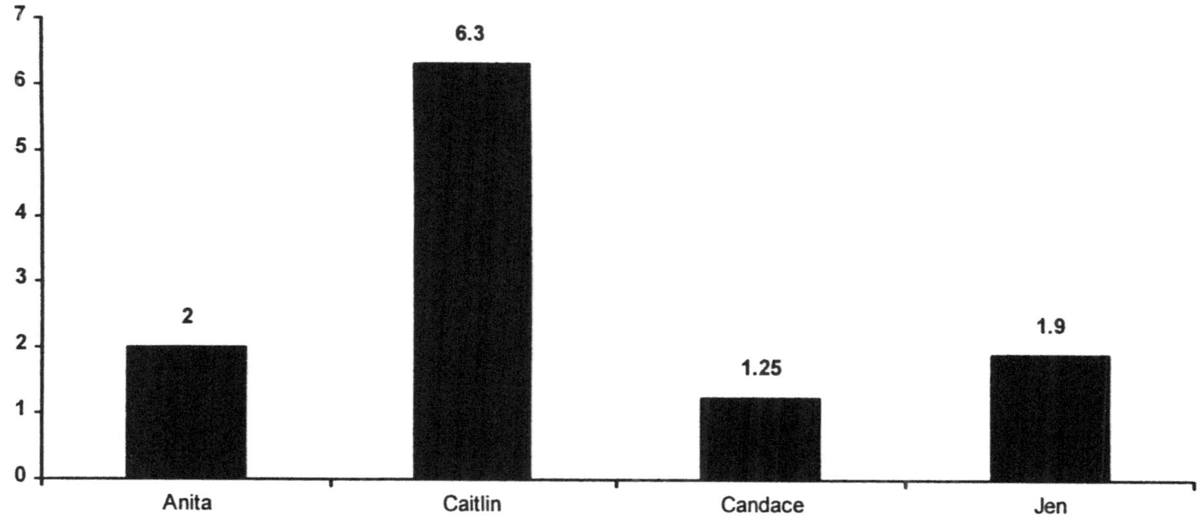

FIGURE 4.8. **Average e-mail messages sent between teachers and students by classroom**

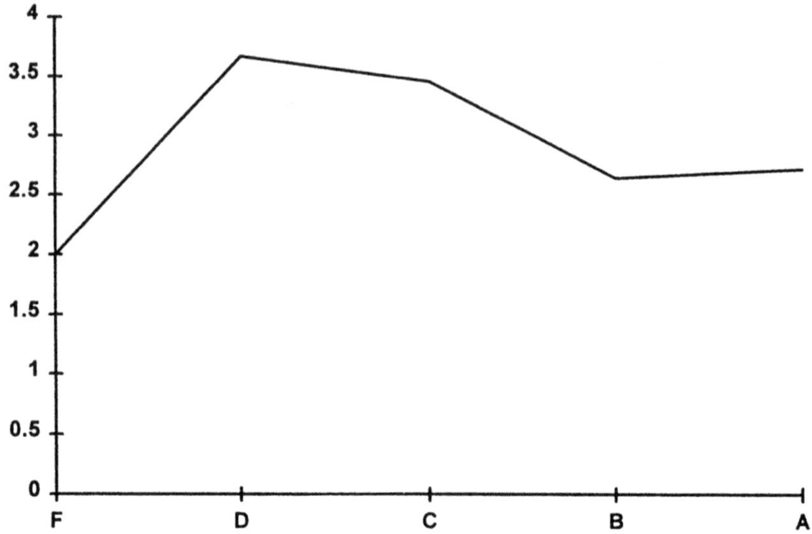

FIGURE 4.9. Average e-mail messages between teachers and students by course grade

> print in front of them made them feel more of an authority, and they had the confidence to send me those messages and say to me, "I want to know what's going on here. Either I don't agree with this grade or I really don't understand what I'm doing wrong." I don't know that other students have expressed that, their disappointment, to me that articulately.

Caitlin, who had the highest average number of electronic mail exchanges with her students, indicated that she encouraged her students to use electronic mail, something the other teachers said they did not do. In her discussion of electronic mail, she indicated that she not only used electronic mail to address issues about class policies and writing instruction, but also to deal with students whom she did not want to confront face-to-face:

> They were mostly when they would write questions to me. And that's what I really encouraged them to do. It's like, "If you have a question, then mail it to me. If you're in the middle of writing your paper and you're sitting in 228 and you have a question at 10:00 at night, you can e-mail it to me immediately. I won't get to answer it immediately, but you'll have asked it when it's fresh in your head." So, I got logistical questions. I got MLA type questions. I got "Can I turn this in on Tuesday? Do you need this piece of paper when I turn in my folder?" Those kinds of questions. I don't recall getting a whole lot of questions about their writing, specifically. They used it more for logistical kinds of things for the course. And I would say that I used it in much the same way. If I was missing something from a student,

> I might drop them an e-mail message. I wrote an e-mail message to a student that I was frustrated with because I was just frustrated enough with him that I couldn't talk to him face to face but I needed to say some things to him about his behavior in class.

Neither the students nor the teachers (except Caitlin) in the Transitions Study used electronic mail extensively. Their reluctance surprises us because an earlier study conducted by Mike found that students and teachers at Carnegie Mellon University were relatively enthusiastic about using electronic mail. After reflection, we conclude that a key factor is the difference in campus culture at the two universities. Carnegie Mellon has long been a highly computerized institution, where students have access to a large number of computers in labs open 24 hours a day and where it is the norm rather than the exception to have networked computers in student dormitory rooms. In contrast, when the Transitions Study was

Teachers Use E-Mail to Encourage Students to Use It:

Your e-mail system should allow you to set up lists of accounts by group so that you only type a message once, yet send it to each student. Check with your system support person if you're not sure you have this e-mail capability. Students may not use e-mail if they don't see teachers use e-mail, so you might want to send several general messages to the entire class at the beginning of the semester.

- Send a general greeting to all the students in your class. Our teachers send messages that welcome students to the class and remind them of office hours.
- Send the class a reminder about Writing Center services and hours.
- Send a general reminder about availability of computers through drop-in labs around campus.
- Remind students of an upcoming campus event.
- If you discuss a class policy in class, summarize your discussion and send students the summary. You could even suggest they print out the e-mail message and append it to your syllabus.
- If you change a deadline in class, send a notice of the change through e-mail.

Once you get to know students and have reasons to send individual messages, do that as well. Remind students at the beginning of the term to check their e-mail because they need to build that into their routine.

conducted, students at Colorado State University had less access to computers and relatively few dorm rooms were networked.

The New Teachers Study, conducted approximately 15 months after we concluded the Transitions Study, indicates that the campus culture at Colorado State has begun to change. In the intervening months, our students and teachers have moved toward wider use of (and easier access to) electronic mail. When we asked Amy about her use of electronic mail in her classes, she indicated that both she and her students used it enthusiastically:

> I really stressed communicating by e-mail because I never go to my office, I never check my [voice mail] just cause I'm never there. Just 'cause there's no computer over there so I do all my work at home so that worked out really well. There were a couple of students that always, you know, especially one in particular, would just e-mail me all the time, asking questions, blah, blah, blah. Quite a few people would e-mail me drafts or they would give me a hard copy and I'd e-mail them comments. And that worked out really well. I had just many, many more chances to deal with drafts, intervention drafts and things like that. That was really, really good for me to do that. And I think it helped them. And I don't, it just felt like the communication

Teachers May Want to Specially Invite Below-Average Students to Use E-Mail

Because some research suggests that students performing below average in composition classes especially benefit from using e-mail, teachers may want to make special efforts to encourage these students to use e-mail. Don't badger students, but do remind them of your availability.
One you identify students that you think might benefit from additional interactions, try these techniques:

- Send e-mail asking about the current paper's progress and if the student has any difficulties a conference might help resolve.
- Early in the work on a paper, ask these students if they are satisfied that their ideas will work in the paper. Often, weaker students have trouble generating ideas and don't know to ask teachers, peers, or Writing Center tutors to help them generate ideas as well as revise rough drafts.
- After you return papers or portfolios, ask students who don't perform well to ask questions about your commentary through e-mail or in a conference.
- Remind these students periodically that extra help is avilable through the Writing Center.
- Remind students to check their mail from time to time.

> was better; there was less confusion going on 'cause they could always e-mail me if they had a question.

As teachers become more comfortable with e-mail communications, and as students become more accustomed to reading and writing e-mail, we expect to see it used much more frequently in student-teacher interactions.

Interactions Among Students

In addition to differences in interactions between students and teachers, we also found differences between the two classroom settings in interactions among students. Specifically, students in the computer classrooms interacted more frequently with each other and, on balance, tended to discuss their writing more often than they discussed social issues. We did not find differences in the number of contacts that students had with each other outside of class, nor did we find differences in the patterns of interaction among students earning different grades for the course.

Students' reports and our observations of the classroom indicate that students in the computer classrooms had significantly higher levels of interaction with classmates during class sessions than did students in the traditional classrooms (see Figures 4.10 and 4.11). The pattern in the two sets of measurements is similar. As we note earlier with student-reported teacher interactions, we sense, based on our observation of the classrooms, that students under-reported the number of interactions that they had with classmates during a given week. We suspect that students remembered whom they talked with, but not necessarily how often they talked with a particular classmate.

We expected similar levels of interaction in the two classroom settings during peer-review workshops. In the Transitions Study, we asked teachers to assign the same essays, with the same due-dates, and to pursue the same primary goals in the two classrooms. We anticipated, and subsequently found, that teachers would schedule similar numbers of peer-review workshops in each classroom setting. However, we found that teachers set aside longer periods of time for workshops in the computer classrooms. In addition, in the computer classrooms teachers engaged in additional, "mini" workshops that lasted for ten or fifteen minutes and occupied time they used for lecture or full-class discussion in the traditional classrooms.

When we asked about interactions during workshops, the teachers indicated that the higher level of interaction among students in the computer classrooms seemed to translate into more productive workshops. Candace indicated that there was a difference in students' seriousness about workshops:

> I think they take it a lot more seriously in the computer classroom. I know they do, and I'm not sure why. But I know that by and large in the traditional classroom after

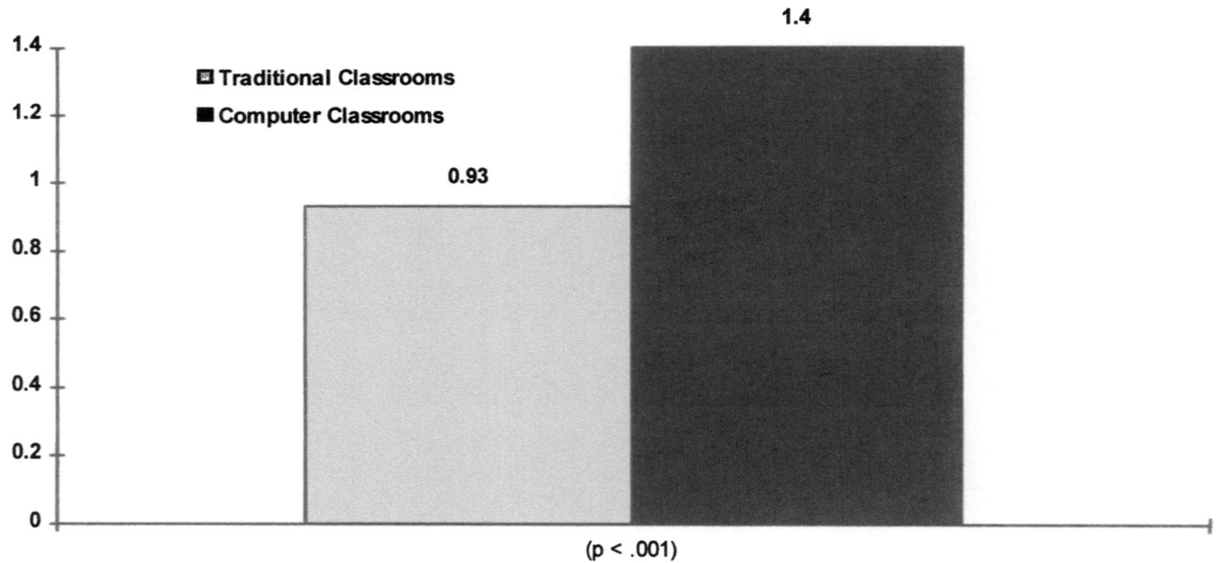

FIGURE 4.10. **Average contacts with classmates per class meeting (from student reports)**

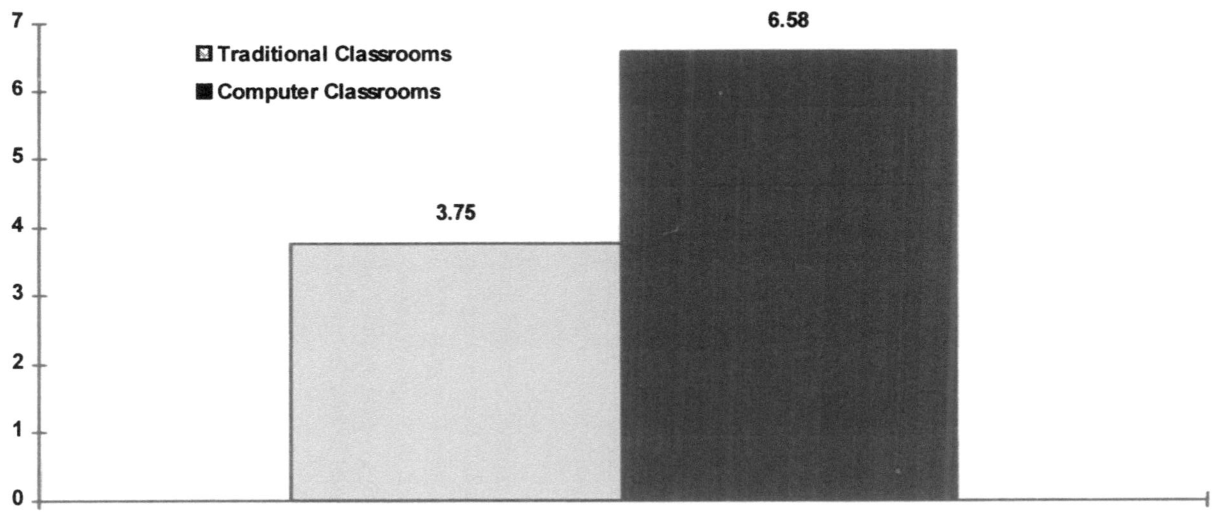

FIGURE 4.11. Average contacts with classmates per class meeting (from classroom observations)

> 15 minutes they're talking about what they did on the weekend or what they're planning to do on the weekend. And in the computer classroom, they're working. And when they finish, they go back to their computers and start revising. I mean, sometimes they'll talk [about social issues], but the degree and frequency is a lot less.

Similarly, Caitlin related the computer classroom's emphasis of in-class drafting to better workshops:

> I think, interaction wise, my students in the computer classroom are more comfortable with workshopping initially than my regular classroom students because they're very used to sitting beside another person who's working on a draft and who says, "Hey Joe, I don't really know what I should do here. What do you think?" And then Joe immediately gives feedback, and so it's something that they've grown accustomed to having happen. Not just at the end of the drafting process, but something that happens continuously throughout the process. It's just there. The student feedback, it's there all the time, and it takes much more effort on the teacher's part to generate that kind of continual feedback in the traditional classroom. I think that's possible, but it does take a lot of work. So, I think that's part of it. The comfort level in the beginning is higher in the computer classroom.

As Candace commented, student interactions in the traditional classroom tended to be social rather than writing related. Student interviews and our observations of the classrooms suggest that students in the computer classrooms appear to have focused their conversations primarily, though certainly not exclusively, on their writing, while students in the traditional classroom were more likely to focus on social issues. In our classroom observations, we noted that the majority of conversations in the computer classrooms concerned student writing. Students asked each other questions about class activities, about upcoming assignments, and about the progress of their papers. Often, students simply asked a classmate to look at a passage in progress. In contrast, students in the traditional classrooms eagerly talked about issues completely unrelated to the goals of the class. In their interviews, students in the computer classrooms reflected on the kinds of conversations they had with their classmates. One remarked that students seemed to feel responsible for working on their writing, while another said that even social talk eventually ended up focusing on writing:

> Mostly there's talk related to class. Of course, there's some social talk. I mean, that's what's going to happen, but most of the time, it is related to class, and if you are getting off task, Ms. S. is right there to get you back on. But I think that most people figure that they're responsible enough to stay on task and they're here to learn so it seems like it was mostly about the writing and the papers and stuff.

> A lot of it is just social talk. You know, did you go to this class? Or this and that. Although a lot of times eventually it does turn to, "Well, how are you doing on this paper? Have you got it done yet? Did you bring your draft today?" And that will sometimes lead to "well, no." And they'll tell what kind of problems they're having, like "I don't have enough research" or "I can't get the documentation down right." Normally, it's almost a really informal workshop because you're actually talking about your paper, and you're getting really indirect feedback on your paper.

In contrast, students in the traditional classrooms indicated that their conversations tended to focus less on writing than on social issues. In the computer classrooms, teachers expected students to work continually on their writing, even when they reached the end of a particular class activity. In the traditional classrooms, students saw the end of an activity as an opportunity to socialize:

> Mostly, and a lot of times within and during class, after you get done with your required work, you tend to slip into a more personal talking mode.

> If we're workshopping, there's going to be a lot of independent conversations, but it's usually about the papers. But after that, there is a lot of social talking, and that's just because there is nothing else to do while we're waiting for everybody else.

> You heard a lot of social talk in here. There was some class related talk, but a lot of it, after you were done was like "what are you doing this weekend?" A lot of it was social talk.

More Contextualized Look at Interaction During Class

One of the most rewarding aspects of the Transitions Study was the opportunity to observe class sessions. As we conducted our observations, we recorded the number of interactions taking place and attempted to identify who interacted with whom. In addition, we also wrote a narrative of what we observed. In some cases, these narratives took the form of brief notes. In others, they took the form of extended prose.

In a classroom observation conducted during the third week of the semester, Jake wrote a detailed narrative description of the two class sessions he observed. As was our practice, he observed the same class session in each classroom, in this case observing two of Caitlin's classes. His narrative description of the two classrooms reveals clear differences in interaction during a DAILY exercise and, later in the class, during a peer-review workshop. We excerpt the lengthy narrative of his visit to Caitlin's computer classroom because it offers insights into differences in interactions between the two classrooms:

> As usual, I arrive at this class early (1:55), only this time I do not realize just how early that is. In fact, what I believe is five minutes early is really fifteen minutes early, since afternoon classes start at ten minutes past the hour. In retrospect, what

might be more remarkable is that I am not the first person waiting in line. Instead, four students are there ahead of me, waiting for the previous class to let out. Furthermore, I am immediately made aware of the fact that these students are all discussing classwork excitedly with one another a full fifteen minutes before the class is even scheduled to begin.

At 2:01 six students and myself enter the classroom. Ms. M. is already inside; she has been observing the previous class. Immediately one of the students rushes up to her in feigned embrace. "Hold that," she responds. "I've got thirteen other things to do first." The student smiles and returns to his computer terminal to start today's lesson.

By five minutes after the hour, ten students are already in the classroom. The room is virtually alive with conversation and work on the computers being done simultaneously. The students are busy logging on and discussing the materials for the next paper, their investigative essay. This is in stark contrast to the scene from this morning where the students sat glued to their seats, silent. One young woman from across the room shouts, "How are you?" to a young man sitting to my right. Drawn in by this friendly remark, the young man quickly bolts from the chair by my side over to the other corner of the room. "Did you get my message?" I hear him asking the woman. He is discussing an e-mail message he sent her between the last class period and this one.

One of the most readily observable facts about this class is that it is in a constant state of motion, and like the two students who discussed the e-mail message, most of the students are actively involved in conversations. Ms. M. seems to be a welcome member of these conversations, but the conversations themselves have a life of their own and are independent of Ms. M's prompting. Several students have apparently been on a trip to Long's Peak over the weekend and now the entire class is participating actively in a recap of the trip. One thing that I notice during this discussion of the Long's Peak trip is that almost all of the students are referring to each other on a first name basis. These students seem to really know one another in a comradely fashion.

By the time 2:10 rolls around many of the students have already completed the DAILY assignment, although there are still quite a few wandering into the room, as well. This state of motion distinguishes this class from the traditional one I observed this morning. It would be virtually impossible to have such a flow of students moving around and coming in and out in the traditional classroom, but here it seems to be working well. To my left, one student is asking another, "Do you mind if I mark on your paper." "Not at all" is the ready response.

By 2:14 there are 21 students present in the class, and Ms. M. asks for everyone's attention. Ms. M. wants to make sure everyone is clear on the assignment she tells them. This brings a hearty laugh from the class and one student makes a remark that

I cannot hear. The message is clear. The students understand the assignment and are anxious to get started on it. Ms. M. is not done with the news yet, however, and so she continues. She reminds the students that she will be out of town for the last half of the week, so if they need to contact her they will need to do by either e-mail or the phone. I am struck by the fact that here is a difference between her morning class and this afternoon's. In the morning class, Ms. M. also mentioned that she would be out of town for the last half of the week, only in that class she only mentioned contacting her by phone, although all students have access to e-mail accounts.

At 2:19, Ms. M. instructs the students to "find a partner and get started" on the assignment. Immediately, the room once again turns to life. As students pair up (most pair up with students that are geographically close to them) and begin work, I notice that there is a lot of checking going on, where one student is looking over the shoulder of the student sitting next to them. "I don't know how to focus my paper," one student says aloud to Ms. M.. She advises him to ask his workshop partner. "All right," the student says, as if by somehow stating the obvious Ms. M. has hit on a previously obscured truth.

As the workshop continues, I notice that there is a great deal of overlap and extension of workshop groups. Although technically the students have only one workshop partner for this exercise, the truth is that students are receiving advice from all of the students surrounding their workstations. Rather than having only one workshop partner, the students have turned the workshop groups into a collection of three to five partnerships each. For example, in the northeast corner of the room is a group of four young women. One student is workshopping another's paper, but when she makes a suggestion for revision, all three join in the discussion. "Your idea is simply no good," two of them chide the third. All four young women laugh in response. Down the row, a group of four young men are having a similarly bantering conversation. One is telling another, "You could have a four paragraph paper here, instead of just two. You have the ideas." Two other students pick up on the remark and all four join into a discussion of how to extend the ideas. These conversations are indicative of others I witness going on around the classroom. The difference between this workshop and the one I witnessed earlier this morning is marked. There, the students remained glued to their workshop sheets, with little interaction with their workshop partners.

Here, in contrast, the exchange of ideas between students is audible and direct.

Closer to me, Ms. M. approaches two young men, workshop partners who have been somewhat absorbed in their own two person group. "Get to know other people, you guys," she warns them, adding that by talking to other students in the class they will improve the feedback they get. Again, I cannot help but note the difference between her interaction with students here and in the traditional classroom, where a far greater number of students seemed to have insulated themselves but without reprimand.

As Ms. M. leaves the two students for the other side of the room, a student catches her attention. His question has to do with how to operate a certain function on the computer. This seems to be a common interaction between the students and Ms. M.. For the most part, computer-related questions seem to go through her first and then to other students. On the other hand, the students seem to ask questions about their papers to each other first, or at least as often as they ask Ms. M.

At 2:30, the room is buzzing with the sound of students. "Boy, you must have learned how to spell 'Hawaii' well after writing this," one is telling another. At the other end of the row, two other voices can be heard. "I don't understand this," one student says to the other. The student does not take the criticism harshly. "I know I need to fix that," she says. "I just haven't had time yet." As I continue to glance around the room only one student seems to be disengaged. He's seated in the north-west corner of the room with his back to the other students, eyes fixed on something going on outside. This pause is, however, only momentary, for in the next instant Matt draws his attention back into the classroom with a question.

Ms. M. is still busy circulating the room answering questions or looking over students' shoulders and giving advice. Apparently, several students have asked a similar question because Ms. M. raises her voice up to speak to the whole class, "Don't get stuck on one question. Remember, you don't have to answer these in order," she says. I again cannot help but notice that this is something she did not do in the traditional classroom. There, questions were kept individualized, compartmentalized. By contrast, here in the computer room there is a clear sense that almost all knowledge is group knowledge. This applies to the students' interactions with one another as well. As mentioned, this workshop is being conducted in pairs, and yet rather than relying only on their group partners, students throw questions out into the air for anyone to answer. As a result questions get answered by a group of students rather than simply an individual. This arrangement at times leads to some disagreement and open discussions among respondents, but all of these discussions seem to be taken openly and not as a challenge to someone else's ego or knowledge.

By 2:40 students are ready to begin printing their workshop responses. They are to make one for the workshop partner and one for Ms. M. A tall male student is the first in line, but his path is impeded by Ms. M. "Are you going to get out of my way, or do I have to knock you down," he jokingly pokes at her. Both know one another well enough to be assured that this is a joke; otherwise, his 6'7" frame might be intimidating. The noise level throughout the rest of the classroom has risen as well as other students are now joining the queue at the printer. "It sounds like some people are finishing up. If so, exchange workshop sheets and discuss what you've found," Ms. M. prompts the class. This quells the noise, but only momentarily. Soon, students are again actively asking one another and Ms. M. questions about their papers. One student turns to Ms. M. and asks, "What's the word I'm looking for?" Three other students are drawn into the discussion by this question and for a moment the four students and Ms. M. brainstorm for the sought-after term. It's Ms. M. who comes up with the correct word: side effects.

Elsewhere around the room two students are discussing the proper placement of quotation marks within a text. Three are discussing a way to format computer files; two are discussing comments on a workshop sheet. Two others are discussing how one of the students might find additional sources. "Look in here," one advises the other. I cannot see what he is pointing out. Again, another student joins the discussion. "Newsbank is a good place to look, too," she adds. This comment, in turn, is heard all the way on the other side of the room and prompts another to ask, "What's Newsbank?"

It's 2:53 and the workshop is winding down. As I look around the room I overhear a student telling Ms. M., "I got torn apart." His voice, however, betrays no malice and before Ms. M. can respond, he adds, "But that's all right. I expected it." He then moves swiftly across the room to discuss a classmate's paper with the writer and another classmate. From across the room, another voice can again be heard. "Is anyone using the printer?"

As class begins to draw to a close, Ms. M. calls everyone to attention. She singles out a student, asking, "What did you learn from your workshopper today?" It is the same question and answer session time that the morning class went through, only this time the students seem eager to share their comments. "I need to organize my examples better," the student responds. "How about you?" Ms. M. asks another student. "I need to provide more evidence," the student responds immediately, without hesitation. "Where are you going to put that," Ms. M. follows up. Again, the student doesn't hesitate but points to a specific place in her paper. This drill reminds me of a sergeant and a bunch of boot camp recruits, only the students seem to be enjoying their experience in this instance. Two more students are next in line. They too respond promptly and with a specific suggestion for improvement in their own papers. The first needs more facts, he says. "How are you going to do that?" Ms. M. inquires. "I'll go back to the library," he responds, although his voice gives away the fact that this is a chore he does not look forward to.

At 3:01 the class dismisses for the day. As the students file out, the air is still filled with conversation, only most of the conversation seems to revolve around the cold outside and who has what class next. As I too leave, three students remain behind to ask Ms. M. a question.

What we find interesting about this observation narrative is not just the level of detail that Jake captured as he observed Caitlin's teaching, but also the human face these descriptions put on our quantitative data showing greater interaction in the computer classroom. Clearly, even after just three weeks of class, students in this computer classroom were building patterns of interaction quite unlike those of Caitlin's traditional classroom students. As the semester progressed, these patterns of interaction contributed to classroom environments that differed markedly.

ALTERNATIVE DESIGNS FOR COMPUTER-SUPPORTED WRITING CLASSROOMS

As experienced teachers know, we can change the dynamics of the classroom if we change its physical layout. These changes, in turn, can shape the patterns of interaction that take place among students and teachers. Some classroom layouts, such as when teachers in traditional classrooms ask students to form a circle or semi-circle with their movable desks, help bring students together. Other layouts, such as clustering desks together, encourage students to work in small groups, isolated from other groups but focused on the classmates in their cluster. Similarly, teachers alter the physical space of classrooms by changing their positions within that space. As Barker and Kemp (1990) describe, some teachers prefer the proscenium model of teaching with the teacher at the front of the room, clearly taking center stage. But writing teachers have long recognized the importance of working closely with students, and so many of us walk around our traditional classrooms. If the room does not have enough space to accommodate a circle or semi-circle, teachers walk up and down aisles. During workshops, we've observed teachers climbing over desks to get to groups that have clustered in the corners distant from the front of the room. In short, experienced teachers in traditional classrooms learn the limitations of those physical designs and adapt numerous techniques to alter spatial features of the room and thus shape student behaviors.

Computer classrooms, on the other hand, look like foreign territory, even to many experienced teachers. Because the computers need constant power and are generally too bulky to move, teachers can no longer move the classroom furniture in ways they want. Moreover, the classroom's architecture imposes limitations on the flexibility of the room by fixing the location of the computers. In this section, we look in some detail at the advantages and disadvantages of alternative computer classroom designs.

Rows, Pods, and Circles

If architects or engineers design computer classrooms without teachers' input, they often fall back on the traditional school model of rows of desks or tables facing the front of the room (see Figure 4.12). Unfortunately, this design is the most limiting for teachers and students in computer-supported writing classrooms. Typically, computer monitors are too high for students to see most of the whiteboard, and even the teacher disappears from view all too often unless the front of

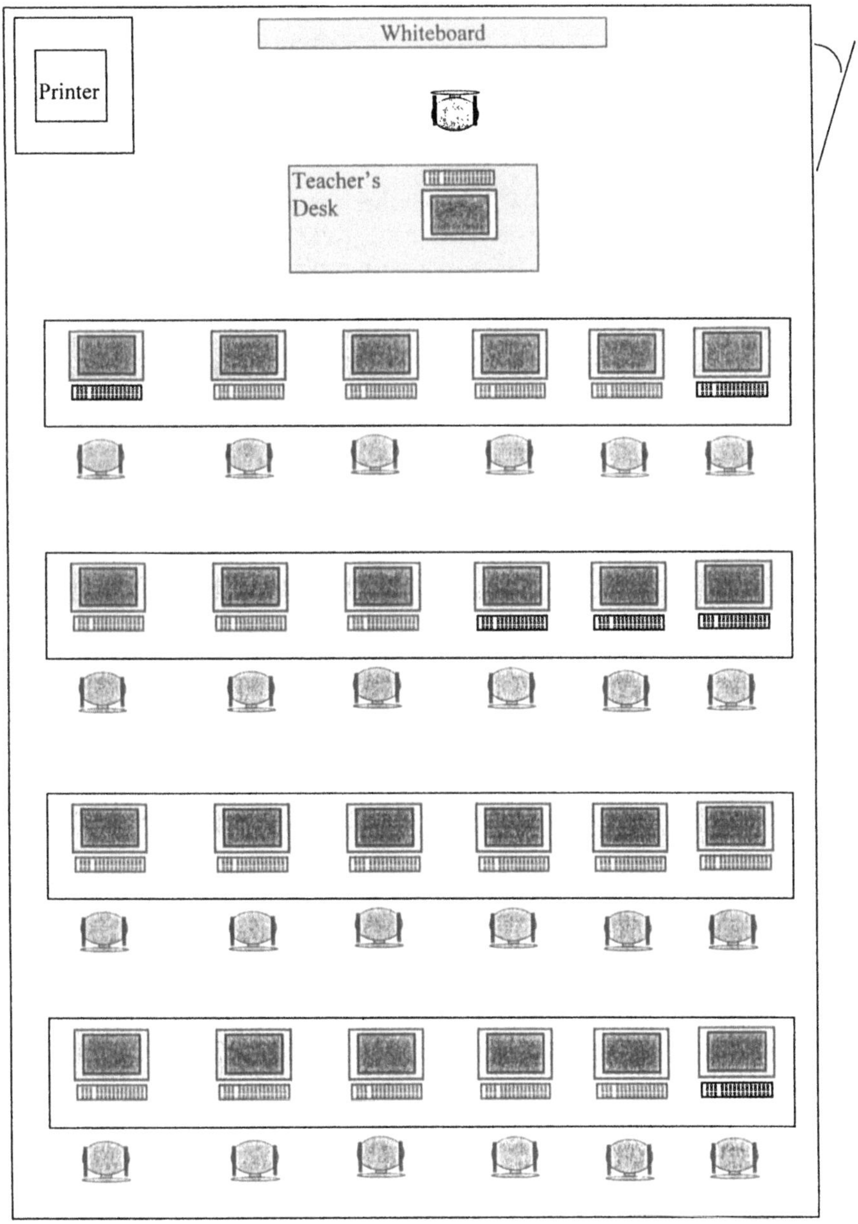

FIGURE 4.12. Computer classroom arranged in rows

the room also has a teacher's platform. Students collaborate with peers sitting next to them but cannot see the computer monitors if they try to work in clusters with other students in a row in front or in back of them. Finally, although most designers allow adequate room for chairs behind each computer, they usually do not allow extra room for someone to walk behind occupied chairs. A teacher who wants to walk along rows to talk to students or to read work-in-progress from their computer screens must squeeze behind each chair or ask students to scoot up.

In effect, this room layout minimizes teacher contact of all sorts: not only are teachers effectively limited in their attempts to go to students, but students have great difficulty even seeing the teacher. We have attended workshops or classes in computer classrooms with this design, and we have reacted much as we expect our students do in similar environments. We play with software rather than pay attention to the teacher; we feel frustrated because the teacher can't see an upraised hand; and we socialize with people sitting next to us when we become bored. Because the computer monitors block the teacher's view of us as well as our view of the teacher, we feel little concern about not paying attention to the teacher. Forward-facing rows, we feel, are the least conducive to productive writing instruction, even when compared to traditional classrooms with immovable desks (e.g., lecture halls).

Rather than reinforce the model of the teacher-centered, *teacher-fronted* classroom, some computer classroom designs help break students out of the assumption that physical space reinforces the teacher's authority over them. Pods and variations of circles all work much more effectively in computer-classroom design.

We define pods as small clusters of computers—usually three or four but as many as eight to a cluster—with the computers facing the center of the cluster (see Figure 4.13). As Carolyn Boiarsky (1990) explains, this arrangement most closely models the newsroom bullpen, where "interaction is not only facilitated, but natural. Looking inward toward each other, students make eye contact easily, extending and accepting invitations for collaboration" (p. 53). Because the pods have enough room between them for comfortable movement, teachers circulate to read over students' shoulders, to set up impromptu conferences, or to answer questions. Because the pods encourage students to look at and talk to each other, they facilitate interactions among students as well. Boiarsky claims that her students ask for help from each other on a full range of writing questions, such as effective openings, appropriate supporting detail, and minor details of editing.

The disadvantages of the pods are obvious. For those occasions when a teacher wants to conduct a full-class discussion, the pods create the same visual blocks that rows of computers do. Students can't see each other or the teacher, and if the classroom has a whiteboard or projector screen, students can't see most of that either. Klem and Moran (1992) explain that teachers in their classroom with a pod design solve the problem when they ask students to move their chairs

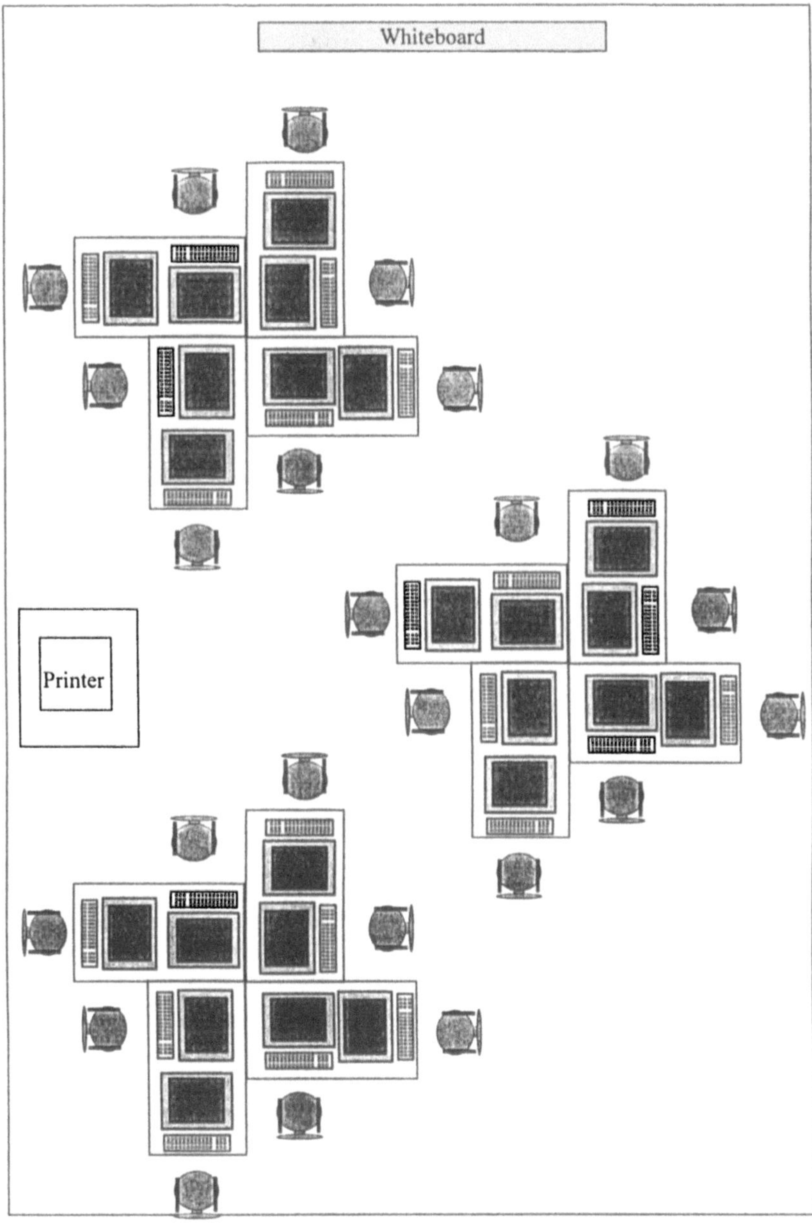

FIGURE 4.13. Computer classroom arranged in pods

into a corner of the room, away from the computers. Although this solution removes the problem of viewing other participants in the discussion, students can't refer to text on the computer unless they first print. Moreover, on our campus, we cannot convert a classroom large enough to accommodate several pods (because they take more floor space than other designs) *and* an area for discussion. Without adequate room at one side or one end of the room, students are jammed into the "discussion" space and are still unable to see each other as they face a teacher directing the discussion.

A circle design, with computers placed around the perimeter of the room, creates adequate space for the computers, for free movement in the room, and for large-group discussions (see Figure 4.14). When a teacher wants to get everyone's attention, no computers block students' view of the teacher, whiteboard, or projector screen. Asking students to participate in discussions from their computers allows them to refer to text on the screen. Or, teachers can ask students to move to the large group of tables in the center of the room for a seminar-like arrangement. Teachers can also separate the tables in the center to accommodate several small groups working on hardcopy of drafts or working with both paper and computer-based texts.

The most glaring disadvantage of this classroom design is that students face the wall as they work. Because students are territorial, they also tend to return to the same computer day after day. In doing so, they learn the names of people sitting on either side of them but may not interact with students on the other side of the room unless encouraged by the teacher. (We take up specific ways to encourage interactions throughout the room in Chapter Seven.)

Learning Names Encourages Student-Student Interaction:

On the first day of class, take a roll of tape and pieces of recycled paper that are still blank on one side. (There are always hundreds of such sheets of paper near the computer printer.) Ask students to fold the paper to make a 3-D triangle. They write their name on one face and then stand the paper on the top of the computer monitor they're working at. As you walk around the room, study names and heads, occasionally interrupting students to look at their faces, too. When students come to the center table, ask them to bring their name placards with them.

To encourage students to take different chairs and to interact with more students in the classroom, collect the name placards after you know students' names. For a week or so, distribute the placards randomly around the room before students arrive. As they get settled, remind them to re-introduce themselves to the students on either side.

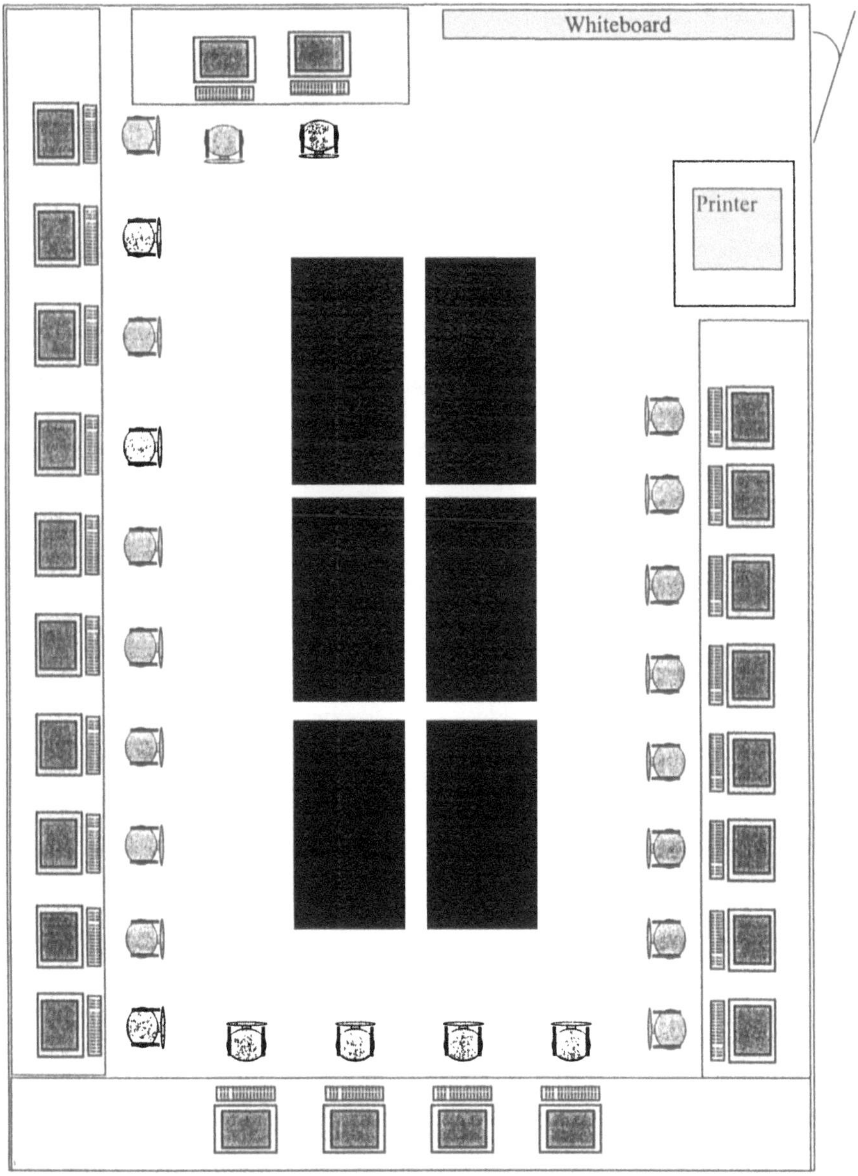

FIGURE 4.14. Computer classroom arranged in circle

Variations of the circle or perimeter design include semi-circles and concentric circles. The semi-circle or "U" configuration better accommodates a teacher position, a possible disadvantage of the pod and full circle designs. The semi-circle allows focused discussion at one end of the room—with a whiteboard, projection screen, and, perhaps, a teacher's desk (see Figure 4.15). Teachers sometimes find having students on all sides in the full circle design disconcerting. Like "theater-in-the-round," the full-circle design means teachers must constantly scan the entire room to see if students have questions. And if the teacher wants to use a projector or whiteboard, some students in the full circle design must either move their chairs or see the board less clearly.

Concentric circles are set up so that students all face the center, in which case the disadvantages of rows come into play. Or they can be set up with one circle of computers facing the center of the room and an inner circle facing the perimeter of the room (see Figure 4.16). This arrangement has the advantages of pods where students look up and make eye contact with other students but requires a large enough room so that teachers and students can move comfortably behind the outer ring. The inner circle might also cut down considerably on the space available for discussion and consultation in the center of the room. Like the pod design, this arrangement requires a much larger room than the other designs.

When we look at these layouts for computer classrooms, it's helpful to think in terms of physical and psychological barriers to interaction. Visualize each of the layouts, for a moment, as a series of bridges and moats. The design based on rows provides bridges between students, but only between adjacent students; moats separate the rows of students from the teacher and from each other. The full circle or perimeter design bridges the space between students and, in effect, joins all the computer users. (This is only one of several good reasons for teachers to have their own computer during class time.) Physically, the moat between the circle of computers and the central tables is much less intimidating than the moat separating students from the front of a proscenium classroom because the tables are shared space, not teacher space. (Interestingly, in the "U" design, students avoid walking in the moat at the teacher's end of the classroom.)

The pod design creates bridges between students in a pod but separates pods with moats. Depending on how freely students feel they can cross these moats as they move around the room, students may become stationary in a pod design. The concentric circle design might appear at first glance to have the least physical intimidation. But, in effect, students, even though they face each other, cannot reach each other across the moat that separates the two circles of computers. Because physical contact is distanced in this design, it seems to have less intimacy than the pod arrangement.

Teachers, of course, have the authority to cross both bridges and moats whenever they desire in the psychological model of classrooms our educational system inculcates from the earliest days of schooling. But in this model, students aren't

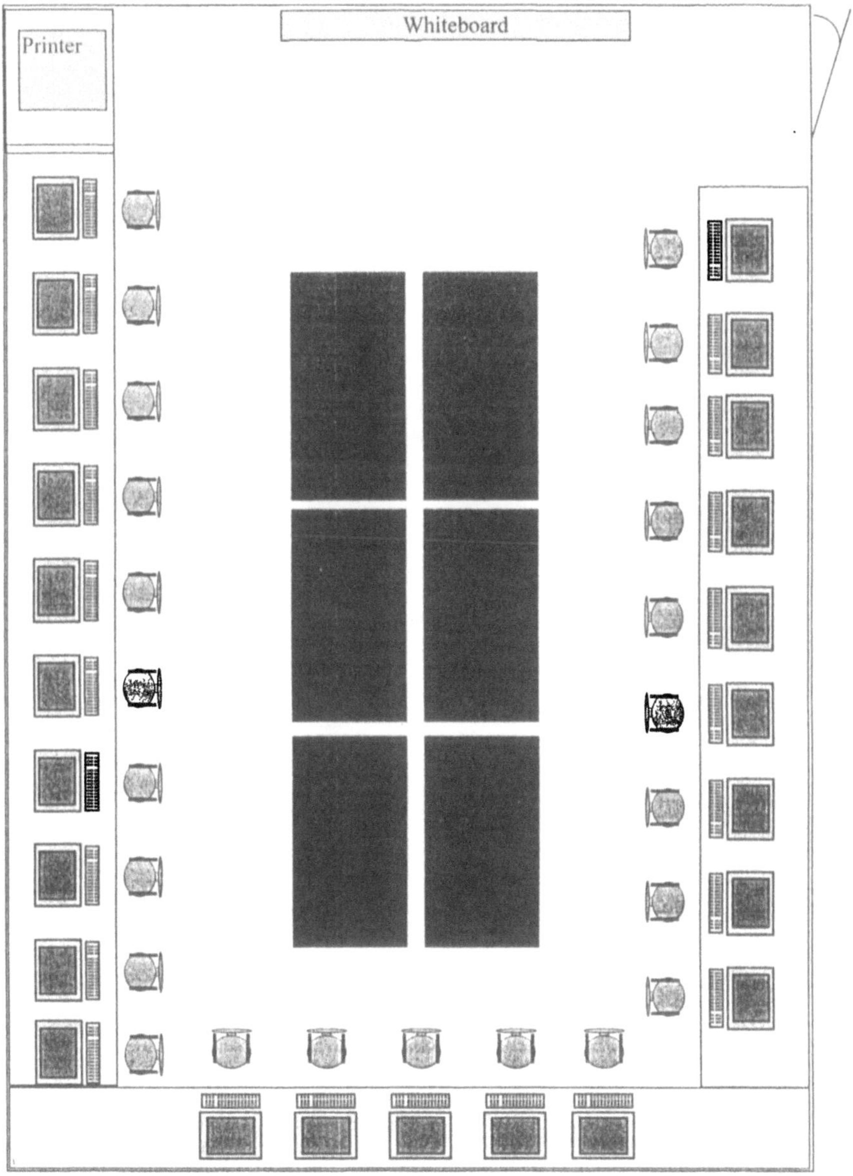

FIGURE 4.15. Computer classroom arranged in semi-circle

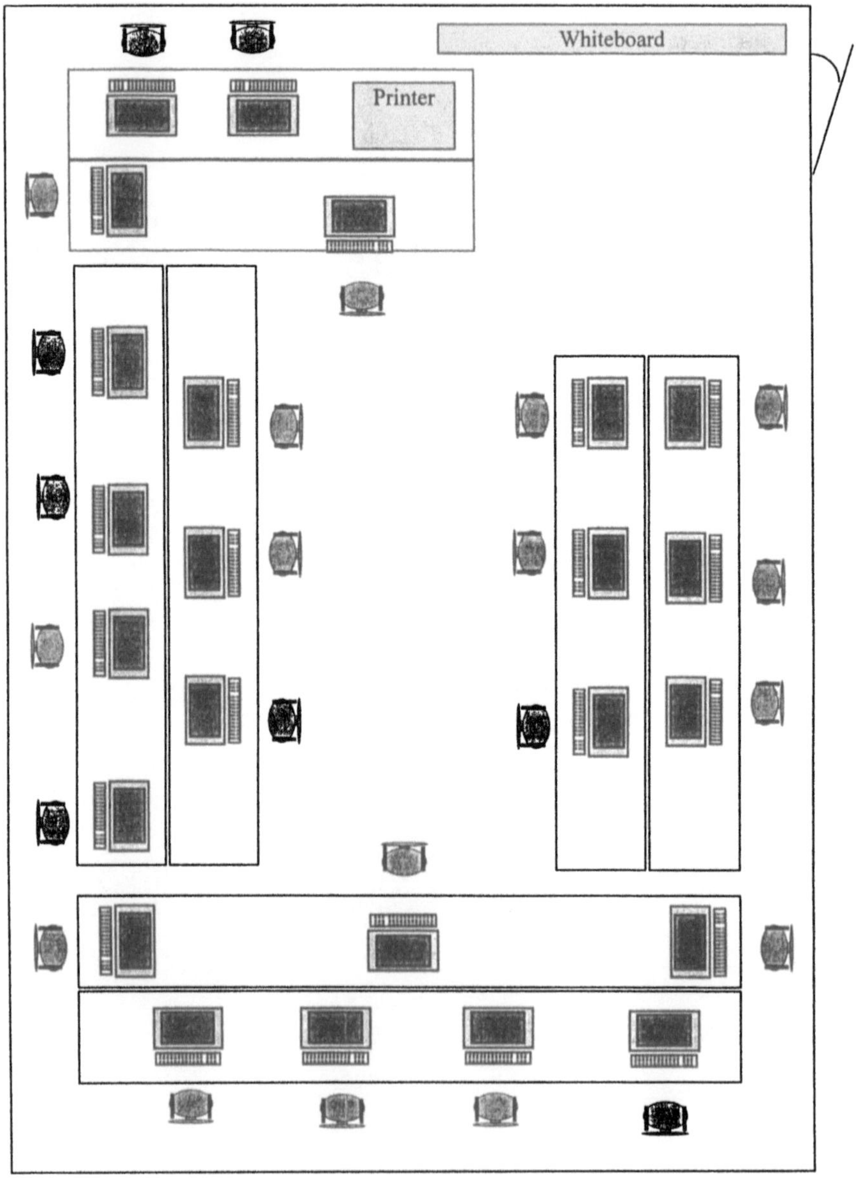

FIGURE 4.16. Computer classroom arranged in concentric circles

Teachers Encourage Face-To-Face Interaction in Any Computer-Classroom Setting:

Design a collaborative activity with pairs of students so that they share one computer and get used to reading from each other's screen.

Set up an activity through DAILY that first asks students to write and then to read from a partner's screen before they return to their own writing to incorporate their partner's viewpoint.

In several early activities, follow up individual writing with small-group activities.

supposed to cross moats, and so the power of the physical barriers in a computer classroom becomes much more obvious.

In sum, when we want students to interact comfortably with their teachers and peers, we must provide not only the atmosphere of community that so many writing scholars discuss, but also a setting that reduces the impediments of physical barriers.

Equipping the Computer Classroom

Computer users always argue about the best hardware (Mac versus PC) and the best word-processing software. Institutional constraints, such as compatibility, cost, and available support systems, always affect those decisions more than any other factors, and so we will not address those points here. Rather, we want to add just a few words about other "furnishings" in the computer classroom that affect the physical space and how teachers and students use it.

As we note previously, designs that foster flexibility seem most advantageous to us. Additionally, flexible furniture allows teachers to adjust the classroom to their needs. Chairs with wheels, for instance, seem like a luxury, but they make movement in the computer classroom so much easier that they are preferable, particularly when they cost no more than chairs with legs. Similarly, a large table in the discussion area provides space for students' books or papers as well as a solid writing surface for those who want to take notes. Several small tables can be pushed together to form a large table or spread apart for small-group work. In our computer classrooms, we opt for the flexibility of several small, movable tables.

Most writing teachers find that they occasionally want to capture the key points of large-group discussion on a whiteboard. Again, we argue for a board on wheels that moves completely out of view when teachers don't need it. Without this feature, teachers and students view the whiteboard as constituting the front of the classroom, and teachers tend to gravitate to a place near the front, just as students tend to avoid it.

One other useful item to consider for a computer-supported writing classroom is an LCD panel or computer display unit. An LCD panel attaches to a computer but fits over the horizontal surface of an overhead projector. Whatever appears on the computer monitor also appears on the LCD panel and is projected onto the wall or pull-down screen in the classroom. Our teachers find the LCD panel particularly useful when they explain or demonstrate new ways to use the software in our computer classrooms. For instance, teachers often use the LCD panel as they connect to the Internet and then walk through a search so that students see how to use search engines.

If you plan to include a whiteboard or a projector screen in your computer classroom, make sure that students can see it. Some classroom designs privilege one-on-one interaction so much that students are at a serious disadvantage when they engage in full-class activities.

Decisions about what software to include in a computer-supported writing classroom is frequently contentious. Some teachers (e.g., see Schroeder & Boe, 1990) believe in a minimalist approach. That is, students need only simple word processing software to write; other software is distracting and expensive. Other teachers argue that the full range of software tools currently available makes the computer-supported classroom the most attractive writing environment for both teachers and students.

Although we understand both arguments, we feel strongly that some kind of networking is far superior to a classroom with stand-alone computers. We are not convinced, however, that the so-called "master-slave" technology is appropriate for writing classes. "Master-slave" setups involve one computer controlling what appears on the other computers. Teachers who advocate this technology frequently cite the advantage of taking an engaging opening paragraph from one student's paper and "projecting" it onto the screens of all the computers in the classroom so that students can read the sample text and discuss its effectiveness. This application sounds appealing and intriguing, and teachers can certainly imagine other positive uses for such network capabilities.

Unfortunately, this remote control network also allows the "master" computer to silently tap into every other computer and monitor student work. In our experience, reading what students write as they compose and revise is advantageous for both students and teachers because students comfortably ask for help and teachers easily determine the best times to intervene. But we feel that "reading over the shoulder" needs to be open and obvious. In our computer classrooms, students know when the teachers walk around the room. If they are drafting a piece too personal to share with the class, they are welcome to turn down the brightness on their computer screen so that no one else can read it. We've also found that students feel comfortable saying to teachers, "Don't read this now; come back in a few minutes." With the remote control technology, students don't know when

Planning Tips:

Although a few colleges and universities mandate integrating computers into the curriculum from the top, most schools will not build or remodel computer classrooms without the impetus of teachers and program directors. In effect, writing teachers who know little about physical layout might suddenly find themselves in charge of major remodeling plans. (Both Kate and Mike have found themselves in this position.) We offer just a few points you might consider as you plan a computer classroom:

- Consider your philosophy of writing instruction. If you expect to schedule classes during which students complete drill-and-practice programs or tutorials, then almost any design works. But if you include classes that emphasize workshops and collaboration, consider carefully the advantages and disadvantages of designs we discuss above.
- Plan for flexibility. The classroom design typically lasts much longer than any single faculty member and perhaps even longer than some courses currently offered at your school. A design that allows for flexible use of the furniture is more comfortable for teachers and students. You'll also find that you will use the room for a wider range of courses than you first imagined. For example, although we designed our room with first-year composition students in mind, we now schedule all levels of writing courses, teacher education courses, small literature courses, and graduate courses in our computer classrooms.
- *Do not* plan for growth. Don't assume that you can add additional machines and shoehorn more students into the classroom at some point in the future. Design the room for comfortable and safe movement of the maximum number of students who enroll in the courses you plan to offer in that environment. Then, limit enrollment so that every student has a computer and everyone has enough room to work comfortably. Don't forget to leave enough room between or beside computers for students to put books and papers. And think, too, about where coats and backpacks get stowed during winter class sessions.
- Think about special heating and, especially, cooling requirements. Although new computers generate less heat than older models, 20 to 25 computers and printers in a room can raise the room temperature over 12 hours of daily use.
- Think about sharing space. If you cannot get a large enough room dedicated for computer-supported writing, ask other departments if they could use a computer-supported classroom in their curriculum as well. If so, you might get a larger or more desirable room because it will be used for more hours of the day. Or you might argue with your administrators that in the hours the classroom is not used for classes, it can function as a drop-in lab.

teachers read their work, and all sense of privacy and control over the writing evaporates. We value student ownership of texts and thus contend that this particular technology can seriously undermine the trust that underlies all effective interaction in a writing classroom.

CLASSROOM DESIGN AND INTERACTION

Although we discuss at great length the importance of the classroom setting on interactions among classmates and between students and teachers, these concerns are not unique to computer classrooms. Writing teachers scheduled into laboratories (with massive stone lab tables) and lecture halls (with 100 or more fixed chairs) always protest that the classroom setting seriously disadvantages students taking a writing course. The questions we raise here are extensions of those affecting all teachers as they consider the physical arrangement and attributes of their classrooms.

The computer-supported writing classroom is unique, however, in that writing teachers often do have a voice in its design, and they certainly choose how to use the space to their advantage. As we have pointed out repeatedly in this chapter, one of the unexpected advantages for students is the increased level of interaction, not just with the teacher, but also with classmates. As we continue to look at the complex interactions of computers and writing students, we need to keep in mind that the physical setting itself is a key component of the instructional context, one that teachers must acknowledge if we are to use it to our students' advantage.

5

Writing in the Classroom: Student and Teacher Perspectives

Writing teachers seem surprisingly uncritical of the fact that little, if any, writing is done in most writing classes. As we've come to understand writing instruction in the past few decades, writing is something that is discussed, critiqued, analyzed, and read during writing classes. It is not, however, something that is *done*. Occasionally, teachers ask students to make brief forays into a writing activity during a class session; brainstorming or free-writing, for instance, are staples of many classrooms. For the most part, however, it is a rare writing class in which writing occurs as the dominant classroom activity. Even classes based on a workshop model generally devote more class time to peer review and critique than to composing or revising.

George Hillocks' "modes of instruction" in writing classrooms underscore the notion that writing, as an activity, is marginalized in the writing classroom. In his meta-analysis of research on writing instruction, published in the mid-1980s as a follow-up to Braddock, Lloyd-Jones, and Shoer's 1963 *Research on Written Composition*, Hillocks (1986) identifies three modes of instruction: the presentational mode, the natural-process mode, and the environmental mode. Hillocks also identifies a fourth mode that, for the purposes of our discussion, is less relevant. In this mode, the individual mode, "students receive instruction through tutorials, programmed materials of some kind, or a combination of the two" (p. 126).

The presentational mode, the most teacher-centered mode, involves front-of-the-classroom activities led by the teacher, a focus on models or rules of writing, and teacher-feedback on written texts. The natural-process mode, the most student-centered mode, stresses out-of-class writing assignments on student-selected topics which are addressed to an audience of peers, extensive use of peer feedback during class sessions, a focus on revision, and high levels of interaction among students during class. Hillocks calls the teacher in the natural-process classroom functions "a 'facilitator' who frees the student's imagination and promotes growth by sustaining a positive classroom atmosphere" (p. 119). Teachers who follow Hillocks' preferred mode, the environmental mode, take a middle-ground position between the prescriptive presentational mode and the reactive natural-process mode. They focus on creating environments in which students engage in processes "important to some particular aspect of writing" and in "activities, such as small-group problem-centered discussions, conducive to high levels of peer interaction concerning specific tasks" (p. 122).

In creating these broad categories, Hillocks draws on work conducted by a number of researchers who share his goal of understanding the factors that contribute to successful writing instruction. What we find most intriguing, of course, is that none of these modes includes writing as the central classroom activity of writing classes. The operating assumption seems to be that class time is best spent preparing students for the act of writing rather than engaging them in that act. This is clearly the case with classrooms that Hillocks characterizes as presentational, in which teachers impart information to students primarily through front-of-the-classroom teaching techniques. But it is also the case in most natural-process and environmental classrooms, where writing—when it is used—is usually carried out as an activity designed to help students explore ideas or develop competence in specific aspects of writing processes.

Regardless of whether we accept Hillocks' categories *in toto*, his characterizations are grounded in the observations and interpretations of writing researchers who have observed a variety of classrooms and discussed teaching with a wide range of teachers. Most experienced writing teachers reject the notion that these categories are mutually exclusive—in fact, most writing teachers use teaching strategies that fall into more than one of Hillocks' categories. For our purposes, we are primarily interested in the assumption—apparently long held by teachers and researchers—that writing is not an activity well suited to the writing classroom.

In this chapter, we explore the role that writing played in the traditional and computer-supported writing classrooms that we observed in the Transitions and New Teachers Studies. We draw heavily on classroom observations and interviews conducted with the teachers and students who participated in the studies. Our discussion focuses on seven related topics:

- drafting as a central activity in the computer classrooms,
- the relationship between in-class drafting and classroom interaction,
- the impact of classroom context on revising,
- the relationship between in-class drafting and student improvement as writers,

- perceptions of empowerment and control over student writing,
- the impact of DAILY writing assignments on student attitudes about writing, and
- the shift during the semester to more writing in the traditional classrooms.

DRAFTING IN THE COMPUTER CLASSROOMS

One of the most intriguing differences in the Transitions Study was teachers' use of in-class drafting in the two classroom settings. Although teachers relied heavily on in-class drafting in the computer classroom, they largely ignored it as a classroom activity in the traditional classrooms. In the traditional classroom, as we point out in the previous chapter and take up in more detail in Chapters Six and Seven, teachers tended to rely on activities that fostered talk about writing rather than engaging students in writing itself. Activities teachers used most frequently in the traditional classroom included group work, peer review, whole-class discussions, and lecture. In contrast, students began most class sessions in the computer classroom with a DAILY writing assignment and frequently worked, either individually or in groups, on writing assignments or writing activities that contributed to progress on a writing assignment.

The difference in the use of writing activities and in-class drafting was particularly apparent early in the semester. As the semester progressed and the teachers began to consider how activities in one classroom setting might transfer to the other, teachers assigned more writing activities in the traditional classrooms. At no point in the semester, however, did the time spent writing during class become comparable.

In our classroom observations, we saw that Candace clearly adapted class plans to emphasize in-class writing in the computer classroom (see Table 5.1 for details on the paired class plans). In February, students wrote responses to DAILY in the computer classroom for 25 minutes, but in the paired traditional class students wrote by hand for only 10 minutes, the remainder of the time being given to large-group discussion. In March, students composed on the keyboard for 30 minutes at the beginning of the computer class and then moved into discussion; in the traditional classroom, students wrote on paper for only 10 minutes of class.

Similarly, the details of Anita's classes showed a marked preference given to students' writing on the keyboard (see Table 5.2). In October, the computer class had a substantial portion of class time (30 minutes) to begin drafting their papers. In the paired traditional class, Anita instead moved students through a series of guided prewriting activities. In other words, students wrote, but about generic topics and in generic ways rather than thinking through and drafting on their own topic. In November, Anita's computer class spent the entire class period working on their drafts-in-progress; Anita did not even offer students the option of collab-

TABLE 5.1.
Candace's Class Plans as Described by Classroom Observers

Traditional class	Computer class
2-16-94	**2-16-94**
guided annotation of assigned essay (10 min)	students write DAILY responses to reading assignment (25 min)
students practice writing a response (10 min)	large-group discussion of reading and their responses (25 min)
large-group discussion of responses (30 min)	
3-9	**3-9**
question/answers on progress with current assignment (20 min)	students write DAILY responses to reading assignment (30 min)
reading professional essay (20 min)	large-group discussion of reading and their responses (20 min)
write-to-learn task (10 min)	
4-13	**4-13**
reading text (20 min)	reading text material (15 min)
large-group discussion of documentation (20 min)	discussion of reading and use of documentation (25 min)
brief workshop on drafts (10 min)	peer-review workshop focused on use of sources (10 min)
5-2	**5-2**
large-group discussion of sample essay (25 min)	large-group discussion of sample essay (15 min)
workshop pairs (25 min)	students drafting individually and consulting in workshop pairs (35 min)

orating on an arguing exercise. In her traditional class, students chose between revising their papers or working on a generic exercise, but the observer noted that many students chose not to revise their work during that class period. In effect, Anita's choices of in-class activities reinforced students' notions that students and their writing were at the center in the computer classroom but peripheral to the traditional classroom.

Jen, who devoted almost all class time to workshop on the days that we observed her class, still made concessions to the different format of the classrooms (see Table 5.3). In February, students wrote on the collecting exercise for almost 2.5 times longer in the computer classroom than in the traditional classroom. If we add the 13 minutes of writing time devoted to DAILY, then we see that her students in the computer classroom spent 43 of 50 minutes writing during class. In addition, the in-class writing superseded large-group discussion in Jen's classes. In February and again in April, we see students spending more time

TABLE 5.2.
Anita's Class Plans as Described by Classroom Observers

Traditional class	Computer class
9-10-93	**9-10-93**
freewriting (10 min)	freewriting (10 min)
modeling peer review on a sample essay (writing, small groups, and large-group discussion) (40 min)	modeling peer review on a sample essay (writing, small groups, and large-group discussion) (40 min)
10-13	**10-13**
large-group discussion of writing a response (20 min)	introduction of response assignment (lecture-discussion format) (20 min)
guided prewriting activities for response (30 min)	students draft response on computers (30 min)
11-17	**11-15***
students worked on an argument worksheet or revised argument drafts (individual and small-group work; mini-conferences) (50 min)	students revised argument drafts and discussed work in progress with teacher and peers (individual work and mini-conferences) (50 min)

Note: *Observers asked teachers to have them attend parallel class sessions. Often, teachers were covering similar material on different days because one class took longer on an activity or teachers were otherwise adjusting their schedules.

writing and less time discussing in the computer classroom than their peers in the traditional classroom.

Caitlin's class plans show not only that her computer classroom students did more in-class writing but also that she built upon that writing in ways that changed the class plan (see Table 5.4). In October, for instance, Caitlin knew that her DAILY task would take up about 10 minutes in the computer class, so she assigned the essay postscript for homework. Students in the traditional class completed the postscript during class instead of writing about the summary/response assignment as did students in the computer classroom. In the traditional class, students did not have a writing task to prime them for a discussion of summarizing, and so their ten-minute question/answer session relied heavily on the teacher's presentation of information. In contrast, students in the computer classroom took 10 minutes to respond to this prompt: "Brainstorm two lists below. One, what are the criteria for an effective summary? Two, what are the criteria for an effective response?" By reading over their shoulders, Caitlin could tell that students knew the key criteria, and so she felt confident about moving them directly from their writing about summary into a workshop on drafts of summaries and beginning their revisions based on peer commentary in the workshop.

Instead of a question/answer session on summary, students in Caitlin's computer classroom substituted a lively discussion about an activity they had com-

TABLE 5.3.
Jen's Class Plans as Described by Classroom Observers

Traditional class	Computer class
2-14-94	**2-14-94**
misc. announcements and introduction of assignment (20 min)	DAILY and introduction of assignment (13 min)
idea-gathering writing activity (12 min)	idea-gathering writing activity (30 min)
large-group discussion (20 min)	large-group discussion (7 min)
3-9	**3-9**
portfolio workshop (50 min)	portfolio workshop (50 min)
4-6	**4-6**
peer review of drafts (45 min)	draft workshop (50 min)
large-group discussion of workshop reviews (5 min)	
5-2	**5-2**
misc. announcements (8 min)	misc. announcements (10 min)
portfolio workshop (40 min)	portfolio workshop (40 min)

TABLE 5.4.
Caitlin's Class Plans as Described by Classroom Observers

Traditional class	Computer class
9-13-93	**9-13-93**
review assignments (10 min)	review assignment (10 min)
lecture-discussion on peer-review techniques (10 min)	workshop on investigating draft (40 min)
workshop on investigating (30 min)	
10-22	**10-22**
students write postscript for portfolio (20 min)	DAILY (9 min)
question/answer session on summary (10 min)	large-group discussion of computer activity (15 min)
workshop on draft (20 min)	workshop on draft (20 min)
11-3	**11-1**
question/answer session about problems with current draft (20 min)	workshop (15 min)
peer-review workshop on arguing draft (30 min)	large-group discussion (5 min)
	mini-conferences during continued revision work (30 min)

pleted during the prior class session: they e-mailed comments on drafts to each other. As the observer noted, "Discussion here is truly outspoken. Everyone seems willing to express their viewpoints at length. . . . It's the students who're keeping this discussion going. Caitlin's not asking questions. The students are building on one another's responses."

In other words, Caitlin used the DAILY assignment in the computer classroom to substitute for what was largely a presentational activity in her traditional class. By incorporating the DAILY into her class plan, Caitlin rearranged the entire lesson to give students a discussion that engaged and stimulated their thinking about peer review and technology. She set students up effectively for their peer-review workshop without laboring over the key concepts of summarizing for students who showed they already understood the writing task.

Caitlin, like Jen, also shifted class time to emphasize writing rather than discussion. In November, students in the traditional classroom discussed their work-in-progress for about 20 minutes, but the parallel discussion only took five minutes in the computer classroom. Caitlin gave students in the traditional classroom 30 minutes for peer review. Students in the computer classroom completed a 15-minute peer-review workshop, and then spent 30 minutes of class time meeting individually with Caitlin or revising their papers, during which time students informally continued to discuss revisions with peers.

The four teachers in the Transitions Study quickly discovered that students in the computer classroom take full advantage of time devoted to in-class writing in ways that students in a traditional classroom do not. No doubt, many writing teachers in traditional classrooms tell students that they can begin drafting or revising, only to have students socialize or pack their backpacks because they assume that class is really over, that the writing is "busy work" or "filler." Of course, some students in computer classrooms also need reminding to attend to the task at hand, but most students turn eagerly to drafting and revising in the computer classroom whereas those in the traditional classroom often need cajoling, as Candace described it. Our teachers' plans throughout the study reflect their increased use of computer classroom time for writing and revising.

We suspect that the greater emphasis on in-class writing in the computer classroom depends, at least in part, on the attitudes students and teachers bring to the two classrooms. The traditional classroom, structured as it is in ways similar to other classrooms that the students and teachers have experienced, does not seem to challenge the teachers or students to treat writing in ways encouraged by the computer classroom, which differs radically from the traditional classroom in design and facilities. The computer classroom allows students and teachers to look beyond their assumptions about appropriate practices in a writing classroom and explore writing as an integral part of the in-class instructional mix. As we claim at the end of our discussion about student and teacher attitudes about writing during class, the shift to incorporate in-class drafting and interaction is not necessarily an easy one: it clearly involves developing a new set of teaching strategies suited to the dynamics of the computer-supported writing classroom.

An additional explanation of differences in in-class drafting in the two classrooms stems from the greater ease with which computer-generated text is integrated into writing outside the classroom. During the Transitions Study, students in the traditional classrooms were vocal about this issue, noting that it annoyed them (at the least) to retype text they had generated by hand during class. Students in the computer classrooms, in contrast, commented that they appreciated the time they could save by drafting during class (an outcome that was not generally intended by the teachers) and the ease of immediately putting to use information they had assimilated from class discussions, group work, or peer reviews. We explore these attitudes in more detail in the next section.

Attitudes about Writing During Class

As we point out in Chapter Three, students and teachers in the two classroom settings had distinctly different attitudes about writing during class. Teachers consistently expressed disappointment with the reactions that greeted them when they asked students to write in the traditional classrooms. In her mid-semester interview, Candace said:

> It's almost impossible to get people to draft with a pen and piece of paper in the traditional classroom. . . If I have students sitting around in a circle doing freewriting by hand, I find that they're resistant. They're lethargic. They roll their eyes. They often don't want to do it.

She picked up on this theme in her final interview, indicating that she'd taken steps to change the classroom setting so that students would be more interested in writing during class. Unfortunately, she learned that even these changes did not increase the interest of her traditional-classroom students:

> You can't keep students engaged writing on paper for a whole hour in a traditional classroom. At least, I haven't been able to so far. There's a lot more fidgeting. There's just a lot more resistance, and I've tried various approaches. I've tried having them write outside. I've taken them to the art gallery. I've done a lot of things to really try to break it up and get them interested. In the computer classroom, we never go anywhere, and they're—it's just a different scene.

The students that we interviewed confirmed the teachers' observations. Noting that her teacher had asked her to write during class, a student from a traditional classroom said:

> It's kind of just boring sitting in class. And taking down notes and sitting there writing on paper because a lot of the time we did have to write our first drafts in class, and I didn't like it. I had to sit there and write everything out.

Although students in the traditional classrooms resisted in-class drafting, students in the computer classrooms typically characterized in-class drafting as one of the most beneficial aspects of the course. When asked about the advantages of learning to write in a computer classroom, a student from a computer classroom identified in-class drafting as the clearest advantage:

> You get more class time to work on your papers. . . . Probably during the portfolio and revision process you get to work on it most. . . . I wouldn't want to be in a writing classroom where you actually have to write [by hand]. It takes too much time.

Similarly, a student from a different computer classroom indicated that she would not have wanted to draft in a traditional classroom:

> I mean, I would not like sitting there having to write out those papers by hand. It would've been very, very tedious and I would not have enjoyed it. I really don't mind sitting at a word processor and typing it.

For these students, the primary advantages of in-class drafting lay in reduced time requirements and ease of revision (an issue we talk about in more detail in the next section). The teachers focused, as one might expect, on the larger issues of student improvement—among them revision, interaction with classmates and teachers during class, and students' sense of control over their writing. For Candace, these issues linked closely to the overall classroom dynamics in the two classrooms:

> In the computer classroom what I would often do is go into the class with a DAILY, which was harder to do in the traditional classroom. So I would put in a DAILY and have them respond to a reading that they had been assigned. So we might start with a DAILY, which would get them writing first thing, which is good, and then we would maybe read some of those and talk about them. Then, we might move on to questions that they had about what they were working on. Then, I would probably let them draft for 15 or 20 minutes, sometimes longer. We might stop at a certain point and have somebody read what he or she had just written and do a mini-workshop before the class went out. That's something that you can't really do in a traditional classroom because you could have students bring stuff in, but again some of the immediacy is lost. They don't have the power to change it just then. They're not willing to do the same kind of work on paper. Maybe they can't see the results as quickly, and they're just not as engaged.

The evidence we collected in the two studies strongly indicates that students in the computer classroom spend a great deal of time during class writing and talking with classmates and teachers about their writing. Our experiences as teachers—and those of many of our colleagues—are also consistent with the notion that computer-supported writing classrooms can shift teachers' and students' perceptions about the role of writing during class sessions. This shift does not come without trade-offs, however. The teachers in the Transitions Study often referred to the idea of "controlled chaos" as a label for the multiple activities, such as drafting, conferencing, group activities, and peer reviewing, that typically took place in the computer classroom. In her interview at the end of the semester, Candace observed that one of the key factors that contributed to "controlled chaos" was her willingness to allow students to work at their own pace and the willingness of her students to see in-class drafting as a valuable classroom activity:

> In a computer classroom, everybody is much more willing and able to come in and do their own work and to work at different paces. I can work with students more effectively because they have the thing tangibly on the screen and, for whatever reason, they're really engaged with that process and they want to be working on it. For example, one student may be having trouble drafting a first draft. Another student may be on a third or fourth draft. You can do that in a computer classroom because for some reason students are a lot more willing to write and people are engaged.

The New Teachers Study suggests that teachers must be willing to reduce their control over classroom pacing to foster student investment in writing during class. In her interview at the end of her second semester of teaching in the computer classroom, Linda indicated that she'd seen clear differences between her first and second semesters in in-class interaction and writing:

> Sometimes they would spend more time at the computer; other times, especially on the last unit, they did a lot of talking together about things. It seems like they did more in Unit 2 getting other people's input more than they did last semester and that seemed to have a lot to do with having the computer there. They seemed to pair up a lot more, you know, as far as the buddies next to'em and look at each other's work on the computer more than I noticed them doing last semester.

Amy, who also participated in the New Teachers Study, balked at giving up some of her control over activities in the computer classroom. A key factor in her unwillingness to do this appeared to stem from a lack of teaching strategies that would have allowed her to focus on global rather than local issues during her discussions with students:

> At first, I didn't want to, but on their midterm evaluations the students asked, "Why can't we have in-class time to work?" I had given them an in-class day for the iden-

tity narrative way at the beginning of the semester. And so I gave them one for the arguing essay [in Unit Two]. I felt they probably didn't think it was a loss, but I felt like it was a loss because there were so many people with specific questions I didn't get to go around and watch over everyone's shoulder and see what they were writing. I spent all my time answering questions about citations or this or that or whatever. And the 50 minutes really isn't long enough by the time they get going and then you answer everybody's little specific question. So I don't know how I'd deal with that. I don't know if I'm going to do that again. It seemed like both times that I did it I got so hung up answering individual questions that I couldn't do what I wanted to do which was go around and sort of read where they were at and see what they were writing and I don't know why that was. I couldn't do the kind of conferencing I wanted to do because I was answering these tiny little specific questions that could have been answered during office hours or before or after class.

The New Teachers Study, thus, reinforces our contention that teachers need time to develop new teaching techniques that foster student interaction and in-class drafting. As Amy explained—and as we notice in our own teaching—it is easy to get sidetracked into discussions that have little to do with the overall goals of the class. Simply asking students to write during class is not sufficient to foster the workshop environment that experienced computer-classroom teachers create in their classrooms. Instead, just as teachers must learn techniques for guiding front-of-the-classroom activities and group work, they must learn techniques for maximizing the benefits of in-class drafting and conferencing.

Student Perceptions of the Advantages of Writing During Class

During the Transitions Study, students in the two classroom settings typically made two sets of observations about the advantages of in-class drafting. As we describe in the previous section, students in the computer classrooms viewed time spent drafting during class as time they did not need to spend drafting out of class. One of the students in a computer classroom was particularly happy about the time savings afforded by time spent drafting during class:

> It was just so much easier because I could just sit there and get everything done right there and then. I could get it printed, and you don't have to worry about anything. . . . If you're in the computer classroom, everything is set up for you. It's just a lot easier.

In contrast, some of the students in the traditional classrooms indicated that they resented re-keying text into the computers or word processors they used outside the classroom. Teachers are unlikely to see reduced time spent drafting as a advantage, but they should take heart in our findings (discussed later in this chapter) that students in the computer classrooms typically produced more rough drafts than their counterparts in the traditional classrooms. In this sense, it appears that the students' perceptions do not necessarily correlate with our understanding of their drafting behaviors.

We are encouraged that students recognize the benefits of *immediately* applying information they gain from a group activity, peer-review session, or whole-class discussion to their writing. Two students from computer classrooms reflected on the benefits of making a direct link between discussions during class and their writing:

> I really did like having the computer. We could talk about something. I could whip around and I could open up my report or my paper or whatever, pull it apart, throw what I want in there. Slam it back together. Print it out. I have a new draft. That, I think, is a must in a writing class. You know, now that I've taken this class, I really would kind of shudder at an actual writing class where you did not have a computer right with you. Where you had to make all the—"Yes, I'll fix this here later." I mean, it's so much easier, so much nicer to just turn around and slap it in. . . . I try to imagine this class without that. That would just be scary.

> It would have been very difficult to work on roughs and stuff like that if we couldn't have them right there on a disk, if we always had to bring them on paper. And with the disk, she gives you a comment and you can go back and change it immediately and have it set right there, not drawn in pencil right above the sentence and go back home and re-enter it in your computer. You can do it right there while the idea's fresh in your head. I feel like that was a very worthwhile tool.

We find these students' awareness of the value of linking discussions during class with in-class drafting and revising as extremely promising, not simply because it validates our expectations about the benefits of in-class writing and interaction, but also because it indicates that these students are well on their way to understanding more about how they learn. In our discussion of student empowerment and control over their writing and learning later in this chapter, we expand on this theme, calling attention to teachers' perceptions of how the computer-supported writing classrooms fostered students' growth as learners. Before addressing that issue, however, we consider the relationship between in-class drafting and classroom interaction.

THE RELATIONSHIP BETWEEN IN-CLASS DRAFTING AND CLASSROOM INTERACTION

In our discussion in the previous chapter, we pointed out the key differences between interaction among classmates and between students and teachers in the two classroom settings. In this section, we extend that discussion by considering how it was related to students' drafting during class.

Interaction with Teachers During Drafting

The teachers that we observed remarked that in-class drafting appeared to facilitate student interaction with teachers. They called attention in particular to their practice of circulating through the room while students drafted, responding to student questions, and initiating discussions with students who appeared to have difficulty with their writing. Anita, who mastered the technique of circulating among students in both classrooms, favored the computer classroom for connecting with her students' writing:

> I always called myself a facilitator in the computer classroom. . . . You can walk around and say, "Oh, this paragraph is effectively written," or "Try this," or whatever. And I was just so concerned about making sure that they were even in the ballpark with the assignment. You can facilitate on assignment concerns in the regular classroom because they can bring in stuff and you can go around and say, "Okay. Where are you at? What are you having troubles with?" But you get to really see more writing in the computer classroom and intervene in the writing, the actual composing of the words and how they work in terms of reader and audience.

Caitlin echoed Anita's comments, noting that the lack of interest in drafting during class among students in her traditional classroom reduced her ability to interact with her students about their writing:

> I look at their papers more often in [my computer] class and see over their shoulder what's going on. And a lot of it's informal, you know. I'll walk around the computer classroom and I'll say, "Well, that's real interesting. Have you thought about how that ties in?" It's much more difficult to do that in the traditional classroom even though I give them time in class to stay there and work.

The practice of circulating around the room was common among the teachers that we observed, particularly at the beginning of class sessions when students typically responded to a DAILY assignment. In our classroom observations, we found that teachers generally allowed students to take 10 to 15 minutes of class time to respond to a DAILY assignment. In addition, since most students arrived at least five to 10 minutes before class officially started, the time devoted to responding to DAILY assignments was sometimes doubled. In our classroom observations, we saw a tendency among teachers to conduct what we call "mini-conferences" in the computer classroom, brief (typically one- to three-minute) discussions with students about their writing. In one observation, we noted that the teacher had conducted a mini-conference with nearly half the students in class. She later told us during an informal meeting (one not recorded) that, although she tended to talk with some students more frequently than others, she made an effort to have extended conversations about writing with each student at least once each week.

Ellen, in the New Teachers Study, indicated at the end of her second semester of teaching that she used the DAILY assignment as an opportunity to interact with her students:

> I walk around and make sure that they're working on their DAILIES, answer questions, and if somebody doesn't have much typed out I ask them if they have a problem with the question in terms of understanding it or if they're just thinking about what they want to write. And, again this semester, people were showing up early for class and working on their DAILIES. I'd walk in and normally 20 out of 24 of the students would be in there already working on their DAILIES. *[Interviewer: How early were they getting there?]* Well, last semester was interesting because they were there ten minutes before class started. This semester some of them were there 20 minutes before class started because there wasn't another class in the room before mine.

One of the key issues that emerges from teachers' discussions of their interactions during class is the danger of making unwanted intrusions into students' writing. The teachers in our studies expressed concern about learning which students did and did not welcome teacher-initiated discussions during drafting. When asked whether students resisted her interventions during drafting and, if so, how she reacted, Linda said:

> You get the look and so I wouldn't hang around as much. And sometimes I would sit on a chair and just scoot around. That seemed to bother them less, but there still are some that just don't want you reading. *[Interviewer: And so what did you do? Just not do it?]* Yeah, I just kinda, you know, do it real fast and go by. . . . Some of them didn't seem to have any real problem with that at all. But . . . . there were a couple of kids who would sit and stare at the screen a long time before anything would come and I tried not to stand around them as much because I think that just added to it.

Amy summed up the other teachers' attitudes about in-class interaction during writing when she explained that her expectations about communication between teachers and students had changed significantly during her transition from student to teacher:

> I don't know why I feel this way because I never really had this sort of communication with my English professors when I was here. But I really thought it was important to have tons and tons of communication. If you have a question you need to ask

> me; the more you communicate with me the better things are going to go. . . . And just the atmosphere of the class, just calling me over or asking me questions. Just because they're freshmen and they get confused, I think it's important that they feel comfortable asking questions and that I can be there to head off problems before they get there.

The importance teachers placed on interaction with students during class sessions, and in particular during in-class drafting, reflects their awareness that the computer classroom offered some unique opportunities over the traditional classroom. The teachers were not alone in attesting to the benefits of student/teacher interaction, however. Students also praised those interactions. One student indicated that interactions with classmates and teachers were important parts of learning to write in the computer classroom. A key factor that contributed to

In-Class Interactions Between Teachers and Students Don't Happen by Accident:

Several years ago, a new teacher in our computer classroom believed that if she simply went to class and asked students to write, they would automatically become focused and productive. Her class ended up chatting in small groups and trying to draw her into social conversations. To avoid this situation, teachers need to set up an atmosphere that encourages interactions that are genuinely focused on writing.

- Early in the term, set specific writing tasks and require "deliverables" after, say, twenty minutes or at the end of class. If students must turn in a list of topic ideas, interview sources, or debatable claims, or if they must produce a summary of a reading or an introductory paragraph, they typically get right to work on that task.
- Talk to students as you look at their work in progress. Students don't mind interruptions when you praise a point or raise a question.
- Circulate! Let students know that you are reading their work as they proceed.
- Some teachers state explicitly that they discuss social topics before or after class, but not during class. Other teachers, when students ask, "How was your weekend?" respond, "Remind me to tell you after class."
- When students ask for a mini-conference in which they're setting the agenda, ask them within a minute what key point in their papers they want your input on.
- When you ask for a mini-conference, stay on task and work through as much of your agenda as possible. Don't let students distract you into socializing at this point in the class session.

those interactions was the presence of computers and an emphasis on drafting during class:

> It was personal. You could get real one on one help, and you could actually know people. You know, know the instructor well. I liked that. You could use the time efficiently in class a lot just because you had the computers there. I think in a regular, lecture-type composition class, you wouldn't be able to—if you worked on a computer, you'd be out of luck if you wanted to do some revising in class. With the computer and all that there, you had a lot of resources at your hands to work with.

When asked why her teacher had chosen to teach in a computer-supported writing classroom, another student echoed the importance of discussing writing with the teacher during class:

> I think the main reason she wanted to allow us to use the computers and for her to teach the computer class is to give us the opportunity to work on our papers in class because that gave her the chance and the opportunity to be able to walk around, read our papers, answer questions right there. I mean she can look at our screen and see our paper, whereas if it was just a regular class and you have all of these papers and all of your articles and resources, and you come to class and you want to ask her a question about my paper and I left that piece of paper at home, you can't ask her. Here everything was just right there. I just think it gave the opportunity to spend more time with each individual student. She learned the weaknesses we all had and our strengths and always seemed able to help us with our weaknesses and always encouraged us with our strengths and said, "Okay. Keep doing this, but you need to add a little bit of this or that or your organization skills need to change." And she would actually sit there on the computer and help us figure it out. Or if we had printed off the copy, she would sit there and—I can't even remember all the times that everyone has just gone up and she's like, "Okay. I'm open for questions. Come up."

Interactions Among Students During Drafting

Data from the classroom observations, interviews, and weekly contact sheets indicate that students in the computer classroom had a much higher level of interaction with classmates during class meetings. This interaction was particularly apparent during drafting sessions, when students asked questions about assignments, socialized, or asked for feedback on their writing. Not only was the level of interaction among classmates higher in the computer classroom, but the conversations primarily focused on writing rather than on issues unrelated to class. It seems clear to us—as well as to the teachers and students whom we interviewed—that emphasis on in-class drafting contributed significantly to classmate interaction in the computer classroom.

Our classroom observations and our interviews during the studies suggest that interactions among classmates in the computer classrooms developed over the course of the semester, as students grew more comfortable with seeking feedback from each other. Typically, groups of students formed in each classroom, often among students who sat next to each other or who knew each other outside the classroom. A student in a computer classroom told us how his interactions had changed over the course of the term:

> In the beginning, it was just I sat next to my roommate because he was the only one that I knew. And then the people I sat around, we generally talked during class and we became friends . . . I had friends all over the class, I guess. The people I sat with—we generally cracked jokes pretty well together and that kind of thing. . . . So, I enjoyed the people I sat with. I felt like they gave me feedback. Just the same comments. "What do I do here?" And I'd get a couple of different answers as far as different from the workshop. You know, it wasn't a formal thing like a workshop was.

Another student echoed this notion of informal interactions throughout the writing process:

> I will ask people in class to read this. How does it sound. . . . *[You say that you would occasionally turn to other people sitting around you and ask them. When in the drafting would you do that?]* I guess throughout. I don't have a specific point that I would say something. If at any time if I was having a problem I would just turn and ask somebody something. Not at any specific point. *[Did you generally find that that was helpful?]* Yeah, It's just like asking anybody. It's just, "What do you think? Should I go on to the next point or should I do this?" It's just input basically to see what somebody would be interested in reading.

Other computer-classroom students told us of similar experiences, but not all the students engaged in such collaborative relationships with their classmates. Of the 19 students from the computer classrooms we interviewed, one told us that he had not spoken about writing with his classmates at all outside of peer-review workshops while two others indicated that they had had only a few discussions of their writing outside of peer-review workshops. The student who had no interactions indicated that he felt that his personality didn't lend itself to those kinds of discussions; outside of workshops, he said, he didn't ask for feedback from either his classmates or his teacher:

> With the workshops we had I didn't mind that, but I don't ask people. *[Interviewer: So outside of that situation where Ms. R. made you do that, you don't feel particularly comfortable going up to somebody and asking them?]* No, I'm on the quiet side really when it comes to asking people. *[Did you ever ask Ms. R. to look either*

> *at a whole paper or parts of the paper while you were drafting it during the semester?]* No. (laughs) I didn't. I should have done it.

One student who admitted that he asked for help infrequently also indicated that his personality wasn't particularly outgoing:

> In that class, there was 20 some odd of us. And you could definitely see people who were more extroverted were real—you know, they talked to each other all the time and, you know, even about papers. And, you know, had a lot easier time knowing each other and working with each other. Where I talked with—I don't know if you looked at my study sheets but I talked with, maybe, three people five times during the course of the semester that wasn't workshop related where we had to talk to them. You know, and not that I don't like talking to them, it's just—I don't know, most of the time I don't feel like I have anything that's worthwhile to say. And if I don't have anything worthwhile to say, I might as well not say it. You know, I think a lot of time it depends on your personality, how much you're going to get in workshops. If you're a real extrovert and you get to know the people in the class well, then I think you're going to get a lot more out of it than introverted people.

Interviews with these three students, as well as with the teachers in the two studies, indicate clearly that teachers must look for students whose personalities or prior experiences in writing classrooms might not lend themselves to interacting with classmates and the teacher. As we note in our overview of survey results from the Transitions Study, students who reported that their previous writing courses had emphasized grammar and mechanics tended to receive lower grades in the computer classrooms, but not in the traditional classrooms. It seems possible that these students may not have been ready for the highly interactive nature of the computer-supported writing classroom and, far from benefiting from it, may have floundered more than they would have in a traditional classroom.

When we asked students in the traditional classrooms about their interactions with classmates during class outside of peer-review workshops, the majority of students tended to focus on social rather than writing-related conversations. Of the 17 students that we interviewed in the traditional classrooms, only one indicated that she discussed her writing with classmates outside of peer-review workshops. Other students provided comments such as:

> We didn't work too close. I mean other than when we were workshopping. That's pretty much the only time we actually interacted with each other.

> I don't think I really worked with anybody in class. Just like class discussions and stuff like that helped.

> *[Interviewer: How did you go about picking those people?]* Just whoever I sat next to most of the time during the semester. Talked to them and stuff. *[Interviewer:*

> *What sort of things might you work with them on or ask them or talk to them about?]* Not the silly class topics. Just general stuff. How's it going.

Again we point out that the dynamics of the computer classroom appear to foster more concentrated effort on writing than do the typical dynamics of the traditional classroom.

THE IMPACT OF CLASSROOM CONTEXT ON REVISING

As you might expect from our discussion thus far, the emphasis on writing during class includes revision. The four teachers in the Transitions Study told us in their interviews—and our classroom observations confirmed—that they typically left time for students in both classroom settings to revise their drafts following peer-review workshops. Some, but not all, of the teachers indicated that they also encouraged their students to revise during class. As we describe above, students in the traditional classrooms tended to resist writing during class—regardless of whether it involved drafting or revising. In contrast, the students in the computer classrooms welcomed the opportunity to revise their papers, not only immediately after workshops (when time permitted) but also during revising days that the teachers sometimes scheduled prior to the due dates for major papers. Most of the computer-classroom students who talked about the advantages of revision focused on two benefits: saving time and making changes prompted by discussions during class. One of those students made a novel comparison to using computers and writing by hand:

> Your editing options are so much greater than by hand. It's like night and day. It's a stone wheel compared to a modern Ferrari. Especially when, in this class, they really want you to pump out a lot of drafts. Rather than having to start from a new screen and do a whole new draft of a paper, you can go through and edit things and fill in parts and delete parts and save it again. Print it out and there's your new draft. Time wise, it's a major help.

As we describe previously, several students in the computer classrooms focused on immediately applying newly learned concepts to an assignment. The teachers, as you might expect, were even more aware of this advantage. Anita picked up on the advantages of immediately applying the theory of writing to the practice of writing:

> If you have them sitting in front of a computer screen it changes everything because it makes everything a lot more immediate. And I think that they can see that there's a way that they can immediately apply what you're talking about.

In contrast, unless steps are taken to integrate writing more fully into the classroom than was done by the teachers that we observed, teaching in the traditional classroom increased the gap between theory and practice. Candace observed:

> In a sense, there's a way in a traditional classroom that you're teaching through a filter, and that filter is the fact that everything that is happening in the classroom just then is sort of removed from (a) their ownership of their writing, unless you have a class that you can really get writing with a pen and paper. And (b), there is no way that you can make immediate changes or feel any immediate results. You can feel the students in a computer classroom can leave in an hour and have three or four typed pages, and they have a file. There's again something about that in which they've got something tangible, something that's in type, something they feel a lot more attached to that they've been working on. Those kids have been writing for maybe 35 to 40 minutes of a 50-minute class, and they may be writing before you even get there. There's something about that that makes them feel like the time is better spent.

One of the clearest indications of differences in revision between the two classroom settings was the number of drafts students produced for each major assignment. In their end-of-the-semester interviews, we asked students about the number of drafts that they produced for each major assignment. We compared the responses by teacher, rather than overall, since the teacher is likely to have the most important impact on number of drafts. Students in the computer classroom reported that they wrote a much higher number of drafts than their counterparts in the traditional classrooms (see Table 5.5). Only students from Caitlin's classes indicated that they produced a comparable number of drafts. Those from the three other teachers reported a higher number of drafts in the computer classrooms.

In their interviews, the students focused on major drafts, but both teachers and students indicated that they produced a large number of what we might call minor drafts. The small changes that might be made in the five to 10 minutes following a peer-review workshop, for instance, did not seem to constitute a major revision and as a result were not counted when they talked about the number of drafts they produced for each assignment. One of the students directly addressed this issue:

TABLE 5.5.
Average Drafts Reported by Students

	Anita	Caitlin	Candace	Jen
Computer	6.00	4.88	3.80	5.25
Traditional	4.25	5.33	2.75	3.67

> *[Interviewer: How many drafts would you say that it's typical for you to write now of a paper?]* Right now, I probably go through a lot more than three, but that's what I end up printing out. Three or four, but we all tend to have this habit because of the fact that we work right on the computer so much that we'll make the changes right on the computer screen and not think, "Well, maybe I should run this off so she can see the changes I've made." She [the teacher] every once in a while will be like, "Are you guys printing things out, so I can see your drafts and stuff." And everybody will look around, "Oh-oh." And then you see everybody running over to the printer and standing there waiting for their drafts to come out because it's so much easier just to make changes, "Oh, this is a new idea." And forget about. Never run off a copy.

Moreover, Candace, along with some of the other teachers in the Transitions Study, observed that students in the computer classroom seemed more serious about revising their papers. When asked in her final interview if there was a difference in the number of drafts done by students in the two classrooms, she said:

> Absolutely. I had students in my computer classroom who went through the initial drafting process, came up with something they thought they were going to hand in, and got rid of it. They didn't even save it on the computer. They just treated it as pre-writing and started over. I would say I had five or six or seven students do that on a regular basis. That to me—I mean, that's something I'm even afraid to do. But that's what they did. These kids just dove in and just started over, and they would consistently do that. That was unheard of in my traditional classroom. It was like pulling teeth to get them to let go of a paragraph. I really had to sit down with them. There was one woman in particular who was a pretty good writer, and she worked really hard. But she came in with something that she really didn't want to let go of

Ways to Ensure that Introverted Students Take Advantage of In-Class Interactions:

- Have students use e-mail to introduce themselves. After exchanging e-mail messages, ask each student to introduce a classmate to the rest of the class.
- Use lots of group activities and be sure quiet students have significant roles to play.
- Identify strengths of the quiet students and pair them up with students who are weaker in those areas.
- Put quiet students in charge of something or draw on some area of their expertise.
- Assign each student to give a presentation, perhaps about a proofreading tip. That person then becomes the expert the teacher refers others to for more detailed answers.
- Make sure everyone turns to face the center for discussions.

> two or three times. So we would talk about it as a class, and I would work with her. And it would take me the whole hour to convince her that there was room for her to go back and re-think what she was working on. She finally did that, but it was really, really a big thing for her. She wanted to get away with the fewest number of drafts possible.

Given the differences between the two classrooms that we have discussed to this point, these differences in revision practices will not come as a surprise. Once again, however, they contribute to an emerging picture of the computer classroom as a setting in which both students and teachers value drafting, revising, and discussions about their writing. In the next section, we extend our discussion by considering the relationship between the two classroom settings and student improvement as writers.

THE RELATIONSHIP BETWEEN IN-CLASS DRAFTING AND STUDENT IMPROVEMENT

Surveys of student attitudes at the end of the semester indicate that those in the computer classrooms had higher levels of writing confidence at the end of the semester than did their peers in the traditional classrooms. We also found that their writing confidence increased significantly over the course of the semester, while it did not significantly increase among students in the traditional classrooms. We suspect that a key factor contributing to these differences is the amount of feedback students received as they wrote during class. In this and previous chapters, we indicate through numerous quotes and other data that students in the computer classrooms received a great deal of feedback on their writing from classmates and teachers during the act of writing. In the same way that a coach can spot and suggest solutions to difficulties that an athlete has, we believe that classmates and teachers in the Transitions Study could suggest strategies for dealing with difficulties that students had with their writing. This practice, in turn, may have contributed to the differences in student writing confidence.

When asked about her interactions with her teacher during class sessions, a student in one of the computer classrooms provided a fairly detailed explanation of the kinds of interactions that we believe contributed to student confidence about writing:

> *[Interviewer: How about talking with Ms. M. about your papers? Did you do that at all this semester?]* Yeah. Pretty often, probably. Probably once a class time, at least. Just because I had questions. *[Interviewer: What sort of questions would you ask her?]* Maybe if I had enough evidence to back up what I was saying or if I was making any sense. Or, you know, if I was sticking to my thesis or whatever. Just basic questions. *[Interviewer: What sort of comments might she make?]* Well, usually, you know, she'd give me ideas on where to get more evidence if I didn't have

> enough. Or she'd tell me that that was good or that, "Maybe you need to expand." And, you know, I mean, she'd tell me when my paper was too long and I needed to shorten it down. You know, make it more concise or whatever. *[Interviewer: Were those comments generally helpful?]* Yes. I'd say so. Because, usually, she'd point me in the general direction that I should go. She'd be specific about where I should work on instead of telling me my whole paper which doesn't really help me out.

The teachers in the Transitions Study were quite clear about their beliefs that students in the computer classrooms improved more over the course of the semester than their peers in the traditional classroom. Candace explicitly linked computer-classroom students' improvement to the writing habits that they learned in the class—habits that were much easier to encourage in the computer classroom:

> I think students [in the computer classroom] left better writers in the sense that they learned better writing habits. And in some cases, there were students who came in "C-" or "D" writers and went out high "B" writers. That did not happen in my traditional classroom.

Jen concurred with Candace' assessment, noting that she'd seen more improvement among students in her computer classroom:

> *[Interviewer: Was there a difference do you think in the quality of the papers between the two classes?]* In the final portfolios I did have in the computer room a few more people who were like "Wow, this person's finally showing me what they can do." And in the traditional classroom, the people who ended up with really good papers and evidently grades as a result were there to begin with.

A commonplace in teaching is the notion that students must be confident of their abilities if they hope to enjoy long-term success as learners. The findings of the Transitions Study suggest that the computer classroom is a setting in which we can build that confidence. So far, we've suggested that interaction, drafting and revising during class, and a more serious attitude about peer-review workshops are linked to student writing improvement. In the next section, we explore an additional factor that may contribute to student writing improvement—the sense of empowerment and control that access to computers during class may help students develop.

PERCEPTIONS OF EMPOWERMENT AND CONTROL

We discuss in detail in Chapter Six the new roles that teachers in the Transitions Study adopted in the computer classroom—roles that moved students in their computer classrooms to take greater responsibility for own learning than teachers asked of students in their traditional classrooms. Strategies such as shifting to a student-centered classroom and establishing student expectations to seek information about class content or to seek feedback on their writing created a setting that differed markedly from many traditional classrooms. Some students in computer classrooms, as we explain in our discussion of student interaction during drafting, did not seek feedback from classmates and students—a reaction that we believe is related to expectations about writing instruction established in previous writing courses. Yet the majority of students in our studies seem to have benefited greatly from this kind of classroom environment, both in improvement as writers and in increased confidence as writers.

In our interviews with students and teachers in the two studies, we engaged in a number of conversations about the impact of the computer classroom on students' sense of control and empowerment. The students, as we expected, couched their discussions in less theoretical terms than the teachers, noting that the presence of computers made them feel, for example, more "professional" about their writing. The teachers invoked Friere, suggesting that the de-centered model they applied to their computer classrooms was consistent with his approach to teaching. In her mid-semester interview, Candace explained that the presence of computers in the classroom enabled her to create a much more student-centered classroom than she could create in the traditional classroom:

> It goes back to Paulo Freire's notion of self-empowerment and the students not being empty vessels that you sit there and fill. I think that having the computer in front of them makes them feel much more empowered and like it's their show, which it is and should be. And they just learn how to be better writers, better revisers. Quite literally they're in the driver's seat. Whereas in the traditional classroom the way it gets set up is—you can do a lot of things to try and de-center yourself, but they're still sitting there looking at you at the front. You know, and I just find more and more I'm trying to get away from that as teacher. It's frustrating because they're so conditioned by everything else that they expect that.

Whether students felt a sense of empowerment as a direct result of the presence of computers in the classroom, or as a result of the combined effects of increased interaction about writing and higher levels of revision is not clear to us. It is clear that students in the computer classrooms ended the semester with greater confidence in their writing than did their peers in the traditional classrooms and that students in the computer classrooms seemed much more serious about their writing. Other authors have made claims about the theoretical advantages of teaching in computer classrooms that seem consistent with our findings. You'll find a list of those authors under the heading, "Theoretical Critiques of Computer-Supported Writing Classrooms," in the list of related readings at the end of this book.

THE IMPACT OF DAILY WRITING ASSIGNMENTS ON STUDENT ATTITUDES

When we looked at the daily plans teachers used in the Transitions Study, we discovered a number of differences, some of which we've already detailed, such as the greater reliance on in-class writing in the computer classrooms and the greater reliance on front-of-the-classroom instruction in the traditional classrooms. As we describe in Chapter Three, the classroom activity that most clearly illustrated these differences was the DAILY assignment. This assignment, used in almost all class sessions in the computer classrooms and relatively infrequently in the traditional classrooms, asked students to respond in writing to a prompt related to the overall goal of that class session. If the teacher wanted students to engage in a peer-review workshop, she might ask her students to identify the strengths and weaknesses of their current draft and to indicate the kind of feedback they hoped to receive during the workshop. Their response could then be printed and shared with the classmate(s) who reviewed the student's draft. If the students were about to begin a new assignment, the prompt might ask students to freewrite about topics of interest.

In our previous discussion of interactions with teachers during drafting, we described how teachers in our studies often used the time students spent working on DAILY assignments to move about the room and talk with students about their writing. For computer classroom teachers, the DAILY provides a wonderful

Our Teachers Use DAILY Files to Set Up a Variety of Individual Writing Tasks:

- as discussion starters, based either on readings or personal experience (for example, have students write about good and bad experiences with group work at the beginning of a unit emphasizing collaborative writing).
- for study questions and reactions to assigned reading in the textbook.
- to generate criteria for workshops.
- to write a monologue about how work-in-progress is coming along; teachers might pose just the general task or ask specific self-reflective questions about where students are in the process and what they need to do next.
- to brainstorm lists; ask student to generate topics for a paper or strategies for tackling the problem.
- to generate audience concerns or audience characteristics.
- to add another dimension to a reading they've already done; for example, after students write individual summaries or responses, teachers ask them to look again at the reading as the class moves into synthesis.

way to begin a class. Students immediately immerse themselves in writing. Teachers use the same time to discuss writing with students and to get a sense of their strengths and weaknesses as writers. Finally, classmates get to catch up quickly with each other as they settle into the more serious business of writing and learning to write.

An added benefit is the repeatedly observed phenomenon (in the two studies we focus on in this book and in our own and our colleagues' experience) that students tend to arrive earlier for class when they know that a DAILY assignment will be assigned. One of the main benefits of the DAILY assignment is that it sets the tone for the class, and indeed for the entire semester, that the writing classroom is a place where writing is done and discussed, both formally and informally. Although we seldom grade a DAILY, many teachers, including Mike and Kate, collect and respond to DAILY assignments so that students see that their teacher values their writing. The time needed to respond to a DAILY assignment is typically quite low. We certainly do not suggest that teachers with heavy teaching loads collect everything that their students write during class. In most cases, Mike responds to a DAILY assignment in under a minute, with more time reserved for students who show that they don't understand the assignment or a particular concept.

For students, the DAILY assignment creates a set of expectations about the class that, if violated, students react against strongly. When Ellen, one of the teachers in the New Teachers Study, decided to forego the DAILY assignment for a few weeks during her first semester of teaching, her students reacted initially with surprise and consternation. Ellen observed as well that, after her students got used to the idea that a DAILY wasn't going to be assigned, they stopped coming to class early:

More Ways to Use DAILY for Individual Writing Tasks:

- use personal experience to set up new rhetorical strategy; for example, ask students to write down the most recent argument they've had, the audience, and what happened.
- illustrate critical reading strategies; for example, ask students to use the word processor's embedded comment function to annotate a passage.
- practice formatting in-text documentation; one of our teachers writes out publication information in a scenario and asks students to put it into correct format; the correct form appears in a hidden comment that they click on when they finish.
- draft a rhetorical prospectus: DAILY asks students to do a discourse analysis of selected excerpts to help the teacher prepare for inquiry or argument essays.

> Most of them would show up to class early through the first part of the semester to start on the DAILIES because they knew they had the DAILIES. They would show up as soon as the class got out which was right before mine and elbow the students out of the way and sit down to write so they would have that extra ten minutes to write over and above the time I allotted of actual class time. And then I noticed that, once they knew they didn't have the DAILIES anymore, they would get to class right at 3:35, just right on the wire.

Ellen indicated that she dropped DAILY assignments because, as a new teacher, she felt that she needed more control over class activities when she felt she had too much ground to cover. Her conclusion, at the end of the semester, was that she would return to using DAILIES and reduce her reliance on lectures. In our discussion of teaching training, in Chapter Nine, we pick up on this issue in more detail. For our purposes in this chapter, her experiences underscore the effect of the DAILY on student behavior in the computer classroom. When Ellen began treating the computer classroom as, in effect, a traditional, lecture-dominated classroom, students shifted back to the models of teaching and learning associated with their prior experiences in traditional classrooms.

Amy, another participant in the New Teachers Study, consistently relied on the DAILY assignment. Her experiences suggest that the sense of routine established by the DAILY increases the comfort level of her students—a comfort level that is even more important given the differences between students' experiences in traditional classrooms and those in the computer classroom:

> I think students want [to have a routine]. Just, you know, like watching the way they get attached to certain computers. And, you know, like they're freaked out if you don't have a DAILY. I think they really, I don't know, they just sort of start expecting it and if you throw them for a loop then they went "AAAH!" So—and it works well for me too, like, just to sort of have them in that mode so they come in and they start working. They know what's going on.

When we asked the teachers in the Transitions Study about their perceptions of the DAILY assignment, they indicated that it encourages students to arrive in class early and that it fosters a greater seriousness about the class. Jen, in her end-of-semester-interview, explained that the DAILY helped her establish a classroom environment in which students saw clear benefits to taking writing seriously:

> I think that they feel that there is this environment where there is work waiting to be done, and that may be just because they come in and they get into DAILY and it's right up there. You know, they get into the habit of seeing this task for the day or whatever, and the computer, because it gives them a place to get a lot of work done if they can get motivated and use their time wisely, I think that they know that they

can come in and get lots done if they stay focused. And so, it almost seems to be like a place where they see that business is going to happen.

Our studies suggest that the DAILY assignment had three key effects. First, the DAILY helped establish a sense of routine. When students knew that their classes began with a DAILY assignment, they arrived at class earlier and focused on their writing as a matter of course. Second, the DAILY provided a venue within which teachers could interact with students and classmates could interact among themselves. Finally, the DAILY immersed students in writing from the start of class and moved them easily into larger discussions of writing or related activities such as peer-review or group activities.

The importance of the DAILY was not lost on students. Picking up on some of the benefits described above, one of the students in a computer classroom described her experiences with the DAILY:

> We would sit down and our assignment would already be on the computer. We would go in and read our assignment for the day. And that would eliminate time from her having to get everyone quiet and say, "Okay. This is what we're going to do today, and this is what's due tomorrow." Because everyone knew that as soon as you come in and sit down, go to DAILY and find out what your schedule is for today or for the week. And so that would give us about, I would say, a good extra 10 or 15 minutes out of the class time everyday. And then she'd have whatever we'd have to do, and we'd start writing or whatever, and then at 11:30 we're going to turn chairs around and discuss this story that you read, or this article, or the next essay that you needed to write. So it's like she used our time very wisely, and she encouraged us to use the time very wisely.

Similarly, another computer-classroom student indicated that the DAILY assignments played an important role in moving students toward the goal of completing the next major writing assignment:

> I think the DAILIES are really good because you go in and you have a set thing that you need to get done before class starts. And you end up talking about your DAILY and talking about how it relates to whatever paper you're doing. So I think that helped out a lot because a lot of times when we just finished a paper we'll go in the next day and brainstorm ideas for the next topic, and then that will help because then you get to figure out what you want to talk about and if you're going to be able to talk about it or not. So that helped out a lot.

The advantages of DAILY assignments in establishing a routine and creating an environment in which writing and talking about writing are the norm seem clear to us, both through the studies we talk about and through our classroom experience as teachers. By helping to establish expectations about the writing classroom as a place in which students are immersed in writing, the DAILY assignment has a profound effect on student attitudes about writing. In the next section, we explore how writing activities such as the DAILY assignment gradually migrated over the course of the semester in which we studied each of the teachers in the Transitions Study from the computer classroom to the traditional classroom.

MOVING TOWARD MORE WRITING IN THE TRADITIONAL CLASSROOM

As the teachers in the Transitions Study grew more aware of the benefits of writing during class sessions in the computer classroom, they told us that they began to explore how to bring some of those benefits to their traditional classrooms. For some of the teachers, this was a major shift. Candace, for example, wanted to use writing in the traditional classroom, but when she asked her students to write during class, as she indicates in some of her quotations earlier in this chapter, she was discouraged by their resistance. In contrast, the more experienced teachers in the study seemed to take student resistance in stride. Anita, the most experienced teacher in the study and the one with the most experience in the computer classroom, told us that she became comfortable with the transition between the two classroom settings—even if some of her traditional-classroom students resented certain teaching techniques:

> One of the things that I've moved back to this year that I didn't do much three years ago is that I have students write in the regular classroom. I mean on their papers. I have them do little activities or ditties or whatever, but I literally have them drag out their drafts and mark on them and write in it and re-write this. . . . One of the first points I make in the class, is that if you think you're going to save all of your ideas until you get to your word processor you're wrong. You're going to be generating text right here in class.

Similarly, Jen commented in her mid-semester interview that she hoped to increase in-class writing activities in both classrooms. She expressed concern, however, about doing so in the traditional classroom:

> I think I'm going to give the computer people more time to draft in class, but then the way I'm interacting with the traditional guys I see no reason not to do that too although I don't think, I'm not sure about getting them to draft as much, because they may still have to go and type it up, so I might end up doing longer workshops or something different than the traditional classroom. While I'm having the computer people spend more time drafting and, you know, I'm looking over their shoulder more.

Caitlin, who was in her third semester of teaching in a computer classroom, had progressed further in integrating writing into her traditional classrooms. She indicated in her mid-semester interview that she had grown much more confident in using writing in her traditional classroom, crediting much of that confidence to her experiences in the computer classroom:

> I start a lot of my classes with a "write-to-learn" type of activity. And in the traditional classroom, it's just on the board and they begin class by coming in and sitting down and writing. In the computer classroom, it's in the DAILY. They come in and they access the DAILY and they get going. And so, I see that's something I didn't do as much in the traditional classroom before I taught in the computer classroom and that's something I think I've carried over.

Still, in her end-of-the-semester interview, her concerns about making assignments like the DAILY work in the traditional classroom echoed those expressed by Jen:

> [In the computer classroom,] the DAILY seems to work exceedingly well for me. That I give them some sort of task. Either to do independently or to do with a partner or something. That they come in. I love the self-guided nature of the concept of the DAILY. And I've tried to implement that in my traditional classroom where they come in and there's some sort of activity that they start the class period with. I don't know if I learned to teach differently in the traditional classroom, but I've never been able to force myself to make it stick.

The difficulties that the less experienced teachers in our study encountered as they attempted to shift to more in-class writing in the traditional classrooms suggest to us that more than class plans must change for that transition to succeed. Teachers must learn additional strategies for working in a setting that does not encourage—in the same physical way that the computer classroom seems to—writing during class. We'll examine some of these strategies in Chapters Six and Seven. In addition, we also believe that teachers will find greater success in making the transition back to the traditional classroom if they clearly define at the beginning of the term their expectations about writing being a part of the class. With the exception of Anita (and even Anita assigned substantially less in-class writing in her traditional classroom), the teachers in the Transitions Study did not establish those expectations early in the semester. As teachers who were relatively new to the computer classroom, they had not yet begun to rethink their assumptions about teaching in traditional classrooms at the beginning of the study. When they asked their students in the middle of the semester to write during class, they encountered resistance from students who must have wondered what had happened to the relatively familiar composition class they'd been taking.

WRITING IN CLASS: A COMPLEX DYNAMIC

We begin this chapter with the observation that teachers seem surprisingly uncritical of the fact that little writing is done in most writing classes. Our discussion focuses on the notion that the computer classroom can break down the stereotype that writing is something talked about in writing classrooms, not *done*. As we explore the issues of in-class drafting, in-class interaction, teaching strategies, student control and empowerment, and attitudes about writing during class, we suggest that they form a web of relationships. Whether one factor causes another is not clear to us, although like anyone else, we are willing to speculate if pressed. However, we strongly believe that these factors function in ways that fundamentally differentiate the two classroom settings. In the next chapter, we explore how these complicating factors shape the teaching strategies used in each classroom setting.

6

Building on Our Strengths: Adapting Teaching Strategies

Thirty-five years ago, writing classrooms looked exactly like any other classroom on a college campus. More important, the activities conducted in them differed little from those conducted in any other classroom—teachers lectured and students took notes. Typically, the professor arrived on Monday morning with a reminder that a paper would be due on Friday and with readings for the week. Students read the professional, usually belletristic samples, and the professor lectured about elements of these samples for the next three days. If the professor saw specific problems with editing in students' papers, a lecture about, say, semicolons would be dropped into the schedule. Students rarely talked with each other in these classes, and teachers rarely talked about how to gather and arrange ideas for the papers due each Friday or how, if ever, to revise papers. Students and teachers alike expected that by carefully examining the model essays, students could produce reasonable facsimiles and would eventually produce acceptable college papers. Teachers often adopted elaborate codes for marking papers that relied on the numbering format of the assigned handbook; teachers rarely commented on the substance of a paper but rather concentrated on problems with proofreading and editing.

But in the late 1960s and early 1970s, scholars who looked at the ways that students actually write proposed sweeping changes in our teaching of writing. As Maxine Hairston (1982) described it, teachers of writing found themselves swept by the "Winds of Change." Hairston outlined 12 principal features (p. 86) of the recently developed process paradigm for writing, of which we'll recap just a few:

- It focuses on the writing process; instructors intervene in students' writing during the process.

- It teaches strategies for invention and discovery; instructors help students generate content and discover purpose.
- It is rhetorically based; audience, purpose, and occasion figure prominently in the assignment of writing tasks.
- Instructors evaluate the written product by how well it fulfills the writer's intention and meets the audience's needs.
- It emphasizes that writing is a way of learning and developing as well as a communication skill.
- It views writing as a disciplined creative activity that can be analyzed and described; its practitioners believe that writing can be taught.

Now, after more than two decades of teaching writing within a process paradigm, most successful writing teachers translate these features into widely shared teaching strategies for the traditional writing classroom:

- *Peer-review workshops* provide students with a rhetorical writing community, short-term feedback on papers, and incentive to read carefully and critically as well as to revise extensively.
- Varied *collaborative activities* in pairs, small groups, and even some large groupings help students draw on each others' knowledge of language, rhetoric, style, *and* content to generate and arrange ideas.
- *Discussion* of readings allows teachers to help students negotiate shared meanings for sample texts as well as attend to matters of audience, writer's intentions and choices, and other rhetorical issues.

In other words, as we work within the process paradigm, writing teachers move off center-stage as the "keepers of writing truth" and involve students much more fully in reading, writing, and thinking activities that encourage students' practice, and thus their mastery, of writing skills.

Yet even as we shift some of the "work" of the traditional writing classroom to students, most writing teachers in traditional classrooms still find it difficult to meet consistently the first of Hairston's principles. Although teachers in traditional classrooms have developed a variety of means to intervene in students' writing process, *immediate* intervention requires seeing students write and revise in front of us. Much of the problem is logistical rather than theoretical: students simply don't want to do very much writing on paper, and so the class time devoted to students' writing remains limited in the traditional writing classroom.

As we note in previous chapters, the computer classroom eliminates that logistical logjam and opens up possibilities for teachers to become true facilitators of students' practice and mastery of writing. Unlike paper, flat on the desk and hidden from the teacher's view, the computer monitors allow teachers to see what their students are writing and to intervene immediately to encourage a line of thought or good use of details, to divert the writer from faulty arguments, or to question a student's understanding of audience, purpose, and task.

Beyond the clear potential for intervening in students' writing processes, however, teachers often express uncertainty about how to translate process-oriented activities developed for traditional classrooms into the computer classroom. They tell us that they want to take with them the benefits of peer review and other collaborative group activities and of open discussions of readings. They want to encourage students' writing to be at the center of our concern. But they worry that new classroom contexts, especially the computer-networked classroom, require them to change some of our most effective and time-tested teaching techniques.

In addition, teachers who have recently begun teaching in computer classrooms express uncertainty about whether activities they've developed for that setting return smoothly to the traditional classroom. These teachers typically don't know from one term to the next if they'll teach in computer classrooms, or if they'll teach in both settings during the same term. They are understandably concerned about how techniques developed for computer classrooms might transfer to traditional classrooms.

In this chapter, we address these concerns by exploring how the teachers in the Transitions Study changed their teaching strategies as they moved between the traditional classroom and the computer classroom. Following this discussion, we explore a variety of teaching techniques for both classroom settings. First, we discuss techniques that need only minimal modification in either setting. Then we discuss how teachers adapt techniques developed for traditional classrooms to computer classrooms. Following that discussion, we explore how techniques developed for the computer classroom apply in traditional classrooms. We close the chapter with a short section in which we consider how the process of adapting classroom activities from one setting to another has the potential to reinvigorate teaching in each setting.

ADAPTING PLANNING AND TEACHING TECHNIQUES TO DIFFERENT CLASSROOM SETTINGS

As we explain throughout the early chapters of this book, the teachers in the Transitions Study typically created different class plans for their traditional and computer classrooms. Our discussions with them and our observations of their classrooms indicate that the computer classroom fosters:

- more time for writing during class,
- a shift toward a student-centered curriculum,
- expectations that students in the computer classrooms take greater responsibility for their own learning,

- greater ease in working with students while they write, and
- a shift away from large-group discussion.

We discuss writing during class in detail in Chapter Five. In this chapter, we take up the other points and then reflect on how these issues affect curriculum design and daily planning in traditional and computer classrooms.

A Shift to a Student-Centered Curriculum

Our interviews with teachers indicate that control issues recur regardless of teaching experience. The teachers in the Transitions Study felt less control over the pacing of activities in the computer classroom because students worked on tasks independently much more often. However, even though the teachers repeatedly call such classes "chaotic," they clearly value the independence that student pacing fosters. In her interviews, Anita remarked that she enjoyed feeling less need "to orchestrate" all the activities going on in her computer classroom. In her view, students in the computer classroom were much more engaged in classroom work: they perceived that what went on in the classroom was serious and worth their commitment of energy and attention. In effect, the presence of computers helped the teachers redefine their roles in the computer classroom so that students assumed more control over in-class activities.

As we describe in our overview in Chapter Three, the teachers in the Transitions Study noticed differences both in how they related to their students and in what they expected from them. In the traditional classrooms, the teachers tended to find themselves—whether they wanted to be there or not—at the front of the classroom and at the center of their students' attention. Candace remarked that although she prefers a student-centered classroom, she typically found herself at the center in the traditional classroom:

> I think that by nature or maybe by practice, maybe a bit of both, I'm not the kind of teacher who likes to go in and be at the front of the classroom and dictate the course of all the events. I really like the course and what happens to come from the students, and for me the computer classroom is really ideal because I think it allows me to work with my strengths as a teacher, which is to facilitate discussion, to facilitate rather than to control. I know that in the traditional classroom just the very structure of the classroom is such that the teacher somehow ends up being in the center of the classroom, and I really think that as far as teaching writing goes that's counter-productive in terms of students feeling ownership of their writing.

Each of the teachers in the Transitions Study indicated that they adopted a more teacher-centered curriculum in their traditional classrooms than in their computer classrooms. Caitlin commented, "I did a lot more leading of activities in the traditional classroom and a lot more whole-class discussion where I was the discussion leader." In contrast, the teachers in both studies adopted student-centered curricula in the computer classrooms. In most cases, they created a loose structure for class sessions that directly involved the students in writing activities and that students found easy to anticipate—typically a DAILY assignment followed by a brief full-class discussion around the center table and then a group activity or drafting session on the computers. The teachers worked within this structure to adapt to the needs of students as they changed. Candace, among others, indicated that she was much more open to changing a daily plan in the computer classroom than in the traditional classroom:

> I guess if you're one kind of teacher you just insist and demand that they're going to have "x" done on "x" day, and they do somehow. But if you're another kind of teacher you realize that these students are not robots, they're human beings. They come in, for example, and they're all struggling. I've had this happen a couple of times. Instead of that day being a waste, I can scrap my lesson plan and have them draft and do something else or pull something out of that hour. In a traditional classroom, it's harder to pull something out when things are going badly.

Like Candace, Anita indicated that she looked to the students in her computer classroom for cues about what they needed to improve as writers and adapted daily plans in response to those cues. In contrast, she tended to set the agenda herself in the traditional classroom:

> I'm more of an organizer in the regular classroom. I'm more of a facilitator in the computer classroom. . . When I facilitate, I'll let the students determine how they need me. In the regular classroom, I have to pre-determine how the students need me and then I have to make that work. In the computer classroom, I let them determine what they need from me more so. If you're a good instructor, you'll make sure you're moving the thought processes toward the end goal—more effective writing. But I find it much more unstructured in the computer classroom.

Echoing Anita's comments, the other teachers characterized the different roles they adopted in the two classroom settings in terms of formality, teacher-centered versus student-centered teaching, and coaching metaphors. In each case, the teachers felt that they adopted the role of leader in the traditional classroom and of supporter in the computer classroom.

Responsibility for Learning in Computer Classrooms

The roles the teachers adopted in the two classrooms imply differences in the expectations that teachers had about student behavior in classrooms. An important difference was the extent to which teachers expected students to be active versus passive learners. In several interviews, teachers raised the issue of students taking responsibility for their learning. These teachers consistently remarked that they expected students in the computer classrooms to take more responsibility for their learning than students in the traditional classrooms. Caitlin noted:

> I think that the way I structure the traditional classroom, I don't expect my students to be as responsible for maybe picking the main points out of an article. I guide them more directly to that. I lead them more by the nose to come to an understanding or to an agreement among the class. In the computer classroom, a lot of that's done individually on computer and they do their response there rather than do their response verbally in class. And that I say, you know, "Chat with your neighbor," or "Switch seats and take a look and see if you agree or disagree." And then the only leading I do with them is maybe the questions I begin with. But I'm not right there involved in their processes saying, "Do you understand this point? What do you think about, how does this point relate to the other point?" I'm not guiding them in the discussion in understanding the same way I do in the traditional classroom. That's where I think that they're more responsible for understanding things and if they don't understand them, they need to come see me and ask or ask the student sitting next to them or something like that.

The notion that students should take more responsibility for their learning is not new for teachers, but it appears difficult for students to grasp, particularly when they find themselves in a traditional classroom. Caitlin noted that even such simple acts as announcing upcoming assignments signal to students a teacher's expectations about their learning:

> [In the traditional classroom,] you walk in the door and they're all staring at you with this concept of "Okay, what do we do today?" It starts from the very beginning with something as simple as giving the assignment. I never gave an assignment once in the computer classroom. Everyday I put the assignment on the DAILY and I might, at some point, in the classroom yell over the top of everyone else, "Hey! Make sure you look at that assignment carefully. Anybody have any questions about the assignment? Make sure you ask me." But I never would go through and say, "Okay now. Remember, your assignment is—" So, in that sense, the technology of the DAILY right there set the different tone for the classroom.

Ellen, in the New Teachers Study, reflected on how she had tried to create an even more student-centered classroom in her second semester of teaching. She provides further insight on how students' experiences in traditional classrooms reinforce the notion that they don't need to take responsibility for their learning. She indicates that, although her students initially resisted her expectations that they take greater responsibility for their learning, they learned to do so by the end of the semester:

> At first, I think that they didn't quite know how to take the class because they're so used to having everything completely structured. And so everything is spoon-fed to them and not having to take any responsibility for their own learning at all. But once they had to do that they seemed to do well with it. I know there are a few that never were quite happy with that, but the majority, I think, really learned how, really learned about learning as well.

A key element in students' taking more responsibility for their learning is teachers' awareness that students interact with each other and with their teachers more frequently in the computer classrooms. The comparative ease of obtaining feedback about writing or class-related issues in the computer classrooms leads to higher levels of interaction with classmates and teachers and a sense that it is the students' responsibility to ask for help when they need it. As Caitlin observed:

> I would say I do a better job of making my students more personally responsible for figuring things out on their own in the computer classroom. . . . I give them a chance to write, to discuss a little bit, with their peers around them and then I ask, "Do you have any questions? Is there anything you feel like we need to talk about?" And then we'll move on. And so they're more responsible, I would say, for saying, "This is a problem, I don't understand this." Or "I don't know what's going on." Where, because I think I have whole- class discussion in the traditional classroom, I feed them more information.

Greater Ease of Working With Students as They Write

In addition to the sense that students in the computer classroom take more responsibility for their learning, the teachers in our studies also noted that students are much more likely to work on their papers, not on exercises that teach abstract writing concepts. For our teachers, concentrating on student work-in-progress means that, as Caitlin explained, "I feel like I spend much less time having a teacher-centered classroom where I'm guiding my students as a teacher through some activity or group work or exercise." As we know from our own writing, when we hit snags, we ask for help because we care about making our writing effective. Students are no different. When they work on papers, they are much more likely to ask for help when they need it.

If students take their writing seriously and want to solicit advice from teachers and take advice offered by teachers, then one additional element of the classroom context makes computer support ideal: students and teachers must see the work clearly. "I can work with them more effectively because they have the thing tangibly on the screen," Candace noted. In the computer classroom, both teacher and student can easily refer to a draft to question its effectiveness or evaluate its evidence, for example. A teacher doesn't need to step into the student's space to read a paper or take the paper physically away from a student in a computer classroom. Rather, the computer classroom, in effect, projects students' text into a safe space that belongs neither to the teacher nor the student. Both can see the text on the computer monitor, and both can look at the same sentence or paragraph without the awkwardness of sharing a piece of paper. In short, the teacher doesn't have to pre-empt control of a piece of paper to read work-in-progress.

Students quickly discover the advantages of asking for help while they write—either for reassurance or for suggestions to overcome a sticky problem. As we point out in Chapter Four, students ask not only teachers but other students to help in the computer classroom. Here, a much freer exchange of writing advice is possible because students can see the writing and can comfortably initiate requests for help from teachers or peers.

Shifting Away From Large-Group Discussions in the Computer Classroom

Our analysis of the Transitions Study—particularly of classroom observation, teacher logs, and interviews—indicates yet another major change that teachers made as they moved from the traditional to the computer classroom. Teachers in our studies held fewer large-group discussions in the computer classroom than in the traditional classroom, and the discussions they did have were frequently shorter than parallel discussions in the traditional classroom. The teachers proposed various reasons for this change.

Caitlin recorded her dissatisfaction with large-group discussion and attributes the problem to lack of focus:

> [W]hole class discussion was just not working in the computer classroom. My students weren't focused in on it; they weren't getting the main points that I wanted them to get out of the discussion. They weren't thinking. And so, I stopped and thought, "Am I doing something wrong because I'm in the computer classroom? Do I need to structure this differently?" And so, I moved away from whole-class discussion [in the computer classroom].

Yet when Mike attended her class in October, he remarked on how successful the large-group discussion was: "It's the students who're keeping this discussion going. Caitlin's not asking questions. The students are building on one another's responses." Mike also noticed that almost every student participated—at length—in the discussion, and that students felt comfortable to challenge one another's reactions and responses to the computer activity.

Can both these reactions to discussion be accurate? In our experience, large-group discussion in the computer classroom relies on a complex dynamic. On the one hand, students are usually well prepared for discussion, often better prepared than in the traditional classroom, because most teachers in the computer classroom ask students to write about issues before they discuss them. Each student, thus, has an opportunity to think about key questions, reread key passages from assigned texts, and capture thoughts in writing. When the teachers use DAILY to prime students for discussion, the discussions tend to be focused and insightful. One of our current teachers in the computer classroom recently remarked that her discussions have never been better because students have more to say and know clearly the points they want to make in large-group discussion.

On the other hand, students who have written their thoughts already feel that they have contributed to the class, particularly if they know that teachers pick up the DAILY writings and read through them. One of Kate's students last semester commented that she felt so much more engaged in class discussions *even when she didn't talk* because she knew that her contributions would be acknowledged. And if the discussion happened to go in a direction she hadn't written about, she could follow the discussion closely without worrying about how to tie back to points she might have made in her DAILY.

In other words, writing before discussion in the computer classrooms helps discussions be more focused but not necessarily more extended. Students may not feel the same anxiety about stating their points aloud if they know that teachers review their thinking on paper after the discussion is over. Shy students, in particular, may feel relieved of the obligation to speak because, by writing first, they know that they don't need to speak up to contribute to the class.

Unfortunately, most of our teachers use DAILY writing in a way that makes the teacher the only reader, and so "class" contributions are still limited to those students who speak up during large-group discussion. On the other hand, as our institutional context changes to support greater use of electronic mail and other forms of network-based communication, more of our teachers supplement face-to-face discussion with electronic discussions on bulletin boards and that students communicate with their teachers and classmates more frequently by e-mail. In this sense, our students appear to take advantage of alternative ways to voice their thoughts to the classroom community.

Another element of the complex dynamic is the topic of discussion. Students in the computer classroom tend to focus intently on their writing. Discussions of material unrelated, in their view, to their work-in-progress could seem much less important to them than getting back to the computer to work on a paper. Because students are so intent on their papers, teachers in the computer classroom have successful discussions when the material is closely and clearly tied to students' work-in-progress. An abstract treatment of a belletristic sample is just as likely to fall flat in a traditional classroom now as it did 30 years ago; the computer classroom just makes the problem more obvious because students know they have alternative ways to spend their class time and, as a result, tend to make their impatience more obvious to teachers.

Certainly another important factor in the dynamic of large-group discussion is the layout of the room. In the traditional classroom, teachers usually ask students face the front of the room as teachers lead discussions, or teachers put desks in a circle or horseshoe so that students see each other and the teacher during the discussion. With either layout, the teacher easily becomes a visual focal point, often the main visual focal point. In our computer classroom, however, teachers do not have the option of creating rows of students facing one direction; they can only arrange students in a large circle. But even when the teacher adopts a focal position in the circle, the computers are always humming on the periphery. The visual and aural cues of the computer classroom constantly remind students that they can shift their attention away from the teacher and onto their writing.

Anita addressed this issue by adapting discussion from a single large group in the traditional classroom to multiple small groups in the computer classroom. As she explained,

> In the traditional classroom, I have more whole-class discussions. I always elicit responses, make them generate information for me. In the computer classroom, I rarely stand up and have them, as a whole class, generate information. They generate it in groups. And I monitor it as I filter around the groups. It seems to be more clustered information instead of whole group or whole classroom reporting.

With this approach, Anita felt that she maintained the advantages of face-to-face discussion without the disadvantages of dispersed attention.

Information from Caitlin's interviews and teacher log suggests that teachers were aware—even early in the semester—of the difficulties of using the same kinds of large-group discussions in both classroom settings (see Table 6.1). In September, Caitlin stated in her interview that she had not yet started adapting many techniques for the computer classroom because she wanted to get basic material under control. But she had already learned that full-class discussion was more difficult to orchestrate in the computer classroom. And so Caitlin added a 10-minute teacher-led discussion in her September 13 traditional class that she

TABLE 6.1.
Caitlin's Class Plans as Described by Classroom Observers

Traditional class	Computer class
9-13-93	**9-13-93**
review assignments (10 min)	review assignment (10 min)
lecture-discussion on peer-review techniques (10 min)	workshop on investigating draft (40 min)
workshop on investigating (30 min)	
11-3	**11-1**
question/answer session about problems with current draft (20 min)	workshop (15 min) large-group discussion (5 min)
peer-review workshop on arguing draft (30 min)	mini-conferences during continued revision work (30 min)

eliminated completely from her computer class. Similarly, Caitlin used a 20 minute large-group question/answer session in the traditional classroom in November that she transformed into a workshop activity in the computer classroom on that day.

Not every teacher finds that the computer classroom so dramatically affects discussion. Candace suggests in her interviews that her computer classroom students seemed better prepared to engage in discussion because they took their writing more seriously. She asserted that she frequently had longer and more productive discussions with her computer classroom students because they seemed more engaged with the material than did her traditional classroom students.

Generally, however, teachers do comment that large-group discussion is more difficult to sustain in our computer classrooms, although other room designs may alleviate aspects of this problem.

The Impact of Classroom Differences on Daily Plans

The differences we discuss in this chapter clearly affected the class plans of both the classes we observed and those the teachers recorded in their logs. In general, most of the teachers began the semester attempting to create similar class plans for the two classrooms. We had asked the teachers, after all, to make the same major assignments, to use the same texts, and to pursue the same overall course goals in the two classrooms. We anticipated that the teachers in the study would begin to use different teaching strategies to meet those goals as the semester progressed—as we had done in our own teaching. As the study progressed, most, but not all the teachers, recognized and adapted to the differences between the two classroom settings.

In general, teachers in the Transitions Study created daily plans that differed substantially between settings (see Table 6.2). This was not true of all days, however, nor was it evenly distributed across the teachers. Anita, the teacher with the most experience in the computer classroom, created daily plans that differed between classroom settings for about half the class days in the semester. Anita's emphasis in the computer classroom consistently favored students' individual and small-group work that fostered their independence in the classroom. The class plans in her teacher log also substantiate the observations Anita made in her interviews—that students in the computer classroom were more likely to write and revise without as much direct instruction from her.

Like Anita, Caitlin indicated in her teacher log that about half of her class plans differed between the traditional and the computer classrooms. Like Anita, Caitlin used the DAILY files to encourage student writing at the beginning of the class session in the computer classroom, and she adapted many of these writing tasks for the traditional classroom as well. Again, like Anita, Caitlin held peer-review workshops in both classes, and many of the classes with the same class plan were workshop or drafting days. Caitlin encouraged students to use the com-

TABLE 6.2.
The Number of Class Plans Changed From Traditional to Computer Classroom

Teacher	Number of classes in which plans differed
Anita	23 of 45
Caitlin	20 of 45
Candace	32 of 45
Jen	10 of 45

puter network for certain in-class activities, and those class plans differ noticeably from the plan of the traditional class. But once again like Anita, Caitlin designed activities in the computer classroom that typically gave students more time to work independently or in small groups on writing tasks directly related to their paper topics.

Candace, the teacher with the least experience in the computer classroom, created daily plans with the most striking differences between the two classroom settings. She seems to have discovered quickly that having students write in the computer classroom made them more responsible for their writing and most effectively de-centered the classroom:

> The fact that they're in a computer class where the emphasis is truly on their writing in the classroom, not outside the classroom, changes it a great deal. As a teacher, that frees you up to do real work with their writing rather than to manage the classroom

Moreover, Candace reacted strongly to the group dynamic in her two sections of CO150. She repeatedly commented in the interviews that the students in her traditional class seemed easily bored. As we note above, she arranged two "field trips" to alternate sites on campus to spark this group's discussion of ideas in the professional essays she assigned. Candace also remarked that students in the traditional class were unusually difficult to motivate when she offered them time to write in class. After some early negative reactions to in-class free-writing, Candace planned more activities that dealt with sample essays (professional and peer works) so that students could sharpen their critical reading through guided annotation and their critical thinking through extended discussion of the texts.

In contrast, in her computer classroom, Candace observed that students were eager to write, and her class plans show that she offered them opportunities to write in class for significant amounts of time almost every day. When we observed Candace's classes, we noted that she consistently focused more class time on individual writing. Throughout her teacher log, this emphasis on individual writing recurs day after day. As she told us in her end of the semester interview:

> There weren't students sitting there with their arms crossed and with an attitude, and it wasn't me having to push the idea of writing. It was them doing their work and being invested in it, and I really believe that the computer classroom makes students feel more empowered. It gives them more control. I think in every way they do more writing. They do more revising.

Of the 13 days that Candace planned the same activities for both classes, five were full-class workshops for peer review of essays-in-progress and four were conference days. In other words, excluding days devoted to workshops and conferences, on only four days out of 45 class meetings in the semester did Candace conduct the same activities in both her computer and traditional classrooms. Clearly this teacher, although lacking considerable experience in a computer classroom, did not hesitate to respond to the group dynamics and the setting of her classes in ways that allowed students in the computer classroom to set their own pace for writing and learning.

Teachers need to allow students to take control, however, and Jen presents a notable contrast from the other three teachers in this respect. Although Jen perceived that the computer classroom fostered greater *student* control of pacing, she was extremely uncomfortable with giving over control. As a result—and at least in part because Jen did not adapt well to the computer classroom—few of Jen's class plans differed between classroom settings. Our experience tells us that some teachers need a relatively long time in the computer-classroom before they become comfortable enough to adapt their teaching techniques. Jen appears to be one of these teachers.

Unlike the other teachers, who used DAILY prompts to set students up for discussion or to draw upon what they had learned from reading the textbook or sample essays, Jen used DAILY almost exclusively to announce homework tasks and to outline the plan of action for that day's class. The DAILY, then, simply replaced the homework notes and class outline that she jotted on the board at the beginning of her traditional class. Jen also used lectures far more often than any other teacher in the study. Except for class meetings devoted to conferences, peer-review workshop, and in-class revising, Jen lectured for at least part of the hour during every class meeting in the computer classroom as well as in the traditional classroom. Although she incorporated small-group activities into both her traditional and computer classes, she generally maintained tight control over the pacing of activities in both classroom settings.

Jen reminds us that not all teachers operate in alternative teaching environments *in the same ways.* Teachers bring with them their predispositions about what activities work best for them and for their students. They also bring with them deeply rooted models of good teaching. If those models and assumptions do not match as comfortably with a new environment, it takes longer for these teachers to see the ways that the new environment calls for change in their teaching techniques. Some teachers decide that the change is too radical because it upsets too many of their assumptions or features of their mental model of good teaching. We have worked with some teachers over the years who simply could not find any way to feel comfortable in a computer classroom. Other teachers, like Jen, enjoy the challenge of the new environment but need longer to adapt to it. We need to give these teachers both the time and the rationale for change so that they can examine their models of teaching to see how they can change, first, their assumptions about teaching and, second, their techniques in the new environment.

What We Can Learn from the Teachers in Our Study

The four teachers in the Transitions Study do not represent the entire range of teaching styles and approaches, but the common elements of their experience match well with reactions from other teachers who work in the two classroom settings. The key changes we discuss in this section are typical of teachers we've trained over the past decade. Computers disperse the focal point of the classroom. It is much harder for a teacher to be at the head of a class in a computer classroom like ours. As a result, alternatives to lecturing or proscenium teaching work better in the computer classroom, and our teachers successfully adapt many of the teaching strategies that we detail in the next section.

CLASSROOM ACTIVITIES FOR BOTH CLASSROOM SETTINGS

Our examination of the teaching logs kept by the four teachers in the Transitions Study suggests two broad categories of techniques that work interchangeably in both teaching contexts: peer-review workshops and collaborative groups. In this section, we briefly examine how these familiar techniques play out in the two classroom settings.

Peer-Review Workshops

Teachers in the Transitions Study used peer-review workshops throughout students' drafting and revising processes. For the most part, teachers used the same workshop prompts and the same logistical arrangements regardless of classroom setting. Only when students were reviewing relatively small chunks of text—for example, introductions or brief summaries of readings—did teachers generally ask students to read the texts on the computer monitors. Typically, the teachers in our study preferred to have students work from paper copies of work-in-progress so that students could write suggestions directly on the page.

On occasion, however, teachers took advantage of the computer classroom to change the dynamic of peer review. Rather than having students work in pairs or small groups at the tables, teachers asked students to exchange papers, read them, and then answer review prompts in a DAILY file. Because students typically type more lengthy comments than they write by hand on pre-printed workshop sheets, students receive fuller responses to workshop prompts when the workshops are conducted via the computer. After typing their commentary, students reconvened as groups and went over their comments together, making additional notes on the drafts of papers.

An alternative approach to workshops that the teachers used during the study involved a commenting feature in the word processing software. Students can read the workshop paper on the screen and embed their comments directly in the electronic text. The comment feature shows all embedded comments in boxes so that the writer and teacher can distinguish between suggestions. (The latest version of this software shows comments as icons in the margins of a text. Writers click on an icon to open a text box containing a comment.) The comment can interrupt a sentence to point out a spelling or punctuation error, for instance, or can appear between sentences or paragraphs. A comment box can accommodate lengthy comments so that peer reviewers (or teachers) can suggest new lines of development, possible rearrangement, major deletions, or audience concerns, and can also explain the rationale for the suggestions. A single keystroke turns all embedded comments into a font unlike the draft's so that the comments are clearly distinctive from the original text.

Use Computers to Encourage Peer Review:

- Ask students to bring up the paper they want reviewed. Then have students move clockwise (or counterclockwise) around the room to read and comment.
- Ask students to bring up the paper they want to have reviewed. Then have students move to the opposite side of the room to begin reading and commenting. When students finish with one paper, they move to an empty computer because students read and comment at different speeds. This technique is particularly helpful because people don't know who's commenting on their draft.
- Have students work on only one segment of an essay, for instance, the introduction or the weakest body paragraph.
- If students are uncomfortable using the comment feature or reading on the screen, remind them that they can annotate the paper itself and talk about their commentary.

By and large, though, our teachers still use peer-review workshops in the same ways and for the same reasons in both traditional and computer classrooms. Teachers and students value the insights and advice that workshops provide as well as the opportunities to revise in light of suggestions from readers.

Collaborative Work in Small Groups

In both traditional and computer classrooms, the teachers in the Transitions Study assigned small-group work that helped students meet several of the goals implicit in Hairston's list of process-paradigm features. In particular, small-group activities in both classrooms helped students

- consider the writing process,
- learn specific strategies for generating and gathering material,
- learn specific strategies for arranging material,
- learn about audience and how targeting specific readers helps writers make effective rhetorical choices, and
- learn *through* writing as well as communicate what they've learned by writing about their insights.

Table 6.3 shows class plans Anita put together for a session on selecting and arranging material. The group work focuses students' attention on writerly choices and effects on readers. Students in the computer classroom used the computers to record and share their observations about the sample essays, while students in the traditional classroom used paper and "sneaker net" to give their comments to group members. The learning activity is the same in both classrooms, but students in the computer classroom left with printouts of their observations. To repeat a point we made earlier, students who type their work in this kind of activity often write more than students who write by hand, and so the computer classroom students are likely to have fuller lists and descriptions than students in the traditional classroom. To compensate for the extra time students needed to write their descriptions in the computer classroom, Anita assigned two

Use DAILY to Organize a Variety of Group Activities:

- to provide detailed instructions for group work.
- to generate criteria for workshops—in small groups or individually and then in small groups.
- to set up round robin techniques; for example, teachers ask student to write an issue for the argument essay and then other students move to each computer and respond to the issues posed.

TABLE 6.3.
Anita's Paired Classes Using Groups to Learn About Essay Arrangement

Traditional class	Computer class
Class 10	**Class 10**
Objectives:	**Objectives:**
1. Look at shaping strategies for investigative essays.	1. Look at shaping strategies for investigative essays.
2. Begin drafting essay (or introduction).	2. Begin drafting essay (or introduction).
During class:	**During class:**
1. Each student will write down shaping techniques that could be used by students as they draft their individual investigative essays and then pass their notes to their first partner. The "first partner" will add shaping strategies he/she discovered and then pass the combined notes to the next partner. Students will first address Quammen's piece and then begin the process again and address Silko's essay.	1. Each student will write down shaping techniques that could be used by students as they draft their individual investigative essays and then pass their notes to their partner. The "partner" will add shaping strategies he/she discovered and then send a copy back to their partner. Students will first address Quammen's piece and then begin the process again and address Silko's essay.
2. If time, as a class we will generate a list of shaping strategies or techniques on the board.	2. If time, as a class we will generate a list of shaping strategies or techniques on the board.

students to each group in the computer classroom and three in the traditional classroom.

Caitlin was also comfortable using small groups in each setting, and like Anita she modified group activities to take full advantage of the setting (see Table 6.4 for Caitlin's paired class activities). Like Anita, Caitlin changed the size of the group because she knew that students working at the computer took longer but produced more commentary on the topic proposals. Unlike Anita, Caitlin kept students together in groups so that they could talk and write at the same time, whether on paper or on the computer. Although Caitlin's class plan looks similar for the two classrooms, the small changes are significant. By the end of the computer activity, Caitlin expected students to have a complete draft of the topic proposal for her to review. In the traditional classroom, Caitlin knew that students would need to take the group input home and revise on paper to prepare a clean topic proposal she could collect at the next class meeting. Moreover, students in the computer classroom would not have time during class to begin generating interview questions, but they were well prepared to do that work on their own because the topic proposals could guide their independent work. In the traditional classroom, Caitlin hoped to guide students' next step into interviewing a bit more closely by reviewing with them—as much as possible—the kinds of interview questions they jotted down in class.

TABLE 6.4.
Caitlin's Paired Classes Using Groups to Prepare Topic Proposals

Traditional class	Computer class
Class 6 **Objectives:** 1. Work on topic proposals. 2. Prepare for independent work on investigating essay. 3. Explain how to interview. **During Class:** 1. In groups, look at topic proposals and work to focus topics and solidify question (20 min) (See group directions below.) 2. Talk about questions you have about the topic proposal (10 min) 3. Discuss interviewing (5 min) 4. Write out possible questions for your interview. Show these to your neighbor and discuss. I'll circulate to answer questions. *Investigating Topic Proposal Group Activity (on transparency)* 1. Get into groups of 3 people. 2. Have the first person share his/her topic ideas and other information from the topic proposal sheet. 3. The other group members should help the first person with any questions she/he may have. Suggest interview possibilities, focusing strategies, sources, maybe help the person choose which topic is most interesting. Person #1 should take notes so he/she can revise the topic proposal. 4. When person #1 feels comfortable (reasonably) with his/her topic, repeat the process with the next 2 group members. 5. On the back of your topic proposal sheets, write down any questions you want to ask me or the rest of the class.	**Class 6** **Objectives:** 1. Finish topic proposals. 2. Prepare for independent work on investigating essay. 3. Explain how to interview. **During Class:** 1. DAILY activity in pairs. (See detailed instructions below.) 2. Discuss any questions about topics. (10 min) 3. Discuss interviewing. (10 min) DAILY: Pull your topic proposal onto the screen. With the person next to you, discuss what you have so far; use the questions on the board to guide your discussion. If you have questions, raise your hand and I'll come over. Maybe ask the person next to you for some input. The goal is for you to finalize your topic proposal and report to me your workable topic that you plan to write your investigating essay on. When you are finished with your topic proposal, save it as a Word Perfect file and then use today's handout to mail it to me. You have 30 minutes to do this.

Each of the teachers in our study often used the same small-group activities in each setting, sometimes without modification. Changes that they made, although not dramatic, helped students in the computer classroom derive additional benefits from the group tasks. In the next section, we turn to techniques that teachers used in both classrooms but felt that they must change significantly to adapt to the setting.

ADAPTING TRADITIONAL CLASSROOM ACTIVITIES FOR COMPUTER CLASSROOMS

Three other common techniques in traditional classrooms—lecture, large-group discussion, and in-class writing—were used by teachers in the Transitions Study in both classroom settings. However, they modified these techniques in important ways to ensure success in the computer classroom. In this section, we explore how the teachers adapted these techniques.

Lecture

As we mentioned above, our computer classroom is not conducive to lectures or extended presentational-mode, teacher-centered activities (teacher-directed question-answer sessions, for example). The computers provide multiple focal points that draw students' attention away from a central "lectern." The computers also raise the level of background noise so that extended lecturing takes a heavy toll on the speaker (resulting in repeated bouts of laryngitis for one teacher several years ago). Thus, we advise teachers moving into the computer classroom to revise wherever possible to limit lecture time.

The teachers in our study generally pointed out in their logs that they could easily substitute other activities for most lectures in the computer classroom. Some topics, such as key criteria for summarizing a reading, could easily be elicited from students during a DAILY task. Once students had individually typed what they knew about the topic, the teacher could ask for a quick recap from students who then compiled a complete list of features on the white board. Teachers might elaborate on a point or two during the large-group discussion, but for the most part, students provided the material and reminded each other of what they already knew.

Class outlines from Jen's classes provide a good example of how a teacher, who might otherwise lecture, discovered a more effective way to use the computers to meet students' needs. Table 6.5 shows that in the traditional classroom Jen remained comfortable with a strategy she had used successfully in the past. She had collected evaluating essays on April 11 and was now ready to return those essays to students on April 25. In the traditional class, then, Jen presented a general commentary on the class' strengths and weaknesses on the essay. Then she continued with a mini-lecture on improving coherence, an area where most students in the class needed to concentrate their attention during revision. As Jen commented in her teacher log,

Alternative Ways to "Deliver" Lecture Material:

- Find a short text that covers the same ground. Assign it as a handout or make it available on your network, even through DAILY.
- Ask two or three students to cluster around one computer. Use DAILY prompts to elicit the information from students. Then ask groups to read responses from each others' screen to check for accuracy and thoroughness.
- Set up an e-mail dialogue. Announce (through DAILY) what the topic of the day is. Then ask students to generate a question about the topic and to include the key point of the question in their subject line. Students sent questions to the class list. Any student who knows about that key point responds to the class list. (You can do the same activity on a bulletin board.)
- Use the three-ring circus strategy described in Chapter Seven. If you must lecture, lecture to a smaller group of students rather than to the class as a whole.

> I really like the instructional opportunities that turning back papers provides. . . . Students seemed pretty attentive during both presentations. It is interesting the way that they really listen during this type of activity. I think the feedback on strengths and weaknesses of individual assignments is a great way to provide reinforcement and clarification as to what the purpose of a specific essay is and how to meet that effectively. I feel as if it gives them something really concrete to work toward.

On the same day in the computer classroom, however, Jen chose a different approach because she knew that students would not listen attentively to 50 minutes of lecture in the computer classroom. Jen returned evaluating essays without the overview and simply asked students to start revising. She circulated to answer specific questions they had about her comments as well as possible directions for their revisions. Unlike the traditional class, this group of students did not need to devote special attention to coherence, and so Jen felt comfortable relying on students' reading of their individual comments rather than on a generalized overview of the class' strengths and weaknesses.

As teachers moving into computer classrooms quickly discover, some topics, like correct documentation format, are not easily replaced with student-based activities. Rather than lecture about these topics, teachers typically combine other kinds of activities to ensure that students know the information. For topics like documentation format, teachers often ask students to review text-based material (most textbooks have sections on documentation) and then to ask questions based

TABLE 6.5.
Jen's Paired Class Plans Leading to Revised Evaluating Essays

Traditional class	Computer class
Class 39	**Class 39**
Objectives:	**Objectives:**
1. To provide students with group feedback on evaluating essays. 2. To provide students with more tips for achieving coherent paragraphs and essays.	To provide you with individual feedback on and have you begin revising your evaluating essays.
During class:	**During class:**
1. Mini-lecture on feedback for evaluating essays. 2. Mini-presentation on useful tips for achieving coherence.	Keep on revising. Remember that I have set aside the whole of this week for your in-class revisions and one-on-one work. Really try to make the most of the time available to you. If you get stuck while working on your own papers and I am tied up with someone else, bounce ideas off your classmates and/or refer back to the assignment sheets and the textbook. I will circulate, giving you feedback and answering questions.

on the text and their attempts to use the information. These questions are guided to a particular partner or team through an e-mail, chat, or small-group activity, or they are posted on a class bulletin board for anyone in class to answer (including the teacher).

When our study teachers discovered a topic that they couldn't convey clearly enough through any other method or combination of methods, then they did lecture. But the teachers in our study typically limited themselves to "mini-lectures" of no more than 10 minutes.

Large-Group Discussion

Teachers in the Transitions Study generally felt that large-group discussion was more difficult to sustain in the computer classroom than in the traditional classroom. As Caitlin said in her interviews, she moved away from large-group discussion early in the term because it wasn't consistently working the way she wanted it to. Yet, an observer saw a class discussion that engaged and challenged students to express themselves clearly. It appears, then, that class discussion can be as effective in the computer classroom as in the traditional classroom. Candace makes this point throughout her interviews when she described her students in the computer classroom contributing more fully and more intelligently to large-group discussions because they had written about the readings before discussing. Although Candace didn't use large-group discussions in every class, she was pleased with the results of discussions she did have in the computer classroom.

The teachers in our study adapted their use of large-group discussion to take advantage of the computers. Most teachers, like Candace, asked students to write about the readings at the beginning of class. (We look at specific prompts in the next chapter.) After students had written for between five and 15 minutes, depending on the complexity of the reading assignment and the number of prompts teachers wanted students to consider, teachers planning a large-group discussion asked students to print out their DAILY responses and then face the center of the room or gather around the tables. Discussion was always easy to start because students could, if all else failed, read the response they had written just moments before. Typically, though, students were primed for discussion and eager to contribute. Teachers then followed up the discussion with some other activity, usually a writing task, in the computer classroom.

This typical sequence is illustrated by Candace's paired class plans for Class 34 (see Table 6.6). Candace had asked both classes to read a sample essay that used in-text documentation and the accompanying explanation of in-text documentation in their textbook. At the beginning of class, students in both classes began discussing the sample essay and raising questions about in-text documentation. In both classes, Candace remarked, "The discussion went well," but in the computer classroom Candace moved from discussion to workshop for a substantial portion of the class period. In the traditional classroom, discussion continued until the last five minutes of class when Candace asked students to review their essays-in-progress for problems with in-text documentation.

Candace clearly kept her goals for the class session in mind: she wanted students (1) to understand in-text documentation and (2) to use it appropriately in

TABLE 6.6.
Candace's Paired Classes Using Discussion About In-Text Documentation

Traditional class	Computer class
Class 34	**Class 34**
Objectives:	**Objectives:**
1. To review in-text documentation based on sample essay and textbook sources.	1. To review in-text documentation based on sample essay and textbook sources.
2. To be sure students know how to use in-text documentation in their current essay.	2. To be sure students know how to use in-text documentation in their current essay.
During Class:	**During Class:**
1. Class discussion of text materials. (45 min)	1. Class discussion of text materials. (30 min)
2. Students review their current essay for problems. (5 min)	2. Students pair up for workshop on their current essay for problems in in-text documentation. (20 min)

their papers. In the traditional classroom, she allowed a good discussion to take up more time because she felt confident that students could make the connection to their writing in a few minutes at the end of the class period. In the computer classroom, she moved from large-group discussion to workshop so that students could take advantage of the computer and workshop partners to begin revising their in-text citations and documentation entries during class time. Both classes met her goals for the class period, and both groups left the class that day feeling more confident about using in-text documentation. Candace met students' needs in both settings with changes in her plan that drew upon the strengths of each setting.

In-Class Writing

Teachers moving from the traditional to the computer classroom encourage students to take more class time for their writing. As we discussed at length in Chapter Five, students in our computer classrooms write almost every day, usually in response to specific prompts presented in the DAILY activities, but they also use class time for drafting and revising substantial chunks of their final papers. Table 6.7 suggests one way that Anita gave students in her class time to write. In the traditional classroom, she asked them to respond to several prompts to help them shape their next essay. She then presented them with an option to look for or read sources that might help them draft the next essay.

Use Computers to Encourage Student Feedback on Writing Process:

- Let students generate their own workshop sheets on computer. They generate criteria individually or in small groups and then evaluate their own papers or peers' papers.
- Form groups to review a paper. Bring up the paper and let a group of students discuss evaluative comments before an assigned typist from the group types comments on the computer.
- After students generate criteria and get feedback on a draft, ask them to comment on which criteria are most helpful and which they do not want to include on the next workshop sheet.
- After a workshop, ask students to use the computer to generate a revision plan.
- On the day that students turn in papers, prepare "postscript" questions that ask student to reflect on their writing process in this paper. Set up specific questions in a DAILY file.
- After you turn back papers, ask students to respond to clarity of comments. Make this a general prompt or set up specific questions in a DAILY file.

In the computer classroom, the same daily plan changed only slightly, but the change is important. By pointing out the "criteria" file among our prewriting template files, Anita gave students access to a computer-based file that guided them through detailed prewriting for an evaluating essay. (Students take as much time as they like with these files; some students take 30–40 minutes to work through them carefully.) Students in Anita's class thus supplemented the general prewriting prompts directed at audience, criteria, and evidence with specific prompts that helped them jot down and arrange the material they had already collected for their essays.

Anita's class plan gives students options for writing in either classroom, but the additional resource in the computer classroom provides those students with class time for guided work on their paper. Moreover, when our observers visited classes on days during which students had free time for writing, students in the computer classroom stayed on task throughout the class period better than students in the traditional classroom. Students noted that they preferred to draft at home rather than in the traditional classroom. But students in the computer classroom never expressed any dissatisfaction with drafting in that classroom. In fact, they often requested additional time for prewriting, drafting, and revising during class time in the computer classroom.

Ideas From Our Teachers About Using Computers During Class:

- I put worksheets on the computer so that it expands for them as they write.
- I use computers to help students generate peer-review criteria. They generate criteria, we use them on a sample, and then they work through a peer's paper at home and bring two copies of their comments to the next class session. I take one copy to look at it and the second copy goes back to the writer. This class is generally devoted to revising, and students will do a lot of checking on peer-review commentary with their teacher, their workshop partner, and their neighbors.
- I set up timed prompts as they generate material. Each prompt has lots of space following it. When I announce that they need to move on, students scroll down to the next prompt. This strategy also works with revision.
- I ask students to loop on the computer, with my verbal instructions to keep them going. They start writing, especially about claims; at the end of the first loop, I ask them to take the one sentence that captures their thinking and copy it into a new space, then keep writing.
- I like to have students freewrite in a letter to themselves that explains what they intend to do on an upcoming paper or write a letter to someone involved with their topic (editor, opponent).

TABLE 6.7.
Anita's Paired Classes Using In-Class Writing

Traditional class	Computer class
Class 32	**Class 32**
Objectives:	**Objectives:**
1. To prewrite for the evaluating essay	1. To prewrite for the evaluating essay
2. To determine how much more library work students need to do.	2. To determine how much more library work students need to do.
During class:	**During class:**
1. Prewrite on evaluating essay. Answer the following prompts. a. Describe and characterize your audience. b. What criteria (or standards for measurement) will this audience need to consider? c. Write an introduction to your evaluating paper. d. What information (or evidence) do you still need to gather to be able to write an effective evaluation? 2. Write a Works Cited page on the sources you have so far. 3. Continue reading and rereading your sources, annotating as you read. Draft, if you are prepared to do so.	1. Prewrite on evaluating essay. Use the "criteria" prewriting template under "prewrite" if you wish. It is fun and should help you consider your audience in relation to your topic. **Also,** answer the following prompts. a. Describe and characterize your audience. b. What criteria (or standards for measurement) will this audience need to consider? c. Write an introduction to your evaluating paper. d. What information (or evidence) do you still need to gather to be able to write an effective evaluation? 2. Write a Works Cited page on the sources you have so far. 3. Continue reading and rereading your sources, annotating as you read. Draft, if you are prepared to do so.

ADAPTING COMPUTER CLASSROOM ACTIVITIES FOR TRADITIONAL CLASSROOMS

In the last two sections, we consider minor changes in techniques as teachers in the Transitions Study adapted classroom activities to computer classrooms. In this section, we explore how teachers adapted computer-classroom activities for traditional classrooms. We focus our discussion on peer-review workshops, collaborative group activities, lecture, large-group discussion, and in-class writing.

Peer-Review Workshops

Peer-review workshops conducted via computer are not an option for students while they are in traditional classrooms. But these students, too, can take advantage of computers when commenting on drafts of peers' papers. Rather than conducting all peer-review workshops during class, teachers might occasionally assign workshops outside of class. Students can use computer facilities on campus or take home workshop prompts to respond to on a word processor. By asking students to use computers to complete peer-review worksheets, teachers take advantage—at least occasionally—of students' tendency to type longer comments than they would write by hand on workshop sheets. Students begin the next class by exchanging worksheets and talking about the commentary with reviewers.

Collaborative Groups

Collaborative groups can also take advantage of computers available outside of class. We can imagine two situations that lend themselves to groups of students working together on writing projects:

1. If students have access to a campus computer network, all participants need not meet for collaborative group work. Students work independently on part of a task and e-mail their individual contributions to each other. As students read each other's mail, they continue to exchange ideas by mailing additional comments and ideas to all the members of the group. One member, designated in advance, brings a print copy of the mail messages to class so that the group can continue to work face-to-face or to synthesize conclusions drawn from all group members' input. For example, suppose the group project involves reporting to the class on how to identify and locate library holdings of books and periodicals on a given topic. Students in the group divide tasks, complete the library leg-work at a convenient time, mail their findings to group members, and then meet briefly to polish the presentation for the class. In this scenario, the electronic exchanges ameliorate a serious difficulty for students—meeting with a group outside of class time. Moreover, as this example suggests, students complete the group work with a print record of their activities so that they present detailed information to the class and also show the teacher their individual contributions to the group activity.
2. When a teacher wants to encourage group activity with all members present, the computer is still a useful medium for organizing and capturing students' work. (Because students often find it difficult to meet regularly with group members outside of class, teachers may want to assign these face-to-face collaborative groups only occasionally.) Imagine that a teacher wants students to participate actively in discussion and decides to have small groups (pairs or triplets) lead discussion of key essays. Before students complete this task, they must meet to discuss what the essay is about (literally) as well as key points that they want to bring up in discussion. The teacher might well decide that students need some guidance about how to proceed, and, thus, prepares prompts to help students with the task. In a computer file available in a computer lab or on disk for students to work together over a computer off cam-

pus, the teacher creates questions that help students work through the literal points of the essay. Then the teacher includes useful questions that generally spark discussion. Students using this file type in their responses to each question, expanding the file as much as necessary as they think about, discuss, and polish their ideas for class discussion. After students complete the file, they have a cleanly printed paper that guides their classroom activity, and the teacher has an easy-to-read record of their work.

Even without working in a computer classroom, teachers can imagine creative ways to encourage students to use computers outside of class, particularly when teachers want to see a neatly printed record of students' group activity.

Lecture

The key feature of lecture that teachers in our computer classroom study agreed they would take with them to the traditional classroom was the time limit. All agreed that mini-lectures were more effective than the occasional longer presentations they had given in traditional classrooms in the past. For some teachers and some topics, limiting lecture time is easier if forced to do so by the computer environment. But even for those teachers who don't teach in computer classrooms, awareness of the short time students listen effectively helps them lecture wisely and sparingly.

Large-Group Discussions

Large-group discussions will always be a staple of the traditional writing classroom. But one benefit seen in our study of the computer classroom reinforces good teaching practice in the traditional classroom. The teachers in our study—and other teachers who have used the same techniques in traditional and computer classrooms—remind us that students who *write before discussing* tend to have greater confidence about their contributions to discussions. The prompts for writing need not take much time for students to respond to, but asking students to reflect on paper about key issues, information, or writing techniques in a reading assignment generally elicits better discussion about the textual material. Similarly, teachers who ask students to write about the key points made in the prior class see students better prepared to pick up where the last class was interrupted. Students who write about their confusions articulate more clearly what they need re-explained or further developed. In short, writing before discussion primes students about what they know and don't know, what positions they take, and what evidence they have for their opinions.

In-Class Writing

Finally, in-class writing fills an important need in the traditional classroom as well as the computer classroom. Anita, the teacher with the most computer-classroom experience in our study, was emphatic in her explanation about re-importing what she had learned from the computer classroom back into the traditional classroom:

> I have students write in the regular classroom . . . I literally have them drag out their drafts and mark on them and write in it and re-write. . . . One of the first points I make in the class is that if you think you're going to save all of your ideas until you get to your word processor, you're wrong. You're going to be generating text right here in class.

Students do need to understand why they are writing, of course, and that their in-class writing adds value to their out-of-class writing. But, as Anita explains, "When you set the expectation for your students, they really don't have a problem." Again, our teachers in the Transitions Study all remarked that they could see ways to include more in-class writing in their traditional classrooms in the future.

USING TRANSITIONS TO REINVIGORATE TEACHING

The computer classroom pushes teachers to imagine different ways to engage students in learning about and practicing writing. However, the lessons of the computer classroom need not apply only in high tech settings. All writing teachers could periodically re-examine effective teaching techniques by imagining those techniques in a different learning and teaching environment. When we adapt our teaching to new environments, we build our strengths as teachers—not only through techniques that we know work, but also through our creativity in expanding and adapting our repertoire of teaching strategies. As we move into new and challenging teaching contexts, we must also build on our fundamental strength: our concern for helping students become confident and successful writers.

7

Curriculum Design: Doing More with Less

In this chapter, we continue looking at the ways the teachers in the two studies planned class sessions. Before we look at specific strategies developed for the computer classroom, we consider briefly the background information we provide for new teachers just beginning to work in a computer-classroom context. Because we discuss these general guidelines with all teachers new to our computer classroom, we need to discuss them briefly here to explicate teachers' choices in designing curricula for the computer classroom.

SOME CAVEATS

Before our teachers begin in the computer classroom, we always remind them of caveats that make their planning easier and more effective:

- You are teaching a writing class, not a class on word processing or general computer use.
- Computer glitches happen (usually when a computer problem can most disrupt the class, a.k.a. *Murphy's law*), but not as often as you might think.
- The design of a computer classroom typically discourages lecturing, so alternatives to lecture are more likely to succeed.
- It is tempting to simply add to your proven repertoire of teaching activities, but doing so can significantly increase students' workload.

Let's look at each of these caveats briefly to see why they are so crucial to success in a computer classroom.

Teach Writing, Not Word Processing

Just as we would never spend time in a high-school or college writing class helping students learn to script with a fountain pen, teachers often mistakenly assume that teaching in a computer classroom means giving up several weeks of writing instruction to teach students how to use a word processor. In fact, over the years we have taught writing in computer settings, the percentage of incoming students who already know word processing skills has risen from less than five percent in 1982 to over 90 percent in 1994. Almost every student who takes a writing class in a computer classroom already has substantial computer skills. Most know at least one word processing program, and some have worked on sophisticated spreadsheet and graphics packages. Many students have used hypertext programs to learn disciplinary information. In short, many students have more technical expertise than their teachers. (Non-traditional aged students may or may not have such extensive experience with computers and may feel more computer anxiety. Talk privately with those students to calm fears, if any, on both sides. If non-traditional students comprise your entire class, a brief class discussion on the first or second day of class helps you establish their backgrounds and dispel their fears.) Although students may not know the specific word-processing program installed in your computer classroom, if they have a conceptual framework for word processing, they will easily learn the keystrokes, commands, or mouse clicks to operate the program you use.

And that brings us to the key reason for teaching writing, not word processing. We all know from practical experience (and many research studies support our common knowledge) that we learn new skills best when they are meaningful. In other words, if we have a real context for learning the skill, we are more likely to learn it. Students can learn word processing functions by rote, but they are less likely to remember them than if they learn them *as they are completing a real writing task.* And so, our teachers always begin their planning by thinking backward:

- What outcome do I hope to see from students at the end of this sequence of my class?
  - What skills does that outcome require from students?
    - What skills s I work on first?
      - How can I give students authentic writing tasks to build those skills?
        - What word processing functions can I introduce students to as they work through the intermediate writing tasks?

In our writing courses at all levels, one of the goals that we stress is the ability to select relevant details and incorporate them into written texts. Using this as an example, a possible first writing task of the semester might ask students to discover details that make people distinctive. Working backwards from our course goal, we can imagine the following scenario that emphasizes writing but that helps students become familiar with word processing:

On the first day of class, every computer has a blank screen ready for students to begin writing. (We don't necessarily ask them to log-in to the system, to access the word processing program, or to load disks.) We ask them to start writing an introduction of the person sitting in the next seat. They can't complete the task without a short interview, and so they begin introducing themselves to each other. After 10 minutes of animated talk, students begin writing. The teacher sees by walking around the room which students already know the word-processing program and which don't. The teacher identifies which students know how to type efficiently. The teacher can encourage some playfulness with the word-processing program even for those students who are simply trying to jot down ideas without correcting spelling. After just a few minutes, every student has learned a key word-processing skill—inputting text—without receiving any direct instruction.

Depending on the skill level of students in your class, you may need to spend time on short, direct writing tasks that allow students to familiarize themselves with the features of your word processor. Our experience is that most students now come into a writing class already knowing the basic features of word processing (inputting text, deleting blocks, cutting and pasting, saving files) and so teachers can clearly concentrate on the *writing* necessary for students to succeed in the class. Through that writing, students quickly learn how to compose and revise comfortably with any given word-processing program.

Computer Glitches Happen

As we point out in Chapter Eight, no amount of preparation can arm teachers for every contingency in the computer classroom. Some problems are specific to a given machine (the one with the bad disk drive, for instance) or a given student (the one who panics when her password doesn't appear on the screen and so she keeps re-keying it). Good communication between teachers about faulty equipment can head off some problems (if a disk drive eats a disk at 10 a.m., the 11 a.m. teacher tells students not to use that disk drive). Technical support is crucial, and if your composition program does not have a systems administrator or a hotline to the computer center, lobby for one immediately!

Some problems are unavoidable. For example, one day a student was writing eagerly in response to prewriting prompts on the screen; she worked furiously for almost an hour and then kicked the computer's plug out of the wall in front of her! When she screamed and explained the problem, everyone in the room groaned, and then they all immediately saved the file they were working on. No one else in that class lost work again that semester—for any reason.

But many computer glitches can be avoided. For instance, before we upgraded the server on our current network system, we discovered that asking 24 students to do the same system request at the same time brought the system to its knees (it wouldn't actually shut down, but it took so long to respond that it might as well have died). As a result, we use as an instructive example the effects of Kate's decision to help students log-in to their accounts several years ago. Students dutifully listened to Kate's instructions and all typed in their passwords at the same moment. About 10 minutes later, the class simply had to give up waiting for the computer that day. Again, no one else has made that computer mistake since we learned this flaw of our system through Kate's well-intentioned mistake. If you're new to the computer classroom, check with the supervisor who trains new teachers or with other teachers who have used the room before. They know the avoidable problems and can give you tips about how to recover if you should make those mistakes.

Some computer glitches, though, just happen. And sometimes they are serious. If you plan your class with specific goals in mind, then you can usually adapt the same task for a non-computer supported activity. Writing activities can shift from the computer to paper. Interactive tasks can translate directly into small-group activities. Stay flexible and don't panic! If you need a few minutes to catch your breath and re-imagine your class plan, say so to students. They won't mind a few minutes to catch their breath, too.

Another technique that comes up in conversations with teachers who have several semesters of experience in the computer classroom is quite simple. Among the many techniques passed on by these teachers is the idea of always carrying a handout on a topic you can lecture on or have a whole-group discussion about. Some teachers prepare a handout on plagiarism or citing sources; others have materials on editing bugaboos; still others take a favorite reading that they like to discuss with the entire class. When the computer system fails completely or when an electrical storm comes up (never let students continue to work on the computers during a thunderstorm because of the potential for electrical shock), bring out the handout. Explain how and why the topic fits into the course or into the particular paper students are working on. Enjoy a few moments—or maybe even the rest of the class—on the diversion. And then tell students that the class will be back on track at the next class session. Preparing for the worst will calm any teacher's fears about coping with a sudden computer failure. But remember to expect the best, too, because computer glitches are becoming less and less common as the hardware and software we purchase improves.

Think of Alternatives to Lecturing

As we discuss in Chapter Four, our computer-classroom layout works against a single focal point for students' attention. As a result, teachers need to spend time re-thinking class plans that center on the teacher as a presenter of information. Moreover, shifting away from presentational mode doesn't always call for a simple or obvious change. Some material is best delivered by the teacher, and so teachers must find alternatives to extended lecture. Other material is adaptable to small-group or individual reading and writing tasks. Deciding which material fits into which category is not always easy, particularly for a new teacher in the computer classroom.

We recommend that new teachers limit any presentational material to about 10 minutes a day. Most teachers find that they can work within this guideline to recast most of the class plan but still retain a portion of lecture for those informational points that simply need to be delivered. As we discuss in detail in Chapters Three and Six, the teachers in the Transitions Study first reshaped those parts of the lesson that fell clearly into group work or some other mode of delivery. Then the parts that weren't clearly transmutable remained as mini-lectures. Over time, as teachers gain more confidence and experience in the computer classroom, most of these mini-lectures also get transformed into non-lecture format.

Again, let us provide a brief example. The one piece of the curriculum that seems to demand presentation mode is the explanation of the policy statement at the beginning of the semester. Our university and our composition program require a written statement of relevant course policies, such as required texts, reading and writing assignments, consequences of absences or unfinished work, and grading scale and percentages. We also urge teachers in our program to include on this handout information about the Writing Center, other support services on campus, and composition program placement procedures. Typically, teachers fill a page or two with information that captures the essence of the groundrules for that teacher and that section of composition. Teachers need to go over this material with students to ensure that they understand the importance of the policies and that the policies themselves are clear. Yet, it is often a tedious 20-to-30 minutes of class time if the teacher does all the talking.

One of the more experienced teachers in our computer classroom has figured out how not to lecture about class policies. First, she asks students to read through her policy statement while she learns their names. Then she asks students to turn to the computer and write the three most important pieces of information they learned from the handout. As she walks around the room reading over their shoulders, she notes which policies seem clearest to students and which still need some glossing. She asks for questions and then turns students to the next writing task (the introduction exercise). While students write, she starts in one corner of the room and asks a student a question about the policy statement. In a few seconds, three students gather around to ask questions about policies. When she answers those questions, she moves down to the next person she has not yet talked to and again asks about a policy. Four students now cluster around.

Although the teacher has to answer the same questions many times, students ask more questions in the small groups than they ever ask when she presents the same information in a large group. Students also seem much clearer about policies, and there are fewer questions about policies as the semester progresses.

Our educational system so often puts teachers at center stage that we sometimes cannot see alternatives to that position. When we ask teachers to imagine alternatives, they typically find creative and exciting ways to engage students in learning and writing, and our computer classroom sets up these alternatives more clearly, we think, than the traditional classroom environment can.

Don't Simply Add Teaching Activities to Your Curriculum

Teachers new to computer classrooms typically—and reasonably—want to continue using teaching activities that have proven effective in their previous classes. This makes sense. Experienced teachers shouldn't expect to start from scratch when they enter a new teaching environment. Yet teachers are also tempted by the wide range of new activities available to them in the computer classroom. Sometimes, rather than weighing which activities (both new and old) are most likely to contribute to specific curricular goals, teachers simply choose to add new activities to their curricula.

For students, this can mean that, in addition to doing assignments typically asked of them in traditional classrooms, they are also asked to do assignments that are appropriate for the computer classroom. Rather than replacing journal writing with posting messages to a class e-mail list or electronic bulletin board, some teachers ask students to complete both activities. Rather than replacing certain items on a library research activity with new items about the World Wide Web and online library catalogs, some teachers add new items to an existing list. In short, students can find that they are asked to do significantly more work in a computer classroom than their peers in other classrooms—both traditional and computer.

Asking students to post messages to a class electronic bulletin board is a case in point. This activity is one that we strongly advocate, both because it allows students to share their perceptions about assigned readings or issues of interest to the class and because it encourages dialogue among students about those issues. We typically find that the number of messages posted in response to classmates' messages significantly outnumber those made in response to the original assignment. Reading and responding to these messages, however, can be extremely time consuming. If 25 students in a class each post a short message it can take an hour or more just to read all the messages. Some students—particularly those whose schedule is constrained by work or family obligations—will find it difficult to find the time to both contribute to the bulletin board and to complete additional assignments. Typically, their performance will suffer in one or more areas.

Most teachers learn fairly early in their careers how much work they can reasonably expect of their students. When they move to the computer classroom, however, they sometimes underestimate the time students need to carry out certain activities. We strongly encourage teachers new to the computer classroom to carefully consider which activities—both traditional and computer-based—are most likely to contribute to specific teaching goals, and then to choose those that are most effective. Simply adding new activities to a classroom can have unintended—and unfavorable—results.

DOING MORE WITH LESS: TEACHERS DO MORE IN *ADVANCE*; STUDENTS DO MORE *DURING* CLASS

"In the computer classroom, there's much more showing and doing, no more telling." When one of our colleagues made this remark several years ago, the teachers who heard him were astounded. This professor generally relies on lecture, in both theory and writing classes. Before he taught in the computer classroom, he tended to talk about writing, and students did little writing in class. After he taught in the computer classroom, he shifted to "more showing and doing." In effect, the computer classroom offers an environment that shifts responsibilities in the classroom. During class time in the computer classroom, students are more likely to engage in writing and collaborative activities focused around the computer. They are much more likely to focus on their own writing rather than professional texts or teacher talk. They have more latitude and, thus, responsibility for concentrating on their work and developing their papers in the classroom setting. When we look at the typical daily plans recorded by our teachers in the study (see Chapter Six), we see the trend over and over—teachers *talk or tell* less, and students *show and practice* their skills more.

Getting students engaged in their writing and learning doesn't happen by accident, however. Teachers who hope to use the computer classroom to foster this shift from telling to doing must plan carefully in advance. Kate often uses the watchmaker analogy—get all the pieces in good working order, wind it up, and let it go! The classroom activities need to be meaningful and carefully sequenced before students engage fully in them. If students don't see the relationship between writing or collaborative tasks assigned in a given class session and the papers they eventually turn in for grading, they will not work with good will in any class, whether it's computer-supported or not.

Because of this, planning needs to allow sufficient flexibility for students to work at different levels and for different lengths of time. Yet it also needs to provide clear connections in the larger sequence leading to the goals for the individual papers and the course as a whole. In Chapter Six, we concentrate on how teachers adapt general teaching strategies for traditional and computer-supported classrooms. In this chapter, we look at specific strategies our teachers develop for the computer classroom to shift the burden of work to students.

NEW TEACHING STRATEGIES FOR THE COMPUTER CLASSROOM

We divide this section of teaching strategies into two general categories. The first category includes those techniques that start students into the new routine of using computers during class time. The second category includes those techniques that fit many different topics as the semester progresses.

Getting Started with the Semester: Logistical Issues

The computer classroom presents challenges unlike those of a traditional classroom, particularly at the beginning of the semester before students become familiar with the new environment. Although some of these problems may diminish in the future as students exploit non-traditional environments throughout their schooling, students are often as new to computer-classroom environments as their teachers. As a result, teachers need to keep a few guidelines in mind:

1. Set clear groundrules.
2. Establish a clear routine for the opening of class sessions, particularly at the beginning of the term.
3. Emphasize strategies for learning names.

Set clear groundrules

After years of schooling, students have clear, if generally unarticulated, expectations about what happens in traditional classrooms. Teachers dominate the space and attention by taking up a key focal point; teachers direct activities; students participate but only in typical and accepted ways. When students walk into a computer classroom, the layout itself undercuts their expectations. They see no focal point for teachers, who sometimes sit with their backs to students while typing at a computer. They see computers that invite student activity unlike that of the traditional classroom. Frankly, most students walking into our computer classroom mistake it for a computer laboratory, and their behavior will reflect "lab" models rather than "classroom" models unless teachers make clear that the computer classroom is indeed a classroom. (If "lab" behavior doesn't bother you, then don't worry about this advice. But many of our teachers find their first experiences with students' unexpected "lab" behavior disconcerting.)

In a lab, students work together and talk while they do so. No problem in a computer classroom. But students also expect to leave when they finish a task rather than wait to see if the teacher has other follow-up tasks or a wrap-up comment for the whole class. They sometimes assume that because lab work is independent they can start it 10 or 15 minutes after the start of the official class hour—particularly if it takes a few extra minutes to finish that last cup of coffee. Students also assume that computer labs in particular are available for dropping into whenever they need to finish typing or printing.

Experienced teachers in our computer classrooms remind us when we train new teachers that it is important to set clear expectations about behavior in the classroom. Because most of our teachers conduct classes (not just open lab hours for students to drop in to write) they ask students to get to class on time. (As we note elsewhere, the norm is for students to arrive early and begin work on DAILY activities. There are, however, students who don't fit the norm.) When teachers are ready to begin a large-group discussion or small-group activity or even individual writing, they want to feel confident that all the students are there and ready to begin work.

Teachers also explain that moving around the room is necessary: groups often include students who typically sit in all parts of the room, and students must move around to collect papers from the printers in the corners of the rooms. Nonetheless, our teachers typically remind students that independent work is not all that goes on in the writing class and that they expect students to stay until the class is dismissed.

Finally, but perhaps most important, teachers remind students that because the room holds classes, students are not welcome to drop in to use an open computer during someone else's class time—not even just to print a paper quickly. We all still have strangers who wander in from the hall to use a computer from time to time, but students quietly inform the stranger that a class is in session and the sheepish stranger exits quickly.

Briefly discussing basic groundrules and their rationale at the beginning of the semester helps teachers and students build clear expectations about comfortable behavior in the computer classroom.

Set a clear routine for the opening of class sessions

Setting a routine for the class also helps students learn how to treat the computer class as a class. For example, one teacher finds that asking all students to log-in as they enter the room but then to move to the center tables allows her to make a few announcements to set up specific tasks for the day, as well as how those tasks fit into a larger context. She then typically asks students to write at the computers, but if she needs to lecture briefly she can count on having their attention. Students learn the pattern and enjoy the community building afforded by the minutes around the table as they share stories of ski trips and basketball games.

Another teacher sets her routine quite differently. She always begins with students dropping drafts of papers into her "IN" basket. They rifle through her "OUT" basket to pick up drafts she has commented on since the last class. Students then read through comments as class members came into the room. When everyone is assembled, this teacher asks for and briefly responds to questions. Selected students then read work-in-progress, often just one student a day, but sometimes several. After the class comments on the pieces that are read aloud, they turn to the computer to complete assigned tasks, to revise, or to draft. Then, the teacher is available for mini-conferences.

The majority of the teachers in our computer classrooms ask students to come into the classroom and log-in. Under DAILY they know to look for a task with that day's date. They work on the DAILY until the teacher calls for students' attention—sometimes in just a few minutes and sometimes as long as 20 minutes into the class hour.

Because students know the routine in each case, they are comfortable coming into the computer classroom and settling in each day. Typically, over just a few days, students become so accustomed to the routine that they no longer notice that they are in a non-traditional classroom.

Emphasize strategies for learning names

All teachers develop tricks for learning students' names quickly, and many of those techniques work in the computer classroom. But teachers should anticipate looking at the backs of students' heads more often than their faces in many computer classrooms. Students stake out preferred territory in the computer classroom as well, and so they learn names and faces for people who sit next to them but not for people who sit across the room. For everyone, then, names are much harder to learn in the computer classroom than in the traditional classroom. Here are few tips our teachers compiled to help learn names quickly:

- During the first week or two of classes, whenever students face the teacher and each other, ask them to say their names when they ask questions or respond to your questions, or call on them by name as soon as you begin to feel confident that you know them. Ask students to address each other by name as well. (Explain why you're doing this so that students don't feel embarrassed by repeated use of their names.)
- Use name placards.
- Play a name game—there are many of these to choose from that work in a computer classroom as well as in a traditional classroom—every day for at least a week.
- Ask students to choose a computer for the first few weeks. Make up a seating chart and study it while students work.
- Circulate a sheet of paper to take attendance. Make sure students sign up in order. Then follow the same order as you go around the room and study heads and profiles.

Students have never objected when Kate touches them on the shoulder to get their attention and to double-check nicknames. And they are pleased to find that teachers care enough to learn their names quickly. They are also embarrassed, however, to admit that they don't know all their classmates' names, and so we keep using public reminders of names until *everyone* learns who's in the class.

Getting Started with the Semester: Taking Advantage of Computer Tools

A teacher new to the computer-networked classroom soon discovers that word processing is only one of several useful tools available to support student writers. Choosing which tools to use and how to integrate them into class depends on the goals of the course and the specific writing tasks you envision for students. Take the advice below, then, and modify it appropriately to fit your specific teaching context.

Two general caveats

We think two pieces of advice apply to every context. As we discuss in greater detail in Chapter Eight, integrate your use of technology into your curriculum. If you can't imagine a meaningful way to use a program to help *students as writers*, then don't use the program. The point of a writing class, after all, is to help students improve as writers, not to introduce them to the latest computer gadgetry. Second, introduce new tools where they seem most appropriate in your assignment sequence. This is really an extension of our first point, but it bears further discussion. Many computer classrooms provide a wide range of programs to use during class. Your goals as a teacher should guide you in when and how to introduce specific programs. While students may ask you for guidance in using programs that they see on their computers, you should feel no obligation to explain the "ins" and "outs" of a program that you won't use until late in the semester, or, for that matter, to go beyond providing them with the basic knowledge to use the program to accomplish class goals. You'll find a more detailed discussion of these issues in Chapter Eight.

Start with word processing; students need these skills to complete their in-class and out-of-class writing

Students become comfortable most quickly with the word-processing program in our computer classrooms when we introduce it in conjunction with meaningful writing tasks. If you use a graphical operating system such as Windows or the Macintosh, students are likely to learn more functions more quickly because icons or button bars are easier to remember and manipulate than the function keys or commands typically used in DOS or UNIX word processors.

Introduce other programs in the context of classroom activities and writing assignments

While students learn the word-processing program, you can also introduce other key computer tools. Because we access our DAILY files through a button on the graphical tool bar in our word-processing program, we get students started using that tool on the second day of class. If you have a more complex method for sending tasks and messages to the entire class, you might want to wait a week until students feel comfortable with the word processor before instructing them on how to find those tasks and messages.

Our teachers generally tell students about electronic mail in the first or second week of class and incorporate an activity that uses e-mail to help students understand its basic functions, including reading and sending mail. Again, our teachers find that a session that incorporates an e-mail discussion about a reading is a good starter. (See details following under R*epeated Strategies*.) Only after students are comfortable with the logistics of sending simple messages do teachers add the complication of attaching and retrieving files.

Besides using e-mail for discussion, some of our teachers encourage students to use e-mail for enhanced communication between teacher and students. One of our colleagues, Laura Thomas, often asks students to write messages at the end of a class with questions about the topics discussed that day so that she can respond individually to questions and confusions. Mike encourages students to attach drafts of their papers to e-mail messages asking for feedback on specific points. He quickly comments on these intervention drafts and returns his comments to students through e-mail.

If you decide to use an electronic bulletin board for the class, explain groundrules for posting (Should students use their names or pseudonyms? Are any topics off limits? Is flaming acceptable?) and whether students are required or simply invited to participate. Some bulletin board programs are temperamental, so prepare students to take a little longer to feel comfortable with the logistics of posting and reading messages.

Use Electronic Bulletin Boards to Extend Classroom Discussion:

Use electronic bulletin boards to extend discussions that begin during class or to create a foundation for upcoming discussions in class. Before you go to your next class, read student postings to identify areas for further in-class discussion. Some techniques:

- Ask students to post questions about the last major discussion in class. Then ask them to respond to one or two of their classmates' questions.
- Ask students to post their responses to an assigned reading. Ask them to read other students posts and identify overall themes.
- Use the bulletin board as an informal discussion list. Ask students to post about general issues related to the class and its content. Use the posts as a way to better target your classroom activities to student needs.
- Divide students into groups and ask them to role play responses to issues raised during class. If you use a class topic, ask students to role-play various positions on the topic. Or ask them to role-play various kinds of readers (e.g., skeptics, true-believers, etc.).
- Ask people from outside of class to join the class bulletin board as "guest speakers." Outside discussion members could be content-area experts, professionals from various disciplines, or students from other institutions.
- Create dialogues among students from different classes, at your institution or at others. Use the interplay between the groups as a springboard for discussion about audience issues, etc.

Similarly, if you decide to use a chat program (or real-time network communication program) for in-class online discussions, integrate it carefully into an assignment sequence and explain the groundrules for chatting. (One teacher recently discovered a student in her classroom chatting during class with a student in the next classroom.) This computer tool takes time not to learn but to learn to use effectively. Without guidance, students will use a chat program to substitute for face-to-face conversations, often about social topics. If your goal in using chat is simply to improve students' typing and have them look at social conversation in print, then you needn't do much more than tell students how to connect with each other. But if you want students to probe ideas and develop critical thinking in writing, then guided assignments are a better way to start using chat. Our teachers also find that developing critical thinking through writing takes several iterations with guided chat discussions, and so you might want to plan to use chat in several related assignments over many class sessions before you expect to see changes in students' thinking and writing.

In particular, our teachers use chat to foster dissensus and to challenge traditional notions of static text. When students "chat" about argumentative positions,

Strategies for Using Chat:

Use network chat programs (and similar programs, such as MOOs, MUDs, and MUSHes) for a variety of purposes:

- to begin discussion about an assignment. Students can print transcripts of the discussion for future reference. Save a copy of the discussion on a network drive and consider editing the transcript into a FAQ (frequently asked questions) sheet about the assignment.
- to role-play reactions to arguments. Students can adopt the role of a "devil's advocate" and challenge the arguments made by classmates in their papers. Students can save and print the transcript for reference during revision.
- to brainstorm topics for an assignment, either as a whole class or in small groups.
- to conduct live "talk shows" with guests from other classes, departments, or institutions.
- to connect with writing tutors in your campus Writing Center. Topics can include help tutors provide, concerns students have with their current assignment, etc.
- to conduct small-group peer review sessions. Students can comment on their classmates' papers and suggest strategies for improvement. Ask student to save and print the transcript for use during revision.

chat helps students see that they can modify their positions as they take into account other students' questions and comments. When our colleague Donna LeCourt explains her use of chat, she emphasizes that students generate more ideas and avoid getting locked into a position when they see their ideas in print.

You'll find that many of your students are familiar with searching for information on the World Wide Web. However, because the curriculum in our introductory composition course doesn't ask students to do library research until the middle of the semester, we typically wait until then to introduce them to the Web browser and our library's online databases. (Teachers of other courses, such as Writing Arguments and Intermediate Writing, introduce Web tools much earlier because students begin research-based writing almost from the beginning of the term.) Regardless of when you ask your students to use the Web, we recommend that you address issues such as how to read hypertexts and, especially, about bias and credibility in WWW sources. Even if students develop an eye for bias in print resources, they sometimes forget to apply the same critical questioning to Web sources.

Teaching Strategies We Use Throughout the Term

Designing the syllabus with an eye to selecting appropriate computer-based tools for students and writing assignments over the course of the term allows teachers in the computer classroom to move from large-scale planning into small-scale planning. We still recommend planning chunks of the class (two- or three-week segments) before planning individual class sessions. But at some point, planning what to do on a given day becomes your primary focus. In this section we describe and illustrate strategies that work well for varied goals throughout the term. In effect, this section constitutes a grab-bag of teaching techniques that our teachers adapt to many different kinds of writing tasks over the entire semester.

Use the Net:

- Step the class through an online search emphasizing your online library catalog. After you demonstrate a particular search technique, ask students to try it. After students have time to practice, do more demonstration if necessary or move on to the next search technique.
- Play stump the teacher. While you use the LCD panel, students can call out topics and watch you try to find material in the online library catalog or with an Internet search engine.

DAILY Assignments

We allude to our DAILY assignments throughout this text, and now we'll give you some specific examples of how we use this indispensable computer tool. But first, a reminder of just what we mean by DAILY files.

On our computer network, teachers access a virtual drive that links certain files to the teacher and the students. The teacher creates a file and saves it on this drive, and then only the teacher and that class can access the file. Teachers create and modify the file (write and read privileges) but students can only save any changes they make in this file under another name in their own directories (read only privileges).

For example, we explained in the last chapter that Jen typically used DAILY to remind students of homework and upcoming due dates. To do this, Jen could cut and paste from her syllabus or plans or she could type out the reminders in a new file. She then saved this file on our network by logging on and indicating that she wanted to save the file on her "y:" drive. (Our system is set up so that files are saved in the appropriate places based on log-in profiles.) When Jen's students came to class, they logged on to the network, opened the word processor, and clicked on the DAILY button we've created on the word processor's toolbar. Jen's students got the reminders Jen had typed into the DAILY file, and not the work intended for students in any other class.

Respond to DAILY Writing:

Students tend to take this writing task more seriously when they know teachers work it into other class activities or an upcoming paper, or respond to it. Here are some quick ways to respond to DAILY so that it doesn't take up too much time:

- Skim the printouts and comment briefly at some point on every page.
- Pick up printouts at the end of class and read responses to only one of the prompts. Jot notes for students or compose a class response to mail or post on the next DAILY.
- Read only one-third of the responses. Just keep groups organized so that every student gets feedback at least one of three days.
- Read with a highlighter in your hand. Simply highlight good points or workable ideas. Then tell students what you highlighted and why when you return printouts at the next class.
- Skim the printouts looking for especially well-developed or skimpy responses. Respond briefly to encourage the enthusiasm of the writers who write more than most and to cajole students who wrote little.

Most of our teachers use the DAILY files for a variety of reminders and prompts. Often, teachers ask students to write for 10 to 15 minutes about the assigned reading for the day. Students quickly learn that they must do their homework because they don't have time to read and respond during class, and teachers enjoy the benefits of discussion based on thoughtful consideration of key points. Below, we include several DAILY prompts that Candace created for writing-about-reading. As you see, the DAILY prompts sometimes act only to get discussion started on general reactions to a reading, but other prompts ask students to develop specific writing and analytic skills:

> Week 3 - Respond, on screen, to "My Daily Dives in the Dumpster." Did you like the essay? Why? Why not? What specific writing strategies (rhetorical strategies) did you find effective? What is your reaction to the content? Repulsion? Disgust? Admiration? Does the author offer you any fresh perspective on American culture?
>
> Week 5 - Summarize the main ideas, in one or two paragraphs, of either Nichols' essay ("Keep it Simple") or Barry's essay ("Why Sports is a Drag"). Next, respond in brief to the essay: do you agree with the author? Why? Why not? Be prepared to discuss the essay by 3:35 today.
>
> Week 5 - Do you agree with Nichols' assertion in "Keep It Simple" that "if everyone else on earth doesn't learn how to keep it simple, I'm doomed anyway. Unfortunately, my well-being is a collective effort"? Support your position with specific examples from your own experience and observations.
>
> Week 8 - Greetings! Well, you have all had a chance to read "No Wonder They Call Me A Bitch," by Ann Hogman. Take a few minutes just now to respond to this essay. What do you think of this essay? Respond to both the writer's subject, her approach, and her title. Try to move past whatever "disgust" you might initially feel and respond to the author's product.
>
> Week 11 - I know you've all been thinking about nothing else but your argument topics, except maybe Edward Abbey's essay, "The Damnation of a Canyon." Take a few minute (10-15) now to respond. . .
>
> 1. In what sentence do you find Abbey's claim? Type it here.
> 2. What kind of appeals does Abbey use in his essay? Find specific examples of argumentative appeals and type them out below.
> 3. Answer PHG #6, p. 350.
>
> We will discuss your responses at 4:30.

Teachers also use the DAILY files for setting up a sequence of activities in class. DAILY files might, for instance, ask students to:

- work in pairs or small groups clustered around one computer. As students discuss the prompt in the DAILY file, one student records the discussion on the computer. Then the DAILY might prompt each student to add his or her interpretation of the small-group discussion.

- respond to peer-critique questions about a sample paper and then compare the commentary with a partner's advice.
- remember key points of information from the text. The prompts function like a quiz without raising the anxiety of a quiz. After refreshing their memories, DAILY prompts go on to ask students to demonstrate their rhetorical knowledge through writing.
- summarize a reading and then compare summaries to determine what key points should appear in a good summary.
- write a zero draft or quick draft (writing down as quickly as possible everything that you now plan to include in your next paper) and then follow specific guidelines for drafting a working thesis statement based on the zero draft.
- prewrite on a topic to remind students what they already know about the next writing task the class will take up, as in this example:

> Good Morning!
>
> Congratulations! Now that you've turned in your Explaining Essay, you have officially made it two-thirds of the way through the semester— and into the next unit of this class. But to get everyone started with the next essay (which will be an evaluation of a solution to a problem) and for a little relief from heavy-duty drafting, I'd like you to take a moment and think about chocolate.
>
> Yes. Chocolate.
>
> What I'd like you to do is write down what your standards are for truly good chocolate—what makes the best chocolate, and what makes the best chocolate-eating experience? Think about your standards first on the level of all your senses. What should the best chocolate look like, feel like (in your hand or on your tongue), smell like, etc.? Then, think about it in terms of more subjective aesthetic criteria. What makes chocolate good for you? What do you look for personally in a chocolate-eating experience? Try to come up with a set of standards that you could use to judge any piece of chocolate (i.e., don't narrow your criteria to one brand—instead, think about the characteristics that brand has that make it your favorite).
>
> So—write them down here, and be prepared to discuss them in a few minutes.

- Prewrite about rhetorical factors affecting upcoming topics. Caitlin's audience prompt is one of the shortest but by no means the only audience analysis that teachers in the two studies assigned through the DAILY files:

> Think, on paper, about the possible specific publications (audiences) for your evaluating essay. Pick one of the topics you came to class with today and freewrite for about 10 minutes, focusing on the following questions.

- What magazine could you publish this evaluation in?
- Who is the audience for that magazine?
- How will that affect the criteria of your evaluation?
- What special considerations do you need to make for this audience?
- Will your audience be receptive or hostile to your topic?
- What other publications could you direct your evaluation to?

In short, any sequence of activities can be previewed, if not specifically set up, by instructions in a DAILY file. We've even seen teachers include in a DAILY specific instructions about how to use a new computer tool that's being introduced that day in class.

Why do we find this tool so valuable? Primarily because DAILY assignments foster independence among students. Students come into the classroom and get started (if that's the routine the teacher has set up) even before the teacher arrives in the classroom. When the DAILY assignment lays out the sequence of the class, students have a good idea of what's coming and what they need to do to meet the day's objectives. Students appreciate having time to write during class, even when all the writing won't necessarily appear in their next paper. DAILY writing also promotes growth in critical reading, writing, and thinking; after a semester of writing detailed responses about readings, students quickly get to key issues and write authoritatively about them. And, as we mention elsewhere, when students have opportunities to write before discussion, the discussions typically produce more insightful contributions.

Musical Chairs

This technique is one of Kate's favorites. When she identifies a writing task that could benefit from many students giving feedback to one student, she uses this technique. Here's how it works:

Imagine that students are working on an argument paper that requires them to state their own position clearly (pro) and identify and refute opposition arguments (con). Most students are good at generating arguments in favor of their position, but many generate only superficial or easily refuted con arguments. Musical chairs addresses this problem by drawing on the argumentative strengths of the entire class.

Each student types his or her proposition (or argumentative thesis) at the top of a new file. Then the student outlines the three or four key arguments that will support this proposition. The teacher asks each student to move one chair to the right. The students read what is already on the screen and add one con argument. After just a minute, the teacher announces that it's time to move again and students repeat the reading/writing tasks. In just 20 minutes of class time, perhaps a dozen students can look at a proposition and generate con arguments.

Not only do students finish this exercise with a good list of arguments to explore for their papers, but they also discover that arguments opposed to their position have real depth and merit. On occasion, students even head off more serious problems by noting that the "argumentative thesis" is not, after all, a debatable claim. Students get feedback from peers that keeps them from spending a great deal of time on an unworkable topic for the paper.

The musical chairs technique works well for a variety of prewriting and revising tasks—in fact for any writing that students can read and react to fairly quickly.

E-Mail Discussion

As an alternative to teacher-generated prompts in the DAILY files, student-generated e-mail discussion provides an opportunity for students to guide discussion of readings or sample student papers. Unlike using a chat program, students who use e-mail for their discussion have time to reflect on each comment before writing their response. All the entries are also saved automatically by the mail function on the network, unlike some chat programs that lack the ability to save a transcript of an online conversation. In addition, unlike an electronic bulletin board, e-mail discussion allows students to direct their comments toward a single reader, thus creating an extended, but private, dialogue with one classmate. Teachers can ask students to create triads or other small groups to participate in the e-mail discussion, but each group retains control of the conversation; other classmates are not invited to participate unless the group members send them the transcript of the e-mail discussion.

It is important, however, to limit the size of the groups participating in such a discussion. If students generate a question about the reading and send it to all their classmates, students suddenly have 20 questions to respond to and several hundred responses to read through. The numbers alone cut off conversation, and so this activity works best with groups of three to five.

Set up in advance which students belong to which groups and remind students of e-mail addresses of other group members. (Some of our students have more than one electronic mail address, so ask students to share their preferred e-mail address with you and their classmates.) Be sure students know the task. That is, should they ask questions about points they didn't understand (i.e., information issues) or should they explore ideas that lead to contrasting interpretations? Should students focus on rhetorical techniques or content in a reading? Should students suggest specific revisions if the reading is a sample essay? Once the task is clear, then students can send messages to each other and respond to messages sent to them. During class, teachers should monitor the exchanges to tell how long the exchanges are productive. Typically, this activity takes at least 20 minutes. Like the guided discussions on chat mentioned above, students improve the depth of their critical thinking and writing when they are able to practice this kind of guided discussion over several writing sessions.

Three-ring circus

Perhaps the most difficult strategy to implement, the three-ring circus is nonetheless well worth the effort. Based on the circus metaphor of several activities occurring at the same time, this strategy allows the teacher to work with a small group of students while the others stay busy with other work.

Typically, we explain this strategy as most workable when teachers have three or four non-sequential tasks for students to complete during a given class session. Students are assigned to group A, B, or C. Group A completes tasks 1, 2, and 3; Group B completes tasks 2, 3, and 1; group C completes tasks 3, 1, 2. For example, assume that students are working on finding library sources for a research paper. Task 1 involves meeting with the teacher in a small group to discuss difficulties finding material and citing sources properly in the paper. (Handling these problems in small groups is much more effective than trying to work with the entire class.) Task 2 involves connecting to the library computer to check availability of items. Task 3 involves reading through the rough drafts of research papers to determine where writers need to cite sources. Students complete these tasks in any order, but by the end of the class they will all have worked through a set of activities that improve their research papers immeasurably. Students work on tasks 2 and 3 individually, in pairs, or in small groups, but the maximum group meeting with the teacher is eight students—a manageable number for dealing with the intricacies of citing sources.

Our teachers discover that this technique works well to substitute for many of the topics they formerly covered in lectures to the entire class. This technique, more than the others, requires careful timing so that all students cycle through the group meeting with the teacher.

Mini-conferences

Although most of our teachers use this technique when students revise a draft-in-progress, it also works well to help students generate ideas for their papers or organize chunks of text that are not yet coherent drafts.

In effect, while students work on DAILY writings or draft or revise papers, teachers make themselves available for discussions of work in progress. Students might bring notes or a draft to a quiet corner of the room and there discuss with the teacher what successes and failures are most notable at this point in the writing process. Or the mini-conferences might take place as the student works at the computer. Typically, we let students set the agenda for these conferences, but some teachers like to tell students that they will meet for progress reports and specify areas on which to focus. Donald Murray has useful advice for making conferences effective in "The Listening Eye," and his advice translates nicely into these classroom mini-conferences.

Read over students' shoulders

This is the most obvious of the teaching strategies in this section, but it deserves just a few comments. Throughout this chapter, we emphasize how so much of the teacher's work in the computer classroom requires advance planning. For the most part, the watchmaker analogy captures the essence of the computer classroom because students *do* so much more work during class time in this environment.

But the success of the computer classroom goes beyond the watchmaker analogy because the teacher in the computer classroom needs to stay in touch with students. By walking around the room and reading over students' shoulders, teachers check that students are on task, clarify tasks that didn't become clear given the first set of instructions, or intervene when a writer needs advice or guidance.

We recommend explaining to students why you read their work on the computer monitor, because some students are protective of their writing until they declare that it is ready for public consumption. Usually, a short discussion of why we want to read as they write suffices to reassure students that we do not keep a Big Brother watch over them but instead try to gauge how much time they need to complete a task, where the discussion might begin based on their writing, or whether they need some help to make progress on their papers.

Kate often uses the example of a student who didn't write at all when everyone else in the room was busily drafting a paper. When Kate asked the student why, it became clear that writer's block was about to ruin this paper for the student. Kate suggested three or four options for dealing with writer's block, and the student broke through the block within minutes. At the end of class, he stopped to tell Kate how grateful he was for the advice because he had spent hours the night before puzzling over the same problem in getting started with his draft.

Just write!

As we make clear throughout this text, students spend a higher percentage of class time writing in the computer classroom than they do in the traditional classroom. Students in the computer classroom definitely draft more of their work in class than do their peers in the traditional class, and this trend is an advantage to both students and teachers. Students, of course, are eager to use class time to complete their assignments, but teachers benefit as well by intervening effectively and efficiently in students' writing process.

Individual drafting is not the only way to encourage students to write in the computer classroom, however. Having students write *before* work in small groups or pairs has the same advantages of writing before discussion: such writing focuses students' attention more clearly on the task at hand and gives them thoughtful ideas to contribute to the group task. Students are also able to get immediate feedback from peers about what they've just written. Having students write *after* work in small groups or pairs allows students to capture the ideas stimulated by the group activity. Especially when collaborative activities are sequenced to help students with particular aspects of the paper they're working on, the opportunity to move immediately from collaboration to writing generally helps students incorporate what they learn from collaborative work directly into their papers.

Nor can we diminish the importance of the teacher's presence while all the collaborative work *and writing* is going on. Because teachers in either the computer classroom or the traditional classroom hear the shared conversation of groups, teachers know that collaborative activities are effective for students. But because teachers in the computer classroom also *see the texts* that precede and follow collaborative activity, they can sequence activities to benefit students as well as intervene to help students learn as much as possible from in-class activities and writing. For these reasons, most teachers in our computer classrooms find that time for writing is part of the sequence of every class session.

FINDING A "COMFORT ZONE" IN THE COMPUTER CLASSROOM

The computer classroom presents tantalizing opportunities for teachers to extend their teaching strategies and for students to experience new technological supports for writing. For teachers to feel successful in the new classroom environment, however, they need to remember that they will want to experiment with the technology to see how it best fits with their teaching preferences and goals. Few of us feel completely comfortable with a new technique the first time we try it in the traditional classroom; we should expect to have the same "breaking in" period for the computer classroom and its wide range of teaching strategies.

Moreover, because the environment is new for students as well, teachers probably need to explain overtly how the technologies support course goals. Encouraging students to join in creative uses of the technology and eliciting their feedback throughout the course can help teachers see how computer supports best aid students as writers.

Finally, we recommend flexibility to all new teachers in the computer classroom. Techniques may not work as we expect the first time we try them, and students may not respond in ways we expect when we first introduce new technologies. By staying flexible, we learn along with our students about the best ways to help them take advantage of computer supports for writing.

8

Technological Complexities: Dealing with the Complications of Computers and Computer Networks

When we train our new teachers in the computer classroom, we usually write two statements on the board. The first, "Less is more," calls attention to the dangers of creating complicated class plans. The second, "Computers can only count to one," calls attention to the dangers of thinking that computers are at all intelligent. Both statements address the same underlying theme: teachers must recognize and take steps to address the complications of using computers and computer networks in a writing classroom. These complications include:

- allowing additional time for classroom activities;
- computers as a distraction to students;
- introducing students to the hardware and software used during class;
- technological problems, such as equipment malfunctions, configuration problems, and network failures;
- student access to technology; and
- human factors issues, such as relative differences in the legibility of text on screen and on paper.

In this chapter we explore each of these issues, drawing on our experiences and on the experiences of the teachers and students in the Transitions and New Teachers studies.

ALLOWING ADDITIONAL TIME FOR CLASSROOM ACTIVITIES

One of the first things that Kate and Mike learned when they began teaching in computer-supported writing classrooms is that time flies when you're using computers. Class plans, typically adapted from traditional classrooms, that depend on moving students quickly through four or five linked activities have little chance of being completed in the computer classroom. Like other experienced computer-classroom teachers, Mike and Kate quickly learned to schedule fewer activities for longer periods of time and to allow extra time for transitions between activities.

The reasons for allowing extra time are fairly straightforward. When students are using computers—whether writing, browsing the World Wide Web, engaging in real-time chat, or working with electronic mail—they usually want to complete what they are doing before moving on to the next activity. Moreover, in our experience, students in the computer classroom get caught up in activities that directly relate to their writing. When this engagement happens, students want to take as much time as possible to capture ideas on the computer. And, as you might expect, students seldom work at the same pace. Some students might take five or 10 minutes longer than their classmates to complete an activity, which leads teachers to suggest alternative activities to faster students, such as a search of the World Wide Web or an online library catalog for sources for their next major paper, while their slower classmates complete the first activity. In turn, students

Check the Details Before Your First Class Session:

Reduce the number of first-day "glitches":

- Test your network account to make sure that everything is working properly. Be sure your login ID and password work, of course, but also see that you can read, write, copy, and delete files from your directories and from any shared directories that your students might use.
- Test your students' log-in IDs and passwords to make sure that they work properly. Check their read, write, copy and delete rights on the network drives and check their access to any shared network drives.
- Make sure that the class e-mail list is accurate.
- Make sure the class electronic bulletin board is set up properly by posting and reading messages on it.
- Use the programs you'll be using in class to make sure that they are configured properly: word processing, chat, Web browser, news reader, e-mail, etc.

who get involved in alternative activities are typically reluctant to set them aside when the teacher asks everyone to move on to the next item on the day's agenda.

Our concept of "less is more" emerges directly from these phenomena. Although a teacher in a traditional classroom can usually get students' attention within a few seconds, it might take a few minutes (sometimes even longer) before everyone in a computer classroom disengages from one activity long enough to attend to the teacher's directions for the next activity. Teachers who typically set up distinct activities through front-of-the-classroom instructions find that this difficulty challenges both their patience and their ingenuity. Although the presentation mode is still a primary means of setting up activities in a computer classroom, many experienced teachers reduce the time needed to set up activities through handouts distributed on paper or via the computer network. When a teacher finally has the attention of the class, setting up a major activity might involve as little as saying, "Get into groups of three and open up peer-review file number seven. I'll circulate among you as you get set up." The computer file or handout can contain information and instructions that teachers in traditional classrooms might otherwise talk through with students. This content might include which roles to assign, goals for the activity, "products" that will be reviewed or collected, and perhaps a tentative time limit.

Alternative strategies for setting up activities work particularly well in the mid-to-late stages of a term, when students understand their teacher's expectations about activities such as group work and peer-review workshops. Initially establishing those expectations, though, typically requires the same investment of time and ingenuity that teachers in traditional classrooms provide. Some of the teachers in the Transitions Study relied heavily on instructions delivered via the DAILY assignment—or on worksheets saved to the same directory—to provide students with the overall goals and sequence of activities for a given class session. Caitlin, in particular, used the DAILY assignment in this fashion:

> They come in. They access a file. It gives them instructions for their day, and they start off, and they do their thing.

"Doing their thing" might involve engaging students in a variety of activities in a class session. Candace allowed students to choose from a list of activities because she recognized that her students worked at different paces, not simply in individual class sessions but in the semester as a whole. Reluctant to force students who had not yet completed a rough draft to engage in peer review, she allowed them to work at their own pace throughout the semester:

> Once they get into the paper it's like I have to let go of the idea that everybody's going to have the same thing at the same time, so it makes workshop chaotic. For example I end up doing workshop with half the class, while the other half of the class is drafting. Half the people are workshopping in pairs and I'm going around

> and speaking with everybody else, and they're speaking with each other. So it's a totally different learning environment.

Candace expressed a great deal of comfort with this decision, but she admitted that it may have reflected her teaching style more than the context of the computer classroom:

> I think that teaching in the computer classroom suits me personally as a teacher, because I'm somebody who has a high threshold for that kind of chaos. Having everybody working at a different level doesn't bother me. I know that some people would rather have everybody doing the same thing at the same time. But I would rather everybody be at a different place. And I think that maybe for that reason the traditional classroom is more of a struggle for me, because it's so much harder to get that going and have it work effectively.

Clearly, one of the most important technology-related complications of the computer classroom is the additional time required for and between activities. Teachers who choose to have all students working on the same activity at the same time find that they must consider how long the slowest of their students will take on that activity and adjust accordingly. Similarly, they need to acknowledge that students may not break away quickly from the computer. Aside from the need to save or print a file or to shut-down a network connection, students find

Strategies that Accommodate Students as They Work at Different Paces:

- As students come into the room at the beginning of class, ask the second, fourth, sixth, etc., student to sit next to someone already there to work on a task set up in a DAILY, the task in progress at the end of the preceding class, a draft in progress, and so on. Students who arrive very late can be added to existing groups to create triads.
- As students come into the room at the beginning of class, ask them to send e-mail about a specified topic related to your goals for the day to the class list. Students should respond to at least the first three mail messages they receive, but students who arrive early or work faster can respond to more messages.
- Ask students to bring up a paper-in-progress on the computer monitor and then move to another computer to comment on it. When students finish, they should be instructed to move to an open computer. (Some students will get feedback from several readers and some will get feedback from only one or two. The teacher can continue this activity as long as it seems productive.)

their attention so wrapped up in what they are doing that they often miss the teacher's call for their attention. Teachers who choose a teaching model that allows concurrent multiple activities may find that they benefit from some time savings, but in turn they need to consider how to keep track of what their students are doing, not only in a given class period but throughout the academic term.

COMPUTERS AS A DISTRACTION

Perhaps we ought not refer to students' productive engagement with their writing as a distraction, but teachers in computer classrooms, like teachers in traditional classrooms, need students' attention as a group at some points during most class sessions. When the teacher needs to deliver instructions, clarify an assignment, or move the class from one activity to the next, then the computers can be a distraction—from the teacher's point of view. In this section, we discuss some of the more serious ways that computers distract students during class.

In almost every class we've taught, some students came with all the skills needed to start software consulting businesses. In some cases, they already have. It is fairly easy to identify these students. They chat with friends in other states, they download files from Web sites, or they update their personal Web pages while other students figure out how to send a file through electronic mail. It's unlikely that they'll be breaking into the institution's central files, although this fear is not uncommon among teachers new to the computer classroom. When we asked Caitlin, in her mid-semester interview, whether any of her students fit this description, she said:

> I have a couple hacker kind of students who are always trying to bust into the Pentagon, but you know, other than that—and you know, I think that's a personality thing with those students. They're computer science majors, they're fascinated by how our system is put together. They want to figure it out. They want to get into my files, you know.

Whether these students ever got into Caitlin's files is unclear. What is clear is that they were probably fairly bored waiting for other students to gain some measure of control over skills that they had mastered long ago. And bored students, as we all know, do not stay focused during class.

As a teacher, you will want to find ways to keep these students focused on their writing. Our experience, and the experience of teachers in the Transitions and New Teachers Studies, suggests that strategies for maintaining these students' focus on writing fall into three broad categories: shutting them down, recruiting them as peer advisors, and providing them with additional work while other students get up to speed (ideally, work that takes advantage of their

Recapturing Students' Attention:

- Don't just have students stop typing but instead ask them to move away from the computers if that's possible in your computer classroom.
- If you have central tables in your classroom, ask students to move to the table to write, especially if your instructions or discussion take more than a minute or two. (Here's another reason to have chairs with wheels.)
- If students seem disinclined to move, invite them by name to join the group at the center table. (Mike even scoots chairs for people on occasion.)
- Install screen savers so that students aren't tempted to read text on the screen during class discussion.

advanced skills). Of these strategies, shutting them down is the least rewarding, since it tends to foster an "us-them" attitude among the students and can create an ongoing pattern of students trying to outwit the teacher. Of the teachers we interviewed, Jen was the only one who consistently adopted this strategy:

> I tend to just address it as soon as I see it. I mean, they know that they can't get away with much with me. They'll try it, but I keep my eyes open and I'll see it.

Other teachers in our studies adopted the second approach, identifying students who were skilled computer users and asking them to help their classmates learn the system. When Ellen discovered a wide disparity in her students' understanding of how to browse the World Wide Web, she set up an out-of-class tuto-

Ways Our Teachers Keep Students On-Task:

- Require some kind of product by the end of class. This might be several paragraphs or new sources. Ask them to check in before they leave.
- Set intermediate deadlines with time allotments even though you may not end the activity in exactly that much time.
- If students start to "play" on the computers, ask them quietly to get back to work or, less confrontationally, ask them what progress they're making. One of our teachers even chats with students about the computer technology for a few seconds before prompting them to get back to work.
- Keep circulating. If students know that you want to look at their writing in progress, they will tend to write throughout class.

rial for students who were unfamiliar with the Web browser used in our computer classrooms. To build rapport with a student who had shown a high level of computer skills, she asked if he would help run the tutorial:

> It's always good to find the one or two resident computer experts in the class that know a heck of a lot more than I do, and he stayed for both tutorials and helped me out. I actually learned some new things from him.

As we pointed out earlier in this chapter, identifying and recruiting experienced computers users as peer advisors can be a great help to teachers, particularly those teachers new to computer classrooms. By doing so, you address two problems: the need to familiarize the class with programs needed to carry out class activities and the need to keep your more skilled students interested and involved in the classroom community. By drawing on the expertise of more experienced students, you focus your energies on teaching students about writing.

A final strategy, related in spirit to the second, is to provide students who already demonstrate that they know a program with an alternative activity that helps them maintain their focus on writing. If you teach your class how to send a paper to someone else using electronic mail, ask students as they master that skill to provide detailed information about their paper and the kind of feedback they'd like to receive. If you teach students how to browse the Web, ask more experienced students to experiment with more complex search strategies. Using this strategy successfully depends on your ability to recognize students' skill levels, which implies that you need to master those skills yourself. However, even when you haven't mastered those skills fully yourself, you can often work collaboratively with a student to develop an ad hoc extension of the activity on which the rest of the class is working. When you find a student reading Usenet news groups while the rest of the class is still posting to the class bulletin board, for instance, ask that student to locate news groups relevant to the next assignment.

As you gain more experience teaching in computer-supported writing classrooms, you'll develop a sense of the strategies you are comfortable with in class. One teacher recently told us that he uses an escalating series of responses when students play with the computers during class activities. He initially uses humor to keep students on task, and then asks experienced students to help less experienced students. When these strategies don't work, he devises alternative activities. When that doesn't work and students refuse to stay on task, he presses the "reset" button on the student's computer. He finds that, after the first "reset" incident, he seldom has to repeat it.

Although we find the "reset" strategy a bit extreme, we think the escalating series of strategies is a good approach. As a teacher, you will find it useful to develop a consistent set of responses for students who want to use class time for computer-based recreation. In most cases, as we suggest in this section, these students are probably just bored. Devising strategies to reduce boredom enables you to eliminate a small but annoying set of problems that can keep you from fully focusing on your primary goal of teaching writing.

INTRODUCING STUDENTS TO HARDWARE AND SOFTWARE

Some of the first questions we hear from teachers new to the computer classroom concern how best to introduce students to new technology. Our experience tells us that:

- students should start using relevant technology as soon as possible,
- technology should be introduced in the service of specific writing activities, and
- teachers should not feel a need to be experts in every nuance of a particular program.

In this section, we explore each of these points, calling particular attention to strategies that we and other teachers use to introduce students to technology. In our discussion, we include stories of success and failure to illustrate these points.

Introduce Relevant Technology as Soon as Possible

Only a few years ago, when we lived in a world of DOS prompts and UNIX networks, we told new teachers to introduce technology slowly to their students. The difficulties of remembering arcane word processing commands such as "Shift + F7, 1" to print a file were enough to intimidate even the most enthusiastic teacher, let alone a student with limited or no experience using a computer. It's no surprise that many DOS software companies provided cheat sheets that fit neatly in the space at the top of computer keyboards. Simply put, it was awfully hard to remember all those commands.

Today, we live in a world of graphical interfaces, or at least the majority of us do. In our computer labs, we no longer need to teach students how to print or save their papers. In our Windows-based word processing program, we use a graphical toolbar with buttons that say "Print," "Save," "Open File," and so forth. And, in place of our UNIX-based real-time chat program, we use a graphical chat program built into our Web browser. Changes such as these significantly reduce both the time needed to introduce new technologies and the fear often associated with doing so.

In our computer classrooms, we typically begin the first class session with introductory remarks about the course, then move into a writing exercise. Some teachers ask students to log into the network, while others save logging-in for the next class period. Typically, teachers ask students to write about their experiences as writers or to interview and write about a classmate. Some teachers ask students to list questions about the course syllabus after a full-class discussion. In all cases, teachers ask the students to print (and, if they've logged into the network, to save) their files. As students write, teachers circulate around the class, noting students who have difficulties, noting others who bring strong computer skills to the class, and often asking more experienced students to help their less-experienced classmates.

If you teach in a networked computer classroom, you may find it useful to ask your students to log into their accounts on the first day. This is a matter of teacher preference, since it introduces a frustrating element into class if student accounts have been set up incorrectly. Doing so, however, allows the teacher to establish a routine from the very first day of class. If students are using a network-based assignment such as a DAILY assignment throughout the semester, getting them into the habit of logging in will be of lasting benefit. Asking students to log in also provides teachers with the opportunity to find out which, if any, student accounts are not properly set up and to report those problems to the computer support staff (assuming, of course, that your institution provides such support).

If you do ask them to log-in, you have the opportunity to choose between using a word processor or network-based applications, such as electronic mail or chat. When we ask students if they have questions about the syllabus, for instance, it makes little difference to them whether they jot down their questions in a word processor or, for instance, an electronic mail message. They can also compose their questions in a word processor, copy the text, and mail it to the teacher for subsequent response.

Our recommendation to use technology from the first day reflects changes in both the ease of use of software and the level of computer-expertise students bring to the classroom. In the mid-1980s, the majority of students who enrolled in writing courses taught in computer-supported classrooms brought little or no

Introduce Your Students to Each Other AND Technology:

Teachers often use a "get to know you" exercise to help students learn about each other. You can also use this activity to introduce students to technology:

- After students interview each other, ask them to create a text file containing information about the person they've interviewed.
- Ask students to send you e-mail describing one of their classmates.
- Ask students to interview each other using chat or e-mail.
- Ask students to post a message about themselves to the class bulletin board; then ask them to respond to at least two posts.

Use Word Processing or E-mail to Identify Student Concerns about the Course, Computers, Writing, and the Syllabus:

Ask students to write about one or more of these issues in their word processors or in electronic mail. Read and respond to their concerns before the next class meeting. You'll also get to know your students better and be in a position to deal with their concerns earlier in the course.

experience to the classroom. Today, the majority may have more experience than their writing teacher (an issue we address later in this chapter). Because of these changes, the challenge of introducing new technology is significantly lower than it was only a few years ago.

That challenge has not, however, completely disappeared. Many of our colleagues, among them the teachers involved in the Transitions and New Teachers Studies, tell us that they have experimented with a variety of strategies for introducing new technologies. Some of them introduce a new program by asking students to work through a particular process step-by-step (for instance, attaching a file to an electronic mail message), addressing questions about each step as they moved through the process. Others experiment with turning their students loose on a new program, observing who has difficulties and who does not and putting the two groups of students together. Still others use detailed handouts about specific tasks, such as sending electronic mail or searching the World Wide Web, while others ask students to create lists of instructions.

Keep in mind, however, that the most carefully considered strategies for easing students into using a new program can still fall a bit short. Jen, who provided detailed handouts to her students, learned that even the best instructions are only as good as their readers. At the end of the semester, she reflected on her use of a handout for electronic mail:

> I gave them foolproof instructions, and if they read them they would get where they needed to get. I discovered a lot of them can't read instructions. They just totally skipped three steps which say, "Now, you've got this on your screen, press this button." And then they wonder why it doesn't work.

Teachers need to develop experience in the computer classroom to learn the strategies that work best for them. As is the case with teaching in the traditional classroom, it may take several semesters before teachers discover ideal strategies. Ellen, reflecting on her experiences in the classroom after two semesters of teaching, indicated that she learned early in her teaching career which strategies work best for her:

> This semester I definitely started them on the computers much earlier than I did last semester. I did it on the very first day, on the day when we go through the course policies and syllabi. And I sat them down and had them log-in right away that first day. And had them actually write some things up for me, basically about their previous writing experiences and fears that they had about the class, etc., and had them save it and print it out. And then the next day I taught them how to use the DAILY right away. That seemed to work a lot better in terms of the course. The people who were really panicked got out, either left right away or realized, oh, this really isn't going to be that bad. *[Interviewer: Did you lose many people?]* I only lost two the first day. And I know one of them was because of a scheduling conflict with work and the other one I don't have any idea; maybe I just scared them out. *[Interviewer: Why did you decide to do it sooner?]* Because it seemed like on those first two days we do so much with just the administrative stuff, just reading through the course policies and syllabus. I figured this would be a better use of time, a more efficient use of time. And then that way the next week I could get them started doing DAILIES immediately. [snaps fingers] And just go on to high gear with the class and with instruction instead of trying to do all that the second week.

Introduce Technology as Support for Writing

We are strongly committed to the practice of using technology as a means of meeting the goals of a writing course rather than as an end in itself. Many of the teachers we work with worry that valuable time might be lost while students are trained in the use of specific technologies. Our response is that programs should be used only at those points in the semester when they serve a clear purpose and only in ways that help students become better writers. Underlying this argument, of course, is the expectation that teachers can develop classroom activities that familiarize students with the relevant capabilities of a particular program in a way that serves the goal of helping students learn about writing. By relevant capabilities, we refer to things such as teaching students how to send a paper through electronic mail as opposed to teaching them how to set up and manage an electronic mail address book. Ellen provides a good example of this practice in her introduction of the search function in our Web browser:

> Each of them already had their topics in mind for their papers. So I had them actually work in terms of their topic. Okay, use this keyword for your search topic. Okay, you're not getting anywhere with this, let's brainstorm other ideas.

In this case, students learn how to use the Web browser in a way that clearly helps them with their writing assignment. The teacher did not feel that she was wasting time by focusing on the search function in isolation. Instead, when she was ready to ask her students to begin researching their topic in greater depth, she asked them to use the Web browser to accomplish that task. In turn, the students learned about a specific program in a way that helped them meet course goals.

Use Out-of-Class Meetings to Familiarize Students with Specific Programs:

In some cases, you'll find that enough students are unfamiliar with a particular program that you'll want to set up meetings outside of class to introduce students to it. Some of our colleagues have asked some of the more experienced students to attend these meetings as well, so that they can act as peer tutors.

An extension of our suggestion that technology be introduced in the service of specific writing goals and activities is that technology be introduced when it is needed and no sooner. Although we believe that students should work on computers as early as possible in the academic term, this doesn't mean that they need to be introduced to all of the programs available to them. For example, when we move into the second unit of our introductory composition course which includes an expanded focus on searching for and using outside sources, we typically introduce students to the Web browser installed on their computers. Introducing browsers in the service of those goals works well. Students who have limited or no experience browsing the Web adapt quickly to the idea that searching the Web for relevant information helps them develop and refine their arguments.

In addition to introducing technology in the context of writing activities, we also find it useful to explain to students how a particular technology enhances their writing processes. This is clearly an extension of a proven teaching technique, but one often overlooked by teachers in computer classrooms. Their motivation for teaching in a computer classroom, we assume, is that some aspect of the classroom experience helps their students learn more about writing. We believe that sharing that rationale with students, not only for the overall decision to meet in a computer classroom, but also for using specific programs in particular ways, helps make them more aware of their learning. When we asked Ellen what she told her students about her decision that they use a Web browser, she said:

> I told them it was like probably the greatest thing that they were going to use, one of the best resources that they were going to have for doing research and it was going to cut down on some of their time and that they were going to find some things that it would probably take them forever to find in the library if they could find it. And [that it would help] to get them some different ideas. Because one thing I was really trying to get them to do with research was to look at strictly academic sources, academic journals, interviews with professors, and then also doing sources outside the academic community, things that they wouldn't normally think about, resources they wouldn't normally think about using. And I think that the Web is a good way to introduce that. You know, here's this whole other world out here to access for

When You Use a Program That is Completely New to Students:

Although your students might know word processing, electronic mail, and browsing the Web, some programs are completely outside their experience. Programs used to create hypertext documents, for example, fit this description. These programs have numerous uses in computer-supported writing classrooms, however, so consider exploring their use in class. When you introduce an unfamiliar program, spend a bit of time explaining why you are asking students to use the program and how it helps meet course goals. You'll probably find that you'll need to spend additional time, as well, acquainting them with the basic functions of the program.

> information. And also, that also tied in with their interviewing people in the field, like say if they were doing a paper that dealt with health in some way, shape or form, they could go out and actually talk with a doctor or a nurse as part of the research. Instead of just sitting in the library. These things are going on the Web. One thing that was really interesting is, for our third unit on analyzing academic writing, one group was [composed of] computer science [majors]. And they actually used the Internet to conduct interviews with people in Germany and England to see if they did the same types of writing there for computer science that was required here.

YOU DON'T NEED TO BE AN EXPERT

One of the most reassuring things that we tell teachers new to the computer classroom is that you don't need to be a technology expert to teach in the computer classroom. Although you need to be familiar with the basic functions of a particular program to use it effectively, you don't need to know all (or even most) of the functions of that program to be an effective writing teacher. If you teach an introductory writing course, you need to know only enough about a word processing program, for instance, to teach your students how to open and save a file, how to print that file, and how to edit text (e.g., copying, cutting, and pasting text). You certainly don't need to know how to insert and manipulate high quality graphics, or how to link your text file to a spreadsheet, or how to create and edit macros. In a more advanced course that emphasizes features such as desktop publishing, you need to learn additional skills, of course, but once again there are numerous features that you never need to know. In this day of "bloated" software, where programs such as Microsoft Word, Word Perfect, and Lotus Word Pro have grown to the point where they occupy 10s of megabytes of disk space, most people using a particular word processing program end up using only about 20 percent of its features.

In a writing class where producing text is more important than "presenting" it, teachers are extremely successful with only a basic understanding of a particular word processing program. When a student, for instance, asks a teacher how to change the background color for a particular paragraph, that teacher can say with a smile (1) "I don't know" and (2) "Learning how to do that is not the point of this class." This is particularly good news for teachers who find that the program installed in their computer classroom is not the software that they've come to know and love. But it's also good news for teachers who don't want to find themselves distracted with answering technical questions that contribute little or nothing to learning about writing.

When teachers find themselves in a situation where they need to know the answer to a particular question or set of questions, or when they know that a particular class activity requires more technical knowledge than they currently possess, they have a number of options. The easiest is to ask a more experienced colleague or a member of the technical support staff (if your institution has such support) to join you in the classroom. The other person can help you teach the class, focusing on the technical issues and allowing you to focus on your goals as a writing teacher. If that kind of support is not available, try to identify students in your class who possess the knowledge needed to make the activity a success. In almost all the classes we've taught over the past decade, we've located one or more students with a great deal of technical expertise. When you recruit these students as assistants for particular activities, you accomplish two things. First, you can successfully carry out the activity. Second, as we discuss earlier, you help such students avoid a few minutes of boredom while other students figure out what their more technologically advanced classmates already know.

Two other techniques are available to you as well. If you create your class plans far enough in advance and your schedule permits, you can learn the program before you assign it in class. We recognize that this is not always an attractive option for teachers with heavy teaching loads. As Caitlin commented:

> When you have 75 students and you're working to keep your head above water, the last thing that you think about doing is using some sort of new technology that would take, maybe, two or three hours for you to sit down and figure out how you're actually really going to make it work in the classroom. It's something that just doesn't happen.

In cases like this, we recommend our final technique: using an alternative activity that helps you meet the same teaching goals. An alternative technique, of course, may not always work because there are only so many ways to search the net and only so many ways to conduct real-time chat sessions. But many activi-

Hold Your Office Hours in the Computer Classroom or Drop-in Writing Lab:

Holding office hours in the computer classroom or lab is a great way to continue working with students while they write. You'll find that many of your students will begin scheduling their drafting times around your office hours, so that they can approach you with questions as they encounter them in their writing.

ties, such as peer-review workshops, work with a wide range of technologies. If you find it difficult, for instance, to teach your students how to exchange papers using e-mail, you can always teach them how to exchange diskettes or print-outs during class. Indeed, as in many other activities, the simplest route to a goal is often the best. Unless a teacher wants to encourage students to exchange papers with each other and with the teacher outside of class, time spent teaching students how to mail papers to each other during class may be time better spent doing other things.

DEALING WITH GLITCHES

Next to not knowing enough about computers, teachers new to the computer classroom seem most concerned about what to do when problems crop up with individual machines or the computer network. Although not an unreasonable concern, problems of this nature have become less and less frequent in the past few years. Still, even the best-maintained computer classroom has problems. Computers that are in use for 10 to 12 hours per day, five or more days a week, wear out. Sometimes even the simplest kinds of problems disrupt a class—as, for instance, when the space bar on a keyboard becomes stuck or a mouse button decides that clicking is no longer part of its job description.

When we talk about computer "glitches" with new teachers, we divide potential problems into three categories:

- equipment breakdowns, such as monitors that no longer work, diskette drives that no longer read floppies, and the keyboard and mouse problems we discuss above;
- software configuration problems that keep programs from starting or running properly; and
- network problems, ranging from mechanical problems such as disconnected cables to breakdowns on a server in the next building.

As teachers, we've had to deal with these kinds of problems more often than we care to remember. This is not to say that breakdowns happen every day, or even every month. Nonetheless, problems continue to crop up, and so we have established several policies and procedures that reduce their impact. To deal with equipment breakdowns, we schedule one fewer student in each computer section than we have computers. In classrooms equipped with 25 computers, we set enrollment limits at 24. Although this doesn't completely eliminate problems associated with equipment breakdowns—obviously, more than two things can go wrong at the same time—it significantly reduces disruptions. In addition, we invest in warranties that promise same-day on-site service. When a hard drive breaks down, we expect a service technician to arrive within 24 hours with a replacement. On-site warranties increase the initial costs of equipment and, of course, they are only as good as the company that stands behind them. But we find, over the long-term, that eliminating on-site service charges in combination with a reliable equipment provider reduces our overall maintenance costs.

To deal with software configuration problems, we standardize as much as possible both the equipment used in our classrooms and the software that runs on them. Typically, we configure a test machine at the beginning of an academic year and run it through every test that we can devise. When we're satisfied with its setup, we configure the other machines in the same way—whenever possible, by using the same configuration files. Then, we test each machine before the semester begins, and cross our fingers, hoping that unexpected problems don't arise.

Problems with the network are often out of the realm of writing teachers. At many institutions, a centralized academic computing unit deals with network issues. If you work at an institution where this is the case, you may find it useful to adopt the following strategies. First, get to know your network service providers. Talk to them about your goals for your students and your ideas about how

Support for Technology-Related Problems Inside and Outside the Classroom:

Use several strategies to reduce time spent on technology-related issues during class:

- Identify computer-literate students and ask them to act as mentors to classmates.
- Ask your technical support people or a more-experienced colleague to join you during the first few meetings of the term.
- Ask the same people to join you when you introduce new technologies later in the term.

you might use network services. You may find that your institution's network service personnel can provide you with suggestions about new network software or advise you about potential problems you might encounter during class sessions. Whatever the case, strive to build a partnership with your network services staff. If necessary, educate them that, yes, English departments do know about and value computers for much more than word processing. We've talked with several colleagues who have had repeated difficulties with obtaining support from network staff at their institutions. In most cases, they tell us that they failed to lay the groundwork needed to build a good relationship with their network personnel. When problems emerged, they found themselves in an adversarial relationship. The writing teachers became angry because an expected level of service wasn't provided and the network personnel became angry because they didn't know those expectations existed.

In some cases, network personnel and writing teachers get off to a bad start for what we'll call religious reasons. A colleague at another institution obtained funding for a writing lab a few years ago. Despite the fact that the majority of computers on campus were IBM PCs or PC-clones, he chose to install an Apple Macintosh lab. Since then, he's found it nearly impossible to get adequate support from an academic computing culture that seems to know little, if anything, about the Macintosh. Observing the difficulties our colleague has had over the past few years, we come to the conclusion that the distractions associated with

Avoid Hardware Problems by Planning Ahead:

Administrators who are enthusiastically supportive of a computer classroom when the computers are new (and particularly when the funds for the new computers come from an outside source) may prove less enthusiastic when they learn that they will need to set aside funds to replace the machines as they wear out. This phenomenon has resulted in a surprisingly large number of computer classrooms and drop-in word processing labs in which machines are so old as to be virtually useless or so poorly maintained that they literally cannot be used.

We recommend that you work with your administrators to create and implement a replacement plan for computer hardware. If your institution can set aside a certain amount of funds each year to replace equipment in a computer classroom, you'll find that you can avoid many of the problems associated with out-dated hardware. Try to implement a plan in which all the machines are replaced, over the course of a three- or four-year period, with new machines. By purchasing a limited number of machines each year, you can avoid making large expenditures during a single fiscal year.

such a battle are simply counterproductive. (Our colleague is having more luck with his university's support staff lately, but it has literally taken years to get to this point.)

If your department or program controls the network you use, teachers have greater responsibility for network problems during class. Although this eliminates the potential difficulties of working with central staff who know, or even care, little about using computers in writing classrooms, you may instead find yourself wondering how to salvage the rest of your class when you lose access to the network.

The strategies we've adopted to deal with network problems are fairly straightforward. First, at the very beginning of the semester, we ask all our students to get into the habit of saving their files to both their network drives and floppy diskettes. Students are human, of course, and don't always do this. But enough of them get into the habit of backing up on floppies that they usually don't lose too much work. Second, we configure our computers so that, if the network goes down during class, they are still usable as local machines. Printing and saving to the network no longer works, of course, and access to electronic mail is not possible, but word processing and other local programs still work. Also, because each computer is set up as an Internet node, students can still browse the Web and access Usenet newsgroups, network chat, and our online library catalog without network support. This level of access is only possible, however, if the problem is with the network software or server rather than with network wiring. If there is a problem with wiring, then access to the Internet is not possible and you'll find yourself limited to word processing and other programs that run locally.

Beyond these strategies, we ask teachers in our computer classrooms to work with support staff to ensure that problems, when they occur, are dealt with quickly. When the network goes down in the classrooms, we ask the teachers to call support staff immediately (a phone is available in the classrooms). When the problem is with hardware or software, we ask the teachers to put a sign on the computer and to send e-mail to our support staff. Similarly, when the problem is with a student or teacher's account, we ask them to contact support staff immediately after class.

Most important, however, is to prepare for problems. Asking students to move quickly to an alternative activity when problems crop up (preferably an activity that accomplishes the same goal as the one it replaces) helps keep students focused on writing even when the network crashes and the technical support staff is on a three-day retreat. If nothing else, teachers who prepare for problems deal with the situation with more poise and humor than teachers who find themselves blind-sided in the middle of class. (We detail specific teaching strategies in Chapter Seven.)

These strategies, developed over a number of years, help us create a relatively trouble free classroom computing environment. The key word in that last sentence, of course, is "relatively." Until computers are as reliable and as predictable in their behavior as refrigerators, writing teachers will need to be ready to shift to an alternative activity when technological complications arise.

STUDENT ACCESS TO TECHNOLOGY

As we note elsewhere in this chapter, limiting student enrollment in the computer sections generally assures that all students have access to computers during class time. But what about student access outside of class?

Like any other resource, computers are not evenly distributed across the academic and social landscape. Some students will have faster and more powerful computers in their homes than they have in the computer writing classroom. Some students will have faster and more powerful computers in their home academic departments than they have in the computer writing classroom. Other students will have no access to computers on campus except through the computer writing classroom. And some students can only imagine the day they have will computers in their homes or communities.

With such unequal access to computers outside of class, the computer-classroom teacher will be pressed to choose between devoting class time to any computer-based writing tasks other than papers or asking students to complete those tasks outside of class, knowing that some students will be disadvantaged by their limited access to computers. Teachers need to be cautious about planning substantial out-of-class writing activities (such as required bulletin board postings) until they have determined how many students are unable to find computers for out-of-class work.

When teachers discover that some students simply cannot locate computers outside of class time, then they should consider several options. First, they can make certain computer-supported writing activities optional. Second, they can ask students to come to class early or stay late to complete activities on the classroom computers. Or they might set up additional hours during which students can use the computer classroom for out-of-class tasks. One of our teachers typically opened the computer classroom for several hours on Sunday evenings one semester so that students could consult with her and use the computers as they needed to. Students gratefully took advantage of her generosity. Finally, teachers might check with other computer labs on campus to determine if writing students could share those labs. No matter which option teachers choose, however, they should also remember that some students have little flexibility in their home and work schedules to take advantage of campus resources, and so teachers may need to extend deadlines for computer-based work to be completed.

Because we are fortunate enough to teach at a university which has adequate computer resources for writing students, we rarely have to remind students that our drop-in computer labs are available approximately 85 hours each week. More often we confront a related issue that causes even more headaches but one that is much less serious in our view—computer compatibility. Students often remind us that our lab and classrooms use PC clones, but they have Macs at home, in the dorm, or in their home departments. They also complain that the software we use doesn't match what they run on their personal computers, or that our software is not the latest release available to them through their home departments.

These students have legitimate concerns, but the level of inconvenience these students face is nothing like that of the student who simply cannot access computers at all. Our advice to these students is generally simple: save any work you do during class as ASCII (or DOS) text so that you can easily convert it when you work on another computer. Be sure, as well, to save work on that computer in ASCII form so that it will load in our computer classroom. We remind students that it is their responsibility to be prepared for class at the beginning of the class session, and if that means being in the building 10 minutes early to convert a Mac file to PC format up in our lab, then students need to find the time to do that.

We occasionally have students who insist that they don't know enough about our computer system and their home computer system to work out incompatibility problems. When we discuss problems with students like this, we provide as detailed an explanation as possible, and then we send them to our systems administrators who are also able to provide some hands-on support as students figure out solutions. When students are unwilling to learn how to solve compatibility problems, then we ask them to drop the class (such problems are easy to spot in the first few days of the term). We explain that students need to be able to write during class time and that they won't want to work at home only from print-outs of their class work. Students quickly see the advantages of learning the solutions to compatibility problems or taking our writing class in a traditional classroom.

A different set of compatibility issues can arise for students trying to use computer tools over a modem. Students logging into our university network from off-campus need to have both a special log-in (separate from the one assigned to them as students in our classes) and network communications software. We encourage students to contact our network personnel about both the log-in and the software, and we remind students that they are always responsible for getting their work finished by stated deadlines regardless of network, modem, and other technological problems they might encounter.

HUMAN FACTORS ISSUES

In addition to glitches, teachers find it useful to anticipate a second class of problems. These problems arise from what scholars call "human factors issues," or more precisely, from problems related to the interaction of human beings with computers. We're referring to:

- external and room lighting that creates glare on computer monitors;
- the impact of chair and desk heights on ease of typing, which contribute to repetitive stress injuries;
- the impact of computers on noise level in the classroom;
- the relative ease of reading on the screen versus reading on paper; and
- the need to support students with physical disabilities.

If you find yourself in the position of designing a computer classroom, take these issues into account before settling on a design or purchasing equipment. If you have a bank of south-facing windows in your classroom, for instance, think about how that contributes to glare. If you can't do anything with the windows themselves, such as installing blinds or coating them with a polarizing film, then consider alternative arrangements of the computers and/or the purchase of glare filters for the monitors.

You should also consider using ergonomic chairs and tables so that students of different heights and reaches can adjust their chairs and tables to individual needs. Chairs with adjustable arm rests reduce the stress associated with holding arms in a typing position. In situations where students sit at computer stations for long periods—as might be the case, for instance, if your computer classrooms are used as open labs when class is not being held—arm rests can be extremely beneficial. The only disadvantage of purchasing ergonomically adjustable equipment is increased costs. If your funds are limited, you might consider purchasing fixed tables, since our experience suggests that few students adjust tables. However, we strongly suggest adjustable chairs. Their overall quality is typically higher than less expensive chairs, which in itself translates into longer usefulness, and students will find themselves better able to concentrate on their writing, as opposed to giving their attention to that uncomfortable feeling in their arms or lower backs.

We also find that chairs equipped with rollers make it easy for students to move from the computers to the table at the center of the room. Because students are physically separated from their computers when they "circle up," we find they are less distracted by their computers. This action helps us create a clear boundary between time spent in full-class or small-group activities and time spent working on the computers. Once again, you may find that rollers add to the cost of the chairs you purchase, but we strongly advise you to consider them.

Perhaps the most familiar human factors issue that teachers find themselves addressing is the difference between reading text on the screen and reading it on paper. Numerous studies explore legibility of text on computer screens. In general, text on paper is clearer and easier to read than text on a screen, but the work of Hayes and Haas suggests that the functional differences (i.e., differences in recall and understanding of text) between a high resolution screen and paper are minimal. Readability issues aside, our experience suggests that students find it more *convenient* to read on paper. Your students will most likely want to print out their drafts at various points in their writing process, perhaps so that they can spread out the pages and get a better overall sense of the argument, or possibly so that they can make hand-written annotations.

Another human factors issue is sound-level in the classroom. The fans used to cool most computers are relatively noisy. In fact, the noise from 25 such fans sets up a background buzz that is difficult to cut through. Our solution is to purchase computers with quieter fans. The "silencer" fans markedly reduce the noise in the classroom. You can reduce still more noise from echoes and create a quieter environment by installing carpet and acoustic ceiling tiles.

A final issue to consider is students with visual, hearing, or other physical impairments. Equal access to education is a legal issue, of course, so you may find that you need to provide equipment that allows students with visual or hearing impairments to use the computers in your classroom. Regardless of legal issues, computers can be configured fairly easily to assist students with hearing or visual impairments. A workstation in our most recently refurnished computer classrooms has hardware and software that work for students in either situation. In addition, the height of the table is raised to accommodate students in wheelchairs.

COMPLICATING THE ISSUE

As we discuss technological "complications" throughout this chapter, we realize that our word choice could create a negative impression of the network-supported writing classroom. We hope, instead, that we are describing in realistic terms the complexities that teachers face when they choose to teach in computer-supported classrooms. The technology clearly adds layers of complexity that can trip up the unwary teacher. By knowing these complications in advance, we hope that teachers moving into the computer classroom will be better prepared to take full advantage of the unique teaching opportunities available in this setting.

9

Training Other Teachers: Creating Teacher-Training Programs for Technology-Based Instruction

. . . [C]omputer technology, of and by itself, does not magically change the ways in which we teach. . . . [W]hen teachers do adapt to the new technology, it will be the result of carefully-designed and extensive staff-development programs (Klem and Moran, 1992).

After looking in detail at our teachers moving between traditional and computer classrooms, we are in a better position to consider how we can best prepare teachers for these two different teaching environments. Our key recommendation follows directly from the discussions in the preceding chapters: *start teacher training far in advance so that teachers can become acclimated before teaching in an unfamiliar environment.* Our second recommendation to both teachers and trainers is not so obvious: *each teacher must take some time to become comfortable in the new teaching environment. No amount of training can eliminate this individual process.*

START TEACHER TRAINING FAR IN ADVANCE

In many ways, new teachers in computer classrooms face the same challenges that teachers of composition in traditional classrooms faced in the 1970s. In that decade of theoretical and pedagogical upheaval, many of us taught writing process never having heard of writing process from *our* composition teachers. We ran collaborative groups when most of us had completed our college programs without having worked in a collaborative group. We used student-centered teaching techniques when most of us had only been exposed to lectures in college—and we continued to experience lectures in most of our graduate courses! In short, many of us who began teaching in the 1970s taught in ways we had never seen anyone else teach based on models of writing that appealed intuitively but that we had never seen worked out in a writing classroom. In short, we had no models of good teaching for the new model of writing, and many of us reluctantly left behind the models we knew.

New teachers in computer classrooms often face exactly this challenge. If these new teachers had no access to computer classrooms in their high schools or colleges, then they arrive in teacher certification programs and graduate-teaching assistant programs without having seen the kinds of teaching that characterize the computer classroom. Moreover, students who dropped out of academe for several years may not even have used computers before they arrive to begin their teacher training. As we pointed out in Chapter One, lack of familiarity with computers causes anxiety about the computer classroom.

If a teacher-training program begins early, teachers have enough time to accustom themselves not only to the equipment but also to the environment as a whole. In addition, and of crucial importance, if a training program begins early enough, new teachers can sit in on classes taught by teachers experienced in the computer classroom before they teach their classes in that environment. Thus, the new teachers can begin to build realistic models of "teacher behaviors" from which to choose as they learn to teach in the computer classroom.

Allow Time for Modeling

Most teachers-in-training cannot afford the time to sit in on a quarter- or semester-long class in advance of their own teaching, but we urge our teachers to visit as many classes as possible so that they observe a wide range of teaching techniques. New teachers can also see the range of possibilities for helping students set routines, for individualizing student work or pulling the class together for a large-group discussion, for integrating writing into a range of class activities, and even for dealing with occasional mechanical problems.

One teacher in training sitting in on one of Kate's classes enthusiastically praised a technique Kate used. Kate had dealt with a printer problem by asking the student who was intent on chatting with his classmates to come over and help with the problem. We probably would have remembered to tell teachers-in-training that this technique works well, but now we could rely on this teacher to spread the word to her colleagues. And she saw for herself how easy it is to draw upon the expertise of our students in solving technical glitches. We also recommend that teachers-in-training observe as many different teachers as they can.

Thus they can see how different teachers handle the same classroom management problems or choose activities best suited to their students' needs and their own teaching preferences.

Even though we've had a few GTAs who have sat in on a class for the entire semester before they begin teaching in the computer classroom, that kind of dedication is rare. Typically, our teachers-in-training visit two to four classes, even though we encourage them to visit more. Their time is precious, and they often underestimate the value of building models for teaching before they begin teaching in the computer classroom. But without fail, the new teachers report in retrospect that their visits were among the most important parts of their training.

Sadly, the teachers who have the most difficulty in adapting to the computer classroom are those who ignore our advice about visiting classes. Those teachers, lacking models of any sort for the computer classroom environment, typically try to transport their traditional classroom techniques without change into the computer classroom. They quickly discover that the efforts are unsuccessful either because they ignore the computers and thus generate student resentment, or they flounder as formerly effective class plans suddenly don't work.

If your training program simply cannot include visits to classes, then consider two key alternatives:

- Videotapes of successful teachers in computer classrooms cannot substitute entirely for classroom visits, because the camera typically cannot pick up the scope of student behavior throughout the classroom. But videotapes can give new teachers some of the flavor of the classroom environment and can help them see some of the activities, writing tasks, classroom management tips, and so on that differ from the traditional classroom.
- Model as many different teaching techniques as possible during your training program. Hold all training sessions in the computer classroom. Incorporate computer use into as many of the training activities as possible so that teachers can begin to experiment with software while trainers are present to answer questions about the programs and about potential classroom applications.

Even if your program includes visits to classes, these last two options can still be valuable parts of a training program.

Teachers* must *get to know the system

Teaching in a computer classroom requires that teachers familiarize themselves with the idiosyncrasies of the system in the classroom *before* they teach in that classroom. One of two key findings in Elizabeth Klem and Charles Moran's (1992) study of teachers in their transition semester into a computer classroom focused on knowledge of the hardware and software. As Klem and Moran explain, "The speed and degree of the teachers' learning [how to adapt to the new teaching environment] may be a function of the extent to which they themselves feel comfortable, as writers and teachers, with the new environment" (p. 19). If teachers are unfamiliar with the computer tools, they cannot comfortably take advantage of those tools to help students learn about clear communication.

Moreover, even if teachers are fully familiar with a word processing program they've used in another setting, they need to use the program in the same classroom that their students use. Teachers-in-training often discover that software they thought they knew well behaves somewhat differently when 20 or more students are all using it at the same time or when a systems manager has to modify parts of the program to run on the classroom hardware or to provide adequate security. Hardware, too, may look familiar but "feel" odd when used in a classroom setting.

For example, in one of our computer classrooms, we had to optimize space because students asked for more room to put papers and books between computers. We decided to get small keyboards that have no number pads. What we discovered is that the keyboards also have small keys and steep pitch between rows of keys. When we ask teachers-in-training to use these keyboards, we hear time and again, "I hate this keyboard!" We point out that now the teachers know what to expect from students on the first days of class, and we ask teachers to pay some attention to how long it takes to accustom their fingers to the keyboards. The teachers then reassure students that, yes, the keyboards are odd at first but that most people adapt to them within an hour.

Teachers also need to be fully familiar with the other computer tools that are available in the computer classroom. New teachers often hear or read about classroom activities involving specific software. Then they discover, usually with dismay at first, that the version running in the classroom they'll teach in doesn't perform as expected. If these teachers experiment with the software available in their classroom before they design a class activity, they can adapt other teachers' techniques. But if these teachers go into class without learning their own system and its software, they may well leave with egg on their faces.

Because of this, we incorporate "play time" into our training sessions to ensure that teachers try out all the software they will eventually use with their classes. We discuss as a group how the various computer tools can be used most effectively with students. The experienced teachers in our training sessions share our fiascoes, and we all brainstorm for specific activities and techniques that help students. We remind teachers not to use the tools just because they're there, but to use the tools when they make sense as aids for writers.

We also ask new teachers in our training sessions to work through at least one set of tasks they intend to give to students when they begin teaching. Most teachers welcome the opportunity to give new techniques a trial run. All of them are surprised to discover that the activities take much longer than they had planned. And many of them decide to work collaboratively—role playing as teacher and small group of students—to try out still other writing assignments and learning tasks in advance. A few years ago, for instance, we installed a new chat program on our network. Several teachers were eager to use the tool in classes, particularly after reading about the successes of the ENFI project. Four of us participated in a session in which we imagined several different classroom scenarios and how our chat program might work in those scenarios. After outlining the scenarios, we role-played students in our classes and were surprised by some of the behaviors of the program and also by some of the writing that emerged. We finally discussed the benefits of the program and the ways in which teachers might use it to encourage writers.

As another part of our training program, we also schedule several hours during which an experienced computer classroom teacher is in the classroom as a resource person but with no set agenda for training. Teachers often like to experiment on their own and then bring ideas back to share with a more experienced teacher. Or sometimes they like to "play" quietly with the computer and ask for help only when they get stuck. Still other teachers want an individual tutorial, a step-by-step walk-through with a particular piece of software and how they might use it in class. For some teachers, then, a quiet session gives them room to explore; for other teachers, a quiet session offers one-on-one support that's not available with a large group.

In our program, we insist that new teachers attend our training sessions, but we provide the flexible support of the additional hours to help teachers become comfortable. The flexibility in our program seems to accommodate both the more and less experienced computer users and teachers in our training program.

Let us emphasize one warning: Do not let your training program become simply the training ground for techies. As Cynthia Selfe (1992) argues, many current teacher education efforts now encourage "a nearsighted and limited focus on the technology itself rather than on the instruction that it supports." Rather, she says, we need to spend our time "teaching educators to think critically about *how* and *when* virtual environments can support the educational objectives of teachers in English classrooms" (p. 24). Teachers do not need to know the "ins" and "outs" of hardware and software just because the classroom has computers. Instead, the training program must emphasize that teachers need practical knowledge of the computer tools. Requiring that teachers be familiar with the hardware and software in their classroom is essential to their performance as *teachers*, for otherwise, how can they choose among alternative methods to help students learn?

Place the computer classroom clearly into the context of the whole writing program

Every writing program that trains teachers for computer-classroom teaching has goals and expectations unique to that program. Secondary teacher-certification programs often prepare teachers for computer-classroom use that includes a focus on literature, composition, or creative writing. University training programs generally focus only on freshman composition. Some programs prepare computer-classroom teachers for basic writing classes at the high school or college level. Some assume that the curriculum is basically the same in every section of the same course while others assume only that reading and writing go on in the sections and that specifics are determined by individual teachers.

Program goals generally reflect far more than the content and audience for the instruction; these goals also embody essential assumptions about how people teach and learn. Klem and Moran (1992) make this point clearly when they explain how their model of the writing process defined the layout of their networked computer classroom:

> The room layout, with its notably absent teacher place, privileged a workshop model of a writing class, and aimed to cast the teacher as a fellow writer and editor—albeit the most experienced writer in the room—rather than as the center-of-the-class authority. Moreover, the network configuration sought to foster a class model in which much of the learning and writing would happen as students collaborated on the in-process drafts. (pp. 14–15)

What Klem and Moran observe, however, is that each teacher's mental model of teaching and learning is far stronger than the environment:

> Our study most clearly showed us that each teacher brings a pattern of behavior—one cultivated by past experience, and by beliefs about what writing is and how it is best taught—into a classroom. Making the change to a computer-equipped classroom environment may challenge a teacher's models more deeply and more subtly than we have heretofore recognized. (pp. 19–20)

The two teachers in their study often work at odds with the networked classroom as they pursue teaching activities and styles that don't make good use of the computer technology, often ignoring the computers altogether.

We, too, see that teachers can have great difficulty in shifting their models of teaching and learning so that they can take advantage of the networked environment. But a training program that explicitly states its assumptions about teaching and learning, about the kinds of students and specific learning goals, and about course content and teaching methods eases the transition for new teachers moving into the networked environment.

For example, our computer-classroom configurations compared with those designed by the journalism department at our University illustrate just how differently our two departments imagine specific teaching and learning processes. As we noted in Chapter Four, our computers face the walls on the perimeter of the room. In the center of the room, small movable tables can be pushed together to form a seminar table or separated to accommodate small groups working away from or collaboratively on a computer. In the journalism department, the computer classrooms used primarily to teach desktop publishing and newspaper writing and editing have computers on tables bolted into rows so that all students face

Consider "Training" Administrators:
In addition to creating an effective training program for teachers, you may want to consider how you can "train" institutional administrators. Will Hochman, who has invested a great deal of energy into building an innovative computer-supported writing curriculum at the University of Southern Colorado, tells us that he devotes a significant amount of time to informing administrators about his rationale for using computers to support writing instruction. By keeping his department chair, dean, and provost aware of his efforts, he has been able to maintain support for his computer-supported classroom and writing lab during a time of significant budget cutbacks at his institution.

At Colorado State University, we have adopted a similar approach. Keeping our administrators informed of our decisions about the direction of computer-supported writing instruction—and in many cases making them partners in those decisions—has helped us fund computer hardware and software, staff support, and software development. In turn, our administrators tell us that their knowledge of our efforts and their understanding of our rationale for using computers to support writing instruction has helped them justify their decisions to support our efforts.

We've found, as well, that many administrators are familiar with the use of technology to support front-of-the-classroom instruction (e.g., multimedia presentations) and even with the "demonstrate and practice" approach that might be used, for instance, in a hands-on statistics course. Administrators are typically unfamiliar, however, with the "studio" approach that we've taken in our classrooms. When you talk with administrators at your institution about teaching and learning in computer-supported writing classrooms, you may find it useful to share in some detail your curricular goals and your rationale for particular teaching approaches.

the front of the room. The instructors in these classrooms spend substantial time lecturing and directing other activities from the front of the room.

The philosophies underlying these computer classrooms could hardly differ more. Our colleagues in the journalism department feel strongly that students learn desktop publishing, news writing, and editing through a carefully controlled sequence of steps. A teacher who masters this kind of writing guides the learners through specific steps for new learning and for additional practice. In contrast, our computer classroom reflects our belief that students in writing classes need to practice writing on their own but that they learn about how readers react to that writing by sharing their work over the network, in small groups, or in large groups. Our classroom fosters a different type of learning that we feel better meets the needs of our composition students.

If we do not make clear our underlying assumptions, however, we do a disservice to new teachers coming into our classroom environment. As teacher-trainers, we cannot expect participants in our training programs to infer our assumptions. We need to explain explicitly how our design decisions at all levels (classroom layout, syllabus, writing tasks) reflect our goals and expectations for the networked classroom.

The teacher-training program, thus, must reflect the goals of the larger program in which the teachers function. However, even if program goals are clearly stated, their implications for computer classroom teachers are often murky. For example, in a program where teachers in a traditional classroom have a prescribed syllabus, should teachers in the computer classroom follow that same syllabus? Based on our discussions to this point, we argue that a syllabus that prescribes particular activities cannot be taught in the same way in both a traditional and computer classroom. And so in this kind of program, computer-classroom teachers need to know where they have latitude to adapt or cut certain tasks.

More often, issues arise in a computer classroom that simply don't come up in a traditional classroom. Several years ago, when computers were first used by composition students, many teachers lamented that they had to give up time that could have been devoted to writing instruction to provide students with instruction in word processing. Teachers still lament the time taken away from writing to help students learn local network commands or even log-in or disk-management techniques. These issues simply do not apply to a traditional classroom, yet we cannot ignore them because students who don't know how to use computer technology must become comfortable with it before they can learn much about writing in a computer environment.

Or perhaps a particular program has set as a goal the professional presentation of final drafts. In non-computer sections, students are expected not only to proofread and edit carefully, but to attend to page layout, inclusion of visuals, and so on. Could a computer-classroom teacher in this same program stress a paperless class that does not similarly emphasize page layout?

Other program expectations and goals might affect far more than a few class sessions. Consider, for instance, a program that has an exit exam from freshman composition or a junior-level proficiency exam for graduation. If students take their writing classes in a computer classroom and become comfortable composing on a computer, are they seriously disadvantaged by a proficiency exam they must complete with paper and pen? Clearly, a training program must address these issues that affect the long-term success of students as well as the classroom pedagogies adopted by teachers.

Thus, program goals can imply specifics that are inappropriate to the computer classroom. A good teacher-training program makes clear how computer classrooms fit into the overall program and what latitude computer-classroom teachers have for shaping class sessions to meet program goals. In other words, a good teacher-training program for computer-classroom teachers must uncover key issues that might limit the computer-classroom teachers' choices and address them early on in the training.

Our advice to trainers: Begin training as early as possible with a large-group session during which you explicitly address program goals and how teachers in the computer classroom might meet those program goals.

COMFORT IN THE NEW TEACHING ENVIRONMENT

Several years ago, Kate met with Dawn Rodrigues, then teaching at CSU, to discuss an in-service computer-classroom session for tenured faculty in the English Department. As they worked through their plans for the session, they agreed how much they had changed as teachers over the years they had worked in a computer classroom. They described a steep learning curve for themselves the first semester in a computer classroom. But they each commented that they continued to learn new things about themselves as teachers even after several years of teaching in a computer environment. Although they had both experienced a steep rise and then a more gradual increase in our learning curves, they noted that some teachers they had worked with in our training program had reported quite different experiences.

When we ask other teachers about how they adapt to teaching in computer classrooms, we hear responses that seem to fit three general models. The steep initial curve followed by a gradual rise typifies Dawn and Kate's experience. A more gradual curve overall reflects Mike's experience (who learned about teaching in the computer classroom one step at a time). And a third curve is best described as "fits and starts" in which rapid learning precedes periods of consolidation and even back-sliding (as when teachers focus so much attention on one set of issues that they fail to fully attend to issues that they've already mastered).

Teachers who progress in fits and starts often do so because they cling tightly to teaching strategies they've mastered in the traditional classroom. One teacher who fit this learning curve admits the difficulty of her first semester in the computer classroom: "[It] was really tough because I was trying to fit in everything from the traditional classroom." Over the next two years, she changed her syllabus and teaching techniques only gradually because, she says, "I need some kind of anchor to hang onto."

When we asked teachers in the Transitions Study how they had adapted over time to teaching in computer classrooms, Caitlin indicated that she had seemed to learn in fits and starts:

> In the beginning, there was a rise and then I leveled off for a while and then there was another rise after I took a look and did an assessment.

Similarly, other teachers in the Transitions Study reported on dramatic breakthroughs in their first weeks of teaching in the computer classroom followed less by gradual learning than by a period of quiescence. As one noted, "My first semester was trial and error, but mostly error."

As we work with teachers year after year, we see these common patterns repeat, but we also see that each teacher adapts to the computer classroom in unique ways and *at a unique pace.* Moreover, teachers we interview consistently report these experiences *after* our training program. Teachers need time and practice to feel fully comfortable with what are often dramatic shifts in teaching techniques and philosophy. No training program, no matter how thorough and well-designed, can substitute for the time that each teacher needs to become comfortable in a new teaching environment.

Part of what makes the process time-consuming is that learning how to use the software for oneself is only half the work for a teacher. Teachers must go on to learn how to use software to teach. Candace, the least experienced of the teachers in the Transitions Study, told us that she chose not to use certain programs until she developed an understanding both of how they worked and how she could use them in the classroom. As a result, she tended to use technology less than some of the other teachers in the Transitions Study:

> I guess my thing was also not letting the technology at any point get in the way of what we're doing, and until I feel really comfortable with that so that I'm not fumbling for 20 minutes during class I'm probably not going to do it. So the onus is going to be on me to get comfortable with it first, rather than going in there and like, you know. Although certainly I know that's going to happen the first time they do it with each other, but until I can really explain what to do when they mess up.

Beyond simply learning the programs and how they support specific classroom activities, teachers moving into a new environment typically reflect on how the setting affects their teaching. They reflect on their daily successes and failures and often spend much time revising their teaching strategies. As Caitlin told us:

> I think it's made me think about using the technology in the computer classroom more. It's made me think about what do I do differently in the two rooms and why? And am I really using what I have to use and the space? And the configuration and all that kind of stuff. Am I using that in the best possible way? And so, I think it's made me stop and think and **assess my own teaching and my own approaches to things more than, maybe, I would have.** (emphasis added)

What we ask teachers to do when they move into a networked classroom, then, involves their own learning about some technical issues and about how software works. It involves, as well, translating learning into practice as they adapt comfortable and familiar teaching techniques to a new environment and as they work out how to use software to advance students' learning. It involves questioning their assumptions about teaching and learning, as teachers identify and modify the models of good teaching they bring with them into the classroom. Finally, the development that teachers go through also includes examining assumptions about the cultural contexts of teaching and learning. As Hawisher and Selfe (1991) point out:

> All too frequently, however, writing instructors incorporate computers into their classes without the necessary scrutiny and careful planning that the use of any technology requires. . . . In many English composition classes, computer use simply reinforces those traditional notions of education that permeate our culture at its most basic level: teachers talk, students listen; teachers' contributions are privileged; students respond in predictable, teacher-pleasing ways. (p. 55)

If we expect teachers to make these dramatic changes in themselves and their teaching practices, we must give them time and support. We cannot expect a training program of a few hours or even a few days to turn out teachers confident and prepared for all contingencies because teachers need to immerse themselves in the teaching environment with their students before they begin to realize all the challenges they will face.

But we can provide forms of training—pre-service and in-service—that help teachers make difficult adjustments to new teaching situations. A good training program almost certainly includes these features that support teachers over the time they need individually to adapt to the networked classroom:

- access to experienced teachers who share insights with new teachers-in-training,
- time to begin a dialogue between new teachers and computer system administrators,
- on-going support that helps teachers solve whatever problems they experience in the computer classroom, and
- a "safe" place to discuss the emotional highs and lows of teaching.

Access to Experienced Teachers

Whenever possible, you should involve teachers experienced with the move from the traditional classroom to the computer classroom (and back again) in the teacher-training program. Not only can these teachers illustrate principles and concepts (such as, "know the software before you use it in the class" or "don't use a computer tool unless you have good reason to believe it helps your students as writers") with specific examples from their recent experiences, but these teachers often share negative experiences that show clearly why the precepts constitute good teaching. Having a number of experienced teachers available guarantees that new teachers will also hear about a range of techniques (as well as students) that will reassure them of the flexibility they can bring into their own classes.

Perhaps even more important, new teachers perceive experienced teachers as less representative of the composition program per se. If the new teachers are GTAs, part-time faculty, or even new regular faculty, then the experienced teachers usually represent the same constituencies. Training advice coming from experienced teachers is just that—advice from experienced teachers—rather than pronouncements from a Composition Director or some other program administrator.

Furthermore, advice from colleagues currently using the same equipment and teaching the same courses often has much stronger impact than advice from administrators who may not teach the same level of students or the same courses.

Creating a Dialogue with Computer System Administrators

We are always surprised at how adamant our systems administrators are about getting involved in our teacher-training program. The systems support staff wants to minimize technical problems, but their contribution goes far beyond pointing out how to avoid potential technical pitfalls. The systems administrators at our schools are the ones we call frantically when the server crashes in the middle of class or when the printer starts printing one character per page. In short, the support staff usually fields frantic calls from frustrated teachers who foresee entire class sessions falling to pieces. The support staff realizes that the sooner they let teachers know what they can and cannot do to help in various situations, the more likely teachers are to relax.

The support staff also has an agenda quite different from the teachers, but one that the teachers nonetheless need to know about. For example, the systems administrators in our computer classrooms are responsible for network security. When we had an "unauthorized" user log-in with a student's password and delete student work from the server, students were furious. But if the support staff had not explained procedures to the teachers in advance, the teachers might well have been furious, too. Because the teachers knew that a student in a class had to have cooperated with the "hacker" and explained that to classes, students realized quickly that they had to take responsibility for their own security and that they should save elsewhere any files they cared about.

By giving the systems administrators time during the training program to discuss the key elements of their agenda, we facilitate good working relationships between the support staff who know most about computers and teachers who know most about students.

Providing On-going Support for Teachers

All teachers, no matter how much experience they have before teaching in a computer classroom or how much experience they have in a computer classroom, have "problems" in a networked environment. Many teachers, especially those with more experience, may want to focus exclusively on the hardware and software problems. But teachers also need a sense that they can continue to discuss pedagogy.

We highly recommend weekly or bi-weekly in-service meetings for all teachers in networked classrooms. Support staff should attend regularly to facilitate clear communication about computer glitches. And experienced teachers should also participate to help brainstorm for solutions to teaching problems and to address the less tangible reactions we discuss in the next section.

Sometimes we announce an agenda for our bi-weekly meetings, usually drawn from points raised by teachers as they encounter problems or uncover issues they want to discuss with the group of computer-classroom teachers. Sometimes our agenda includes discussion of a new network tool that teachers want to learn more about before they use it in their classes. Sometimes the agenda is driven by technical difficulties that arise between meetings. Support staff is crucial in providing input during these sessions. But sometimes we have open meetings with no agenda so that teachers can simply talk about what seems to work and not work for them and their students. These discussions often lead to more fundamental philosophical issues that teachers might not otherwise have time to discuss with colleagues.

By continuing our training sessions throughout each semester, we invest heavily in the professional development of our teachers—both regular and temporary faculty. But what we gain as a program, through the contributions of each teacher sharing with colleagues and through each teacher becoming a better teacher for students, more than outweighs the cost in time for training-program supervisors.

A "Safe" Place to Discuss the Emotional Highs and Lows of Teaching

The teacher who told us that her first semester in the computer room was "trial and error, but mostly error" admitted a feeling that teachers rarely share with program administrators or teacher-training supervisors. Yet because all teachers experience both frustrations and accomplishments as they go through the challenging transition to the computer classroom, they need to feel confident that all their experiences are viewed positively. If teachers talk about their emotional highs and lows in the transition period, it helps them to proceed with the self-assessment necessary for a successful transition to the new teaching environment. Such support also, of course, makes them feel more positive about the larger teaching context (the program or school) and encourages them to contribute to that program as an experienced teacher who can pass along successes and failures.

We also observe that teachers who have a venue for discussing the "valleys" of teaching tend to project more positive attitudes toward students. By having a safe place to discuss their frustrations, teachers vent their aggravation and move on to consider positive solutions to problems. Finally, when teachers openly discuss what they consider their failures, they are often able to put those experiences into perspective (we almost all have a story to top that disaster!) and to gain from their own and their colleagues' combined expertise in the classroom.

INVESTING IN TRAINING

Knowing that teachers need time for training both before and while they teach in a computer classroom, we need to structure teacher training programs to support long-term professional development. And then perhaps we can meet the goal of life-long learning that Hawisher and Selfe call for:

> Our view of teaching and of how students learn invariably shapes our behavior in the classroom. The metaphors we build to house our professional knowledge exert powerful influence over us. Few of us, we would argue, construe our role as that of "controller," "gatekeeper," or "guard." We are more likely in the context of the writing class to think of ourselves as "teacher," "writer," and perhaps "expert" . . . . We can, if we work at it, become learners within a community of other learners, our students. But the change will not happen automatically in the electronic classroom anymore than in a traditional classroom. We have to labor diligently to bring it about. (1991, p. 64)

Designing and maintaining effective training programs does, in fact, require diligent labor. The effort seems highly worthwhile, however, when it helps teachers move effectively between classroom environments—and most importantly when it results in well-designed and well-taught classes.

10

Pondering the Future of Computer-Supported Writing Instruction

As each new facet of computer technology has appeared in recent years (word processing, local area networks, chat programs, hypertext, access to the World Wide Web) some teachers have looked to computers not as a diamond in the rough but as the Hope diamond—glistening and polished. "*This* new computer application," they assert, "provides the breakthrough to help students learn to write well. *This* use of computers in the classroom finally solves the annoying problems that have kept teachers and students from reaching their full potential."

What our years of experience as computer users, teachers in computer classrooms, and teacher-trainers suggest instead is that computers will always be a *tool* that teachers can use to help themselves and their students. Sadly, computers do not hold mystical answers for improving teachers' instruction or students' learning. To return to our initial metaphor, computers fit into the total picture of an instructional context, but they cannot be the focal point of our hopes for improved student writing.

A GALLOPING HISTORY

When computers first began appearing as tools in *writing* instruction in the early 1980s, computers in education more generally already had 20 years of research and pedagogy to support their limited claims as instructional aids. In many disciplines, those claims focused on using computers as aids for drill and practice activities or for testing students' factual knowledge. Most teachers who used computers for writing instruction realized quickly that personal computers or small numbers of networked terminals didn't help writers if the instruction focused on drill and practice. As a result, the early reports of using computers for writing instruction are dominated by explanations of word processing as the most important software for classroom or laboratory writing instruction. Throughout the 1980s, articles reporting research and teaching practices debated what seemed then to be long-term issues of great importance—what typing skills students must have to take advantage of word processing, whether students should be allowed/compelled to compose on the keyboard, which word processing packages were easiest for students to learn or use, whether students' attitudes toward computers affected their attitudes toward and improved performance in writing, and most crucial, whether word processing enhanced or short-circuited revision.

Interestingly, most of these issues subsequently dropped out of sight as teachers and students became more familiar with computers as writing tools. We no longer worry about students' typing skills in high school and college because more and more students learn to type and use a mouse in elementary school (or even before formal schooling). With the dominance of graphical user interfaces (GUIs) such as the Windows and Macintosh operating systems, we now read little in the professional literature about the competing claims of the Macintosh versus DOS or about which word processing program is most useful for students. Similarly, students' increasing familiarity with computers makes it difficult to assess positive or negative attitudes because computers are now deeply rooted in the "given" of students' educational lives.

The question of revision, then, seems to be the only long-lived question first posed in the early 1980s that we still concern ourselves with today. The focus of this question, however, changes over the years. Instead of asking if computers foster or retard revision, researchers and teachers have turned their attention to the *ways* that students compose and revise regardless of the software medium. In other words, we have come back to the point of looking at the composing process itself rather than the technology of composing.

In much the same way, the early questions posed by users of networked computers often focused on less important elements that arose from teachers' sincere but often short-sighted concerns. What we see more often now in the literature is not focused on specific networking software or other technical considerations, nor even on students as users of particular technologies, but rather on students' behavior as writing students.

In our view, the important questions about the newest technologies, hypertext generally and use of the World Wide Web specifically, will also eventually focus on fundamental points:

- how do we identify information to be learned,
- how do we evaluate the credibility of sources,
- how do we learn and remember, and
- how do we read, how do we write?

But we cannot ask these fundamental questions if we allow the technology to take center stage. Focusing on technology rather than on learning leads to questions with a short shelf-life because technology and our uses of it change so rapidly.

A FUNDAMENTAL PREMISE

If we move the technology from the focal point of the picture into the background, we can still ask useful questions about how to use technology and how to train teachers to take advantage of its potential. But by moving the technology from foreground to background, we also establish what we think of as the fundamental principle of computer-supported writing instruction:

- The computer *supports* instruction but does not dominate or dictate it.

OR

- Because the interactions of teachers and students are the integral elements that must be at the center of instruction, all the instructional aids and tools play supporting roles when they are appropriate.

OR

- Computers and their related technologies are helpful tools to advance what teachers and students could do in other ways.

In other words, we believe that computers are valuable teaching and learning tools, but they are just that—tools. They are not the focus of instruction, nor can they replace the interactions of caring teachers and students. Computers can facilitate, but as soon as they become the focal point of a writing class, then less writing instruction is going on.

It's helpful, we think, to recall a point Mike, drawing on Ong, often makes: composing with pen and paper is a technology that makes composing easier than remembering oral "texts." Composing with a typewriter changed the dominant technology of writing in the middle of the last century, but did it change composing? Composing with a computer, word processing program, and access to library sources all over the world via the Internet constitutes a different dominant technology for writing, but does this new technology changc composing?

ARE WE HYPOCRITES?

If we don't believe that computers change composing, then why have we written this book? If the technology is to take a back seat, why spend time reading and writing about it at all?

As we know from watching young children, stories are easy to compose at an early age. Those same children, fluent in spoken language, often struggle with the technology of pencil and paper, the oddities of English spelling, and the awkwardness of eye-hand coordination. Children need support as they move from completely oral language to print literacies, and so the role of "teaching" technology begins early in our lives as readers and writers.

The various roles of teachers, students, and technologies are not simple, and their interactions create complex webs of learning. We believe that teachers, as well as students, need guidance about the best ways to get the maximum benefit from those complex interactions.

The short answer to the question posed above is—no, we really aren't hypocrites. We think there is great value in studying the ways in which technology does and doesn't work. But we ground this belief in our strong sense that technology is not the reason for looking at those interactions in the first place.

A SKETCH OF THE FUTURE?

In their published work on computer-supported writing in the early 1980s, Hugh Burns (1984) and Bill Wresch (1983), among others, expressed hopes that computer software might replace certain teacher functions. Although prompting software that helps students generate and arrange ideas continues to be developed and refined, we believe that these approaches to computer-supported writing are less common than once thought.

We also take exception to Charles Moran's (1992) view of the electronic or virtual classroom that supersedes physical classrooms. Because of the social nature of learning and especially the collaborative nature of writing instruction, we feel that computer-supported writing will continue within the confines of a classroom setting even while it expands beyond those boundaries.

What do we imagine the future holds for computer-supported writing instruction? And how do we foresee teachers preparing themselves for this dynamic challenge? As Cindy Selfe (1992) points out in "Preparing English Teachers for the Virtual Age," teachers must expect to be lifelong learners themselves. The technology continues to change, obviously, and will change in directions we cannot now predict. Teachers, then, need to know not only what is available right now to support writing instruction, but they need to know how to learn as new applications appear.

We add, however, that teachers' learning will not focus on technology *per se*. Rather, teachers will want to learn new technologies to see how they can use them *to support writing instruction*. Lifelong learning, then, will include not just new information about technology as it changes, but also new information about teaching strategies, writing process, social interactions and learning, and so on.

Learning about technology will be just one facet of the lifelong learning teachers will become accustomed to in the next century.

Rae Schipke (1995) describes a "constructivist approach" to computer technology that challenges teachers to give students the opportunities to create their own learning. As she describes it:

> When students sit down at a computer and create documents collaboratively, research on CD-ROM, discuss ideas and concepts in an open-ended fashion using interactive writing software, explore resources and join discussions on the Internet, they can examine, test, and discuss ideas with innumerable experts and peers. When students discover challenging and inexplicable facts, ideas, and discussions online, they can be eager to learn more. As they learn more using computers to explore, comprehend, and focus on real problems as they relate to English language and literature, they can become both technologically educated and literate. They also can care more about their work and take it more seriously, because they are exploring and collecting real data, information, and life ideas to be shared with others. (p. 1)

The challenge for teachers, she notes, feels overwhelming because of the lack of confidence, resources, and time. How the teachers of the computer-supported writing environments of the future take up this challenge will define in large part what the picture of computer-supported writing looks like in 20 years.

The educational contexts we now take for granted will also undoubtedly change. We believe that as we move into the next century, telephone, video, and computer text will be transmitted simultaneously. We can imagine, for instance, a pop-up screen on the teacher's computer that shows the student calling for information. The pop-up screen can include not just the student but also the student's text. While the teacher talks to the student, he or she might also comment in writing on the draft of the text. The same capabilities may become available on our television sets, so that students calling teachers at home might want to initiate impromptu conferences while we're relaxing in front of a baseball game.

In combining communication technologies, "computers" will support different kinds of interactions among students, teachers, and texts. More important, these interactions are more likely to occur in less formal settings, thereby expanding the "instructional setting" to include far more places than we now consider. As teachers and students take advantage of these technologies, writing instruction will change, and teachers will adapt new techniques that allow these technologies to support students as they learn about writing.

Just as these communication technologies blur the "place" of instruction, they are likely to blur the "time" of instruction. A student in Vermont working on a paper in the evening could ask for help with her writing from a Writing Center tutor in California. A night-owl in California could conceivably ask for help from an early-morning tutor in Vermont. Individual teachers will not take "calls" 24 hours a day, but support services could be set up across the country to help students through most hours of the day. A National Writing Center? It's not impossible if we imagine a virtual center staffed by writing tutors physically housed on campuses across the country and linked electronically to a single Writing Center Internet address.

A necessary precursor of this kind of writing support, however, is cooperation among teachers across the country. Part of the lifelong learning mentioned above might also include keeping current with the philosophies and pedagogies of various support services provided by the virtual Writing Center. Can teachers possibly agree on what tutors from all across the country should say to students about papers? An interesting future indeed!

Another element of a virtual Writing Center is already with us. Multimedia writing supports are available on the Internet around the clock. Virtual handbooks, dictionaries, and rhetorics are available for students to consult. Some universities are contributing other tutorial software to help students with common writing problems. Nor do these computer-based tools rely solely on text. Videotapes and sound recordings enliven the explanations of argumentation, uses of semicolons, and so on.

Most important, the future of computer-supported writing instruction will depend on the continuing efforts of teachers to use new computer tools in ways that help writers. We see a dynamic future with teachers actively engaged in practical efforts and classroom research to help shape constructive uses of new technologies.

Even if these kinds of writing support do not become commonplace in computer-supported writing in the future, several points are certain. Despite the optimism reflected in Moran's article, "Computers and the writing classroom: A look to the future," and Kate's article, "Computers and teacher education in the 1990s and beyond," teachers will face real challenges as they continue to integrate computers into a composition curriculum. We believe that:

- Even if the pace of technology change slows, teachers will still feel hard-pressed to keep up with computer technologies.
- The costs of maintaining hardware and software will fall inequitably on certain teachers and certain schools. In other words, the gap between the haves and have-nots will almost certainly widen in coming years.
- Teachers will feel frustrated in coping with increasing claims on their time. As one of our colleagues recently explained, when graduate students began working on thesis projects on word processing, he was called upon to read and return drafts much more quickly. "And then the X#@% revised drafts come back again in two days!"
- Questions about the quality and quantity of face-to-face versus electronic contact will rise to the fore. Just how often will teachers need to meet with students as a class to build a sense of community among writers? Can students substitute small-group interactions for large-group interactions without loss of

instructional quality? Can students and teachers substitute online tutorials for office conferences without loss of instructional quality?

- Perceptions of difference based on gender, race, and ethnicity will not automatically disappear when students and teachers use electronic communications more frequently than face-to-face communications. Building a community of writing will continue to challenge teachers of writing, even computer-supported writing.
- Teachers will continue to grapple with the questions of authority and power relationships in their classes, whether those classes meet primarily in a physical or virtual classroom.

We need not end on a negative note, however, because teachers are facing the challenges provided by computer technologies in their classroom. A great deal of research and classroom observation will continue into the future. What we learn from teachers and students today will help us to train teachers more effectively in the future. The final certainty about computer-supported writing in the future is that its practitioners will be better trained and better prepared to accept the challenges of creative teaching and learning throughout their careers.

Appendix

Materials Used in the Transitions Study

STUDENT SURVEY ADMINISTERED AT THE BEGINNING OF THE SEMESTER

General Instructions: We are interested in your writing and computing experiences and attitudes. Please take a few minutes to complete this survey. In general, when you are presented with a scale next to a question, please put an X over the number that best corresponds to your answer. For example, if you strongly agreed with the following question, you might put an X through the number 5. If you agreed moderately, you might put an X through number 4, if you neither agreed nor disagreed, you might put an X through number 3.

Example Question:

	Strongly Disagree				Strongly Agree
I like to read magazines like TIME or Newsweek.	1	2	3	4	5

As is the case with all of the information we are collecting for our study, we will keep all the information you provide to us completely confidential. Your teacher will not be made aware of any of your responses. Thanks for your help.

Your Name: ______________________________
Your Instructor's Name: ______________________________

Expectations about Writing:

		Very Little				Very Much
1.	In general, how much writing do you think will be required in your classes at CSU?	1	2	3	4	5
2.	How much writing do you think you will be required to do after you graduate?	1	2	3	4	5
3.	How important do you think writing will be to your career?	1	2	3	4	5

Grades:

4.	In this class, I expect to receive a grade of	A	B	C	D	F
5.	In previous writing classes, I have usually received a grade of . . .	A	B	C	D	F

Attitudes about Writing:

		Strongly Disagree				Strongly Agree
6.	Good writers are born, not made.	1	2	3	4	5
7.	I avoid writing.	1	2	3	4	5
8.	Some people have said, "Writing can be learned but it can't be taught." Do you believe it can be learned?	1	2	3	4	5
9.	Do you believe writing can be taught?	1	2	3	4	5
10.	Practice is the most important part of being a good writer.	1	2	3	4	5
11.	I am able to express myself clearly in my writing.	1	2	3	4	5
12.	Writing is a lot of fun.	1	2	3	4	5
13.	Good teachers can help me become a better writer.	1	2	3	4	5
14.	Talent is the most important part of being a good writer.	1	2	3	4	5
15.	Anyone with at least average intelligence can learn to be a good writer.	1	2	3	4	5
16.	I am no good at writing.	1	2	3	4	5
17.	I enjoy writing.	1	2	3	4	5
18.	Discussing my writing with others is an enjoyable experience.	1	2	3	4	5
19.	Compared to other students, I am a good writer.	1	2	3	4	5
20.	Teachers who have read my writing think I am a good writer.	1	2	3	4	5
21.	Other students who have read my writing think I am a good writer.	1	2	3	4	5
22.	My writing is easy to understand.	1	2	3	4	5

Experiences in Previous Writing Classes:

Strongly Disagree	Strongly Agree

23.	On some of my past writing assignments, I have been required to submit rough drafts of my papers.	1	2	3	4	5
24.	I'v taken some courses that focused primarily on spelling, grammar, and punctuation.	1	2	3	4	5
25.	In previous writing classes, I've had to revise my papers.	1	2	3	4	5
26.	Some of my former writing teachers were more interested in my ideas than in my spelling, punctuation, and grammar.	1	2	3	4	5
27.	In some of my former writing classes, I've commented on other students' papers.	1	2	3	4	5
28.	In some of my former writing classes, I spent a lot of time working in groups.	1	2	3	4	5
29.	Some of my former teachers acted as though the most important part of writing was spelling, punctuation, and grammar.	1	2	3	4	5

Please indicate the TIMES PER MONTH or HOURS PER WEEK you engage in the following activities:

Writing Activities: How many TIMES PER MONTH do you ...

30.	Write in your journal	0	1	2	3	4+
31.	Write poetry on your own	0	1	2	3	4+
32.	Write letters to friends or family	0	1	2	3	4+
33.	Write fiction	0	1	2	3	4+
34.	Write papers for class	0	1	2	3	4+
35.	Write for publication	0	1	2	3	4+

Reading Activities: How many HOURS PER WEEK do you ...

36.	Read the newspaper	0	1	2	3	4+
37.	Read fiction for pleasure	0	1	2	3	4+
38.	Read magazines	0	1	2	3	4+
39.	Read for class	0	1	2	`3	4+

	Attitudes about Computers:	**Strongly Disagree**				**Strongly Agree**
40.	The challenge of learning about computers is exciting.	1	2	3	4	5
41.	I am confident that I can learn computer skills.	1	2	3	4	5
42.	Anyone can learn to use a computer if they are patient and motivated.	1	2	3	4	5
43.	Learning to operate computers is like learning any new skill-- the more you practice, the better you become.	1	2	3	4	5
44.	I feel apprehensive about working with computers.	1	2	3	4	5
45.	I have difficulty in understanding the technical aspects of computers.	1	2	3	4	5
46.	It scares me to think that I could cause the computer to destroy a large amount of information by hitting the wrong key.	1	2	3	4	5
47.	You have to be a genius to understand all the special commands used by most computer programs.	1	2	3	4	5
48.	If given the opportunity, I would like to learn about and use computers.	1	2	3	4	5
49.	I have avoided computers because they are unfamiliar and somewhat intimidating to me.	1	2	3	4	5
50.	I feel computers are necessary tools in both educational and work settings.	1	2	3	4	5
51.	I own my own computer.	No				Yes
52.	I don't own my own computer, but I regularly use my parents' or a friend's computer.	No				Yes

Student Survey Administered at the End of the Semester

General Instructions: Please take a few minutes to complete this survey. This survey is similar to the survey you filled out at the beginning of the semester -- many of the questions are the same, but we have added some new questions as well. In general, when you are presented with a scale next to a question, please put an X over the number that best corresponds to your answer. For example, if you strongly agreed with the follow' .g question, you might put an X through the number 5. If you agreed moderately, you might put an X through number 4, if you neither agreed nor disagreed, you might put an X through number 3.

Example Question:

	Strongly Disagree				Strongly Agree
I like to read magazines like TIME or Newsweek.	1	2	3	4	5

As is the case with all of the information we are collecting for our study, we will keep all the information you provide to us completely confidential. Your teacher will not be made aware of any of your responses. Thanks for your help.

Your Name: ____

Your Instructor's Name: ______________________________________

Expectations about Writing:		Very Little				Very Much
1.	In general, how much writing do you think will be required in your classes at CSU?	1	2	3	4	5
2.	How much writing do you think you will be required to do after you graduate?	1	2	3	4	5
3.	How important do you think writing will be to your career?	1	2	3	4	5

Grades:

4.	In this class, I expect to receive a grade of	A	B	C	D	F

Attitudes about Writing:		Strongly Disagree				Strongly Agree
5.	Good writers are born, not made.	1	2	3	4	5
6.	I avoid writing.	1	2	3	4	5
7.	Some people have said, "Writing can be learned but it can't be taught." Do you believe it can be learned?	1	2	3	4	5
8.	Do you believe writing can be taught?	1	2	3	4	5
9.	Practice is the most important part of being a good writer.	1	2	3	4	5
10.	I am able to express myself clearly in my writing.	1	2	3	4	5
11.	Writing is a lot of fun.	1	2	3	4	5
12.	Good teachers can help me become a better writer.	1	2	3	4	5
13.	Talent is the most important part of being a good writer.	1	2	3	4	5
14.	Anyone with at least average intelligence can learn to be a good writer.	1	2	3	4	5

Attitudes about Writing (continued)		Strongly Disagree				Strongly Agree
15.	I am no good at writing.	1	2	3	4	5
16.	I enjoy writing.	1	2	3	4	5
17.	Discussing my writing with others is an enjoyable experience.	1	2	3	4	5
18.	Compared to other students, I am a good writer.	1	2	3	4	5
19.	Teachers who have read my writing think I am a good writer.	1	2	3	4	5
20.	Other students who have read my writing think I am a good writer.	1	2	3	4	5
21.	My writing is easy to understand.	1	2	3	4	5

Collaborative Writing Processes		Strongly Disagree				Strongly Agree
22.	Outside of class, when I was working on papers for this course, I usually asked someone to read them and tell me what they thought about them.	1	2	3	4	5
23.	During in-class drafting sessions, I usually talked informally about my writing with some of my classmates.	1	2	3	4	5
24.	Workshops in this course helped improve my writing.	1	2	3	4	5
25.	I would have preferred to work on my writing assignments without having to sit through in-class writing workshops.	1	2	3	4	5
26.	I found that comments from my classmates resulted in significant changes to my papers.	1	2	3	4	5
27.	During this semester, I talked outside the classroom with some of my classmates about my writing.	1	2	3	4	5
28.	I found it easy to talk with my instructor about my writing for this class.	1	2	3	4	5
29.	I asked my instructor questions during class (during discussions, during workshops, or as I was working on a paper) several times this semester.	1	2	3	4	5

Please indicate how HELPFUL you found each of the following:		Not at all Helpful				Very Helpful
30.	Hand-written comments on my papers from my classmates.	1	2	3	4	5
31.	Hand-written comments on my papers from my teacher.	1	2	3	4	5
32.	Spoken comments on my papers from my classmates.	1	2	3	4	5
33.	Spoken comments on my papers from my teacher.	1	2	3	4	5
34.	Computer-based comments (e.g., WordPerfect, Electronic Mail) on my papers from my classmates.	1	2	3	4	5
35.	Computer-based comments (e.g., WordPerfect, Electronic Mail) on my papers from my teacher.	1	2	3	4	5
36.	Face-to-face discussions about my writing outside of class with my classmates.	1	2	3	4	5
37.	Face-to-face discussions about my writing outside of class with my teacher.	1	2	3	4	5
38.	Electronic mail as a means of contacting my classmates.	1	2	3	4	5
39.	Electronic mail as a means of contacting my teacher.	1	2	3	4	5
40.	The telephone as a means of contacting my classmates.	1	2	3	4	5
41.	The telephone as a means of contacting my teacher.	1	2	3	4	5

Helpfulness (continued):		Not at all Helpful				Very Helpful
42.	Office hours as a means of contacting my teacher.	1	2	3	4	5
43.	Informal discussions immediately before and after class as a means of talking with my classmates.	1	2	3	4	5
44.	Informal discussions immediately before and after class as a means of talking with my teacher.	1	2	3	4	5

Please indicate the TIMES PER MONTH or HOURS PER WEEK you engage in the following activities:

Writing Activities: How many TIMES PER MONTH do you ...

45.	Write in your journal	0	1	2	3	4+
46.	Write poetry on your own	0	1	2	3	4+
47.	Write letters to friends or family	0	1	2	3	4+
48.	Write fiction	0	1	2	3	4+
49.	Write papers for class	0	1	2	3	4+
50.	Write for publication	0	1	2	3	4+

Reading Activities: How many HOURS PER WEEK do you ...

51.	Read the newspaper	0	1	2	3	4+
52.	Read fiction for pleasure	0	1	2	3	4+
53.	Read magazines	0	1	2	3	4+
54.	Read for class	0	1	2	3	4+

Attitudes about Computers:		Strongly Disagree				Strongly Agree
55.	The challenge of learning about computers is exciting.	1	2	3	4	5
56.	I am confident that I can learn computer skills.	1	2	3	4	5
57.	Anyone can learn to use a computer if they are patient and motivated.	1	2	3	4	5
58.	Learning to operate computers is like learning any new skill-- the more you practice, the better you become.	1	2	3	4	5
59.	I feel apprehensive about working with computers.	1	2	3	4	5
60.	I have difficulty in understanding the technical aspects of computers.	1	2	3	4	5
61.	It scares me to think that I could cause the computer to destroy a large amount of information by hitting the wrong key.	1	2	3	4	5
62.	You have to be a genius to understand all the special commands used by most computer programs.	1	2	3	4	5
63.	If given the opportunity, I would like to learn about and use computers.	1	2	3	4	5
64.	I have avoided computers because they are unfamiliar and somewhat intimidating to me.	1	2	3	4	5
65.	I feel computers are necessary tools in both educational and work settings.	1	2	3	4	5
66.	Since I completed the first survey, I purchased or was given my own computer.	No				Yes

Classroom Observation Form

Classroom Observation Form
Classroom Study
Spring 1994

Teacher:______________________________
Setting: _____Computer ______Traditional
Date and Time:____________________________
Observer: ______________________________
No. of Students in Attendance: ______________

Time:	Narrative:

Teacher Initiated Discussion with Student	**Student Initiated Teacher/Student Discussion**	**Student/Student Interaction (circle off task)**

STUDENT INTERVIEW QUESTIONS AT THE BEGINNING OF THE SEMESTER

One of the key issues we're interested in is how you write and what you think about your own writing skills.

- What's your most comfortable approach toward writing a paper?
- How might your approach to writing differ from that of other writers?
- What specific approaches, resources, or techniques do you draw on in your writing?
- Tell me what you think are your strengths and weaknesses as a writer?
- What are the most important things you've learned in previous writing classes?

At CSU, most teachers encourage students to get feedback on papers—from peers, Writing Center tutors, or teachers.

- What do you think in general about asking other people to help with a paper?
- Have you ever asked for help on a paper? From whom? In class or out of class? At what point in the writing? What kinds of help did you get?
- When teachers ask you to work in groups to review papers, do you find that you get helpful comments to revise your paper? Why? What kinds of comments?
- Would you prefer to pick your partner or group members for in-class peer review or be assigned to groups by the teacher? Why?
- How do you pick the people you choose to work with in class? Out of class?

We're also interested in how you get in touch with classmates and teachers.

- Are there any faculty, staff or students here that you've worked with closely through the past year?
- How do you typically get in touch with your classmates or teacher outside of class?
- Do you ever use electronic mail? When? (inside or outside of classroom?)
- Have you ever sent a paper by e-mail to someone for comments?

And finally, we would like to know about your experiences writing on a computer.

- Do you own a computer or word processor? What kind?
- Have you ever written on a computer or word processor?
- Do you prefer using a computer or word processor to writing by hand or vice versa?

STUDENT INTERVIEW QUESTIONS AT THE END OF THE SEMESTER

One of the key issues we're interested in is how you write and what you think about your own writing skills.

- How does your approach to writing differ now from the beginning of the semester (if at all)?
- What specific approaches, resources, or techniques did you learn this semester and now use in your writing?
- Tell me what you think are your strengths and weaknesses as a writer?

At CSU, most teachers encourage students to get feedback on papers—from peers, Writing Center tutors, or teachers.

- What do you think in general about asking other people to help with a paper?
- During the semester, did you ask your teacher for help on a paper? In class or out of class? At what point in the writing? What kinds of help did you get?
- During the semester, did you ask a classmate for help on a paper? In class or out of class? At what point in the writing? What kinds of help did you get?
- When your teacher asked you to work in groups to review papers, did you find that you got helpful comments to revise your paper? Why? What kinds of comments?
- Would you prefer to pick your partner or group members for in-class peer review or be assigned to groups by the teacher? Why?
- How do you pick the people you choose to work with in class? Out of class?

We're also interested in how you get in touch with classmates and teachers.

- Are there any faculty, staff or students here that you've worked with closely this past semester?
- How do you typically get in touch with your classmates or teacher outside of class?
- Did you ever use electronic mail? When? (inside or outside of classroom?)
- During this semester, did you send a paper by e-mail to someone for comments?

And finally, we would like to know about your experiences writing on a computer.

- Do you prefer using a computer or word processor to writing by hand or vice versa?
- If you had it to do over again, would you choose a computer or a traditional classroom for CO150?

Additional Post Questions

- What have you learned in this class?
- What suggestions would you give your teacher to improve this class next semester?
- We noticed when we observed classes this semester that students often talked with each other during class. If you talked with classmates during class, were you typically talking about a paper, the class activities, or something else? In what ways were these conversations useful to you as a writer?

***ASK THESE QUESTIONS ONLY OF COMPUTER CLASSROOM STUDENTS:**

- In what ways, if any, has the computer classroom affected your learning this semester?
- Your teacher wanted to teach in the computer classroom. Why do you think your teacher finds a computer classroom to be a good teaching environment?
- What advantages do you think your teacher feels it has over the traditional classroom?

TEACHER INTERVIEW QUESTIONS AT THE BEGINNING OF THE SEMESTER

One background area we're interested in is how you write and what you think about your own writing skills.

- What's your most comfortable approach toward writing a paper?
- What specific approaches, resources, or techniques do you draw on in your writing?
- Tell me what you think are your strengths and weaknesses as a writer?
- What do you think in general about asking other people to help you with a paper in progress?
- At what point have you asked for help when writing a paper? From whom? What kinds of help did you get?
- Do you own a computer or word processor? What kind?
- Do you prefer using a computer or word processor to writing by hand or vice versa?

We also want to know about your teaching background, experience, and preferred approaches.

- How long have you been teaching composition? In what settings? (e.g., high school, middle school, community college, university)
- How long have you taught writing in a computer-classroom?
- What advantages, if any, does the traditional classroom have over the computer classroom?
- What advantages, if any, does the computer-classroom have over the traditional classroom?
- Which specific teaching methods change for you as you move from traditional to computer classroom?
- Briefly explain some of your most effective teaching strategies in the traditional classroom.
- Briefly explain some of your most effective teaching strategies in the computer classroom.

And finally, we would like to know about specific computer applications and their usefulness to writing teachers.

- How long have you used e-mail? For what purposes?
- Have you used e-mail to communicate with students?
- Have you used e-mail to send comments on students' papers?
- Do you use other computer applications to comment on students' drafts or final papers? Please describe in detail.
- Which computer applications (software) are you most comfortable adapting for your teaching needs?

TEACHER INTERVIEW QUESTIONS AT THE END OF THE SEMESTER

We'd like to ask questions about differences between the two classroom settings and changes that have taken place since our last interview.

- What advantages, if any, does the traditional classroom have over the computer classroom? Has your notion of advantages changed based on your teaching this term?
- What advantages, if any, does the computer-classroom have over the traditional classroom? Has your notion of advantages changed based on your teaching this term?
- Which specific teaching methods change for you as you move from traditional to computer classroom?
- Briefly explain some of your most effective teaching strategies in the traditional classroom.
- Briefly explain some of your most effective teaching strategies in the computer classroom.

And we would like to know about specific computer applications and their usefulness to writing teachers.

- Has your use of e-mail changed over the course of this semester?
- Have you used e-mail to communicate with students?
- Have you used e-mail to send comments on students' papers?
- Do you use other computer applications to comment on students' drafts or final papers? Please describe in detail.
- Which computer applications (software) are you most comfortable adapting for your teaching needs?
- As you reflect generally on the semester, what stands out as most significant in your teaching, your relationships with students, your use of the technology?
- What are the key differences between the traditional and computer classrooms?
- Were there differences between the classes (level, motivation, participation)?
- Your students signed up for a class in 228 ("Computer-phobes beware!") Why do you think your students wanted to be in the computer classroom?
- Do you think those expectations were met?
- Now that they've completed the semester, what advantages do you think your students see for the computer classroom over the traditional classroom? What disadvantages?

PROMPTS FOR TEACHER LOGS

Reminders for teachers logs—You don't need to answer each question separately, but try to cover the territory at some point in your log entry.

- Which students did you talk to before or after class today?

Date	Name	Length of time	Initiator	Topic

- Which students did you talk to in your office today or during office hours?

Date	Name	Length of time	Initiator	Topic

- What did your class concentrate on today?
- What kinds of in-class activities did you do today?
- Which activities involved groups? How large were the groups? Did you assign students to groups or did they choose members themselves? If students grouped themselves, did you notice any patterns to the member selections?
- What went well in today's class? What didn't?
- Did you do anything you didn't anticipate before class began? What? Why?

Please remember to keep all e-mail and collect papers for us to photocopy.

Your Name:______________________________

Week o
Fall, Ms. M, CO15

As part of our study of student writers at CSU, we're interested in whether or not you discuss your classwork with classmates, writing center tutors, or instructors inside or outside the classroom. Please note that your instructors will not be shown any of the information you provide below. All information you provide will be kept strictly confidential.

	Out-of-Class Contact			**In-Class Contact**		
	In the past week, how many times did you discuss your coursework with a classmate or instructor outside of class?	**Did you talk face to face, use the telephone, or use electronic mail?**	**What did you discuss?**	**In the past week, how many times did you discuss your coursework with a classmate or instructor during class?**	**Did you talk face to face or use electronic mail?**	**What did you discuss?**
Ms. M						
Writing Center Tutor						

Notes

[1]Throughout *Transitions*, we use aliases to refer to teachers who participated in the Transitions and New Teachers Studies. Our use of aliases is in accordance with conditions specified by our University's Human Subjects Research Committee.

[2]Throughout this chapter, we will quote from the interviews conducted with teachers in the Transitions Study. Each teacher was interviewed at the beginning, middle, and end of the semester she participated in the study. All interviews were taped and transcribed exactly. We use ellipses only when we have deleted text from the full quotation.

[3]We have adopted the convention of using a "—" to indicate that interviewees changed direction in mid-sentence.

[4]This item was not used when we compared helpfulness of comments from teachers across classroom settings.

[5]This item was not used when we compared helpfulness of comments from classmates across classroom settings.

[6]Our training program for new graduate teaching assistants includes several components. GTAs attend a week-long orientation session prior to the beginning of the semester. They take a three-credit graduate seminar that directly supports their teaching for the first semester in which they teach. They are observed three or four times during the semester and required to participate in three or four grading reviews. And they attend all meetings of an "audit section," in which they observe an experienced teacher teaching the same syllabus that they are using.

List of Related Readings

SELECTED THEORETICAL TREATMENTS OF COMPUTERS AND WRITING

Barton, E., & Ray, R. (1989). Developing connections: Computers and literacy. *Computers and Composition, 6*(3), 35–45.

Faigley, L. (1992). *Fragments of rationality: Postmodernity and the subject of composition.* Pittsburgh, PA: University of Pittsburgh Press.

Gerrard, L. (1991). Computers and compositionists: A view from the floating bottom. *Computers and Composition, 8*(2), 5–15.

Gerrard, L. (1993). Computers and composition: Rethinking our values. *Computers and Composition, 10*(2), 23–34.

Haas, C. (1996). *Writing technology: Studies of the materiality of literacy.* Hillsdale, NJ: Lawrence Erlbaum Associates.

Hawisher, G.E., Selfe, C.E., Moran, C., & LeBlanc, P. (1996). *Computers and the teaching of writing in American higher education, 1979–1994: A history.* Norwood, NJ: Ablex.

Hawisher, G., & Pemberton, M. (1991). The case for teacher as researcher in computers and composition studies. *Writing Instructor, 10*(2), 77–88.

Hawisher, G.E, & Selfe, C.L. (1991). The rhetoric of technology and the electronic writing class. *College Composition and Communication, 42*(1), 55–65.

Hawisher, G.E., Selfe, C.L., Moran, C., LeBlanc, P. (1996). *Computers and the teaching of writing in American higher education, 1979–1994: A history.* Norwood, NJ: Ablex Publishing.

Heilker, P. (1992). Revision worship and the computer as audience. *Computers and Composition, 9*(3), 59–69.

Joyce, M. (1992). New teaching: Toward a pedagogy for a new cosmology. *Computers and Composition, 9*(2), 7–16.

Kaplan, N. (1991). Ideology, technology, and the future of writing instruction. In G. E. Hawisher & C. Selfe (Eds.), *Evolving perspectives on computers and composition studies: Questions for the 1990s* (pp.11–42). Urbana, IL: National Council of Teachers of English.

Kelvin, P., & Leonard, S. (1992). Computer-assisted writing classes: Problems among the promises. *Bulletin of the Association for Business Communication, 55*(4), 21–25.

LeBlanc, P. (1990). Competing ideologies in software design for computer-aided composition. *Computers and Composition, 7*(2), 7–19.

Moulthrop, S. (1991). The politics of hypertext. In G. E. Hawisher & C. Selfe (Eds.), *Evolving perspectives on computers and composition studies: Questions for the 1990s* (pp.253–271). Urbana, IL: National Council of Teachers of English.

Moulthrop, S. & Kaplan, N. (1991). Something to imagine: Literature, composition and interactive fiction. *Computers and Composition, 9*(1), 7–23.

Selfe, C., & Wahlstrom, B. (1988). Computers and writing: Casting a broader net with theory and research. *Computers and the Humanities, 22*(1), 57–66.

Selfe, C.L., & Selfe, R. J., Jr. (1994). The politics of the interface: Power and its exercise in electronic contact zones. *College Composition and Communication, 45*(4), 480–504.

Selfe, C.L. (1988). Computers in English departments: The rhetoric of technopower. *ADE Bulletin, 90*(6), 67

Selfe, C.L. (1988). The humanization of computers: Forget technology, remember literacy. *English Journal, 77*(6), 69–71.

Slatin, J.M. (1990). Reading hypertext: Order and coherence in a new medium. *College English, 52*(8), 870–883.

Takayoshi, P. (1996). Writing the culture of computers: Students as technology critics in cultural studies classes. *Teaching English in the two-year college, 23*(3).

Tuman, M.C. (1992). *Word perfect: Literacy in the computer age.* Pittsburgh: University of Pittsburgh Press.

SELECTED EDITED COLLECTIONS THAT ADDRESS COMPUTERS AND WRITING ISSUES

Boschmann, E. (1995). *The electronic classroom: A handbook for education in the electronic environment.* Medford, NJ: Learned Information.

Bruce, B., Peyton, J.K., & Batson, T. (1993). *Network-based classrooms: Promises and realities.* New York: Cambridge University Press.

Gerrard, L. (1987). *Writing at century's end: Essays on computer-assisted composition.* New York: Random House.

Handa, C. (1990). *Computers and community: Teaching composition in the twenty-first century.* Portsmouth, NH: Boynton-Cook.

Hawisher, G.E., & Soter, A.O. (1990). *On literacy and its teaching: Issues in English education.* Albany, NY: State University of New York Press.

Hawisher, G.E., & LeBlanc, P. (1992). *Re-imagining computers and composition: Teaching and research in the virtual age.* Portsmouth, NH: Boynton-Cook.

Hawisher, G.E., & Selfe, C.L. (1989). *Critical perspectives on computers and composition instruction.* New York: Teachers College Press.

Hawisher, G.E., & Selfe, C.L. (1991). *Evolving perspectives on computers and composition studies: Questions for the 1990s.* Urbana, IL: National Council of Teachers of English.

Holdstein, D.H., & Selfe, C.L. (1990). *Computers and writing: Theory, research, practice.* New York: MLA.

Myers, L. (1993). *Approaches to computer writing classrooms : Learning from practical experience*. Albany, NY: State University of New York Press.

Selfe, C.L., & Hilligoss, S. (1994). *Literacy and computers: The complications of teaching and learning with technology.* New York: MLA.

Selfe, C.L., Rodrigues, D., & Oates, W. (1989). *Computers in English and the language arts: The challenge of teacher education.* Urbana, IL: National Council of Teachers of English.

Shostak, R. (1984). *Computers in composition instruction.* Eugene, OR: International Council for Computers in Education.

Tuman, M.C. (1992). *Literacy online: The promise (and peril) of reading and writing with computers.* Pittsburgh: University of Pittsburgh Press.

Wresch, W. (1984). *The computer in composition instruction: A writer's tool.* Urbana, IL: National Council of Teachers of English.

Wresch, W. (1991). *The English classroom in the computer age: Thirty lesson plans.* Urbana, IL: National Council of Teachers of English.

SELECTED STUDIES OF TEACHING AND LEARNING IN COMPUTER-SUPPORTED WRITING CLASSROOMS

Bruce, B., Michaels, S., & Watson-Gegeo, K. (1985). How computers can change the writing process. *Language Arts, 62*(2), 143–149.

Bruce, B., & Rubin, A. (1993). *Electronic quills: A situated evaluation of using computers for writing in classrooms. Technology in education series.* Hillsdale, NJ: Lawrence Erlbaum Associates.

Carbone, N. Daisley, M., Federenko, E., McComas, D., Moran, C., Ostermiller, D., & Vanden Akker, S. (1993). Writing ourselves online. *Computers and Composition, 10*(3), 29–48.

Collins, T., Engen-Wedin, N., & Margolis, W. (1988). Persistence and course completion. *Computers and Composition, 6*(1), 27–32.

D'Agostino, K.N., & Varone, S.D. (1991). Interacting with basic writers in the computer classroom. *Computers and Composition, 8*(3), 39–49.

Delmaramo, M. (1992). Microcomputers and the writing process: A survey and critique (Doctoral dissertation, Bowling Green State University, 1991). *Dissertation Abstracts International, 52*, 3845.

Douglas, J.Y. (1994). Technology, pedagogy, and context: A tale of two classrooms. *Computers and Composition, 11*(3), 275–282.

Gunn, C. (1991). A descriptive study of a developing computer-supported writing environment in a first-grade whole language classroom. (Doctoral dissertation, University Of Oregon, 1990). *Dissertation Abstracts International, 51*, 3710.

Hartman, K., Neuwirth, C.M., Kiesler, S., Sproull, L., Cochran, C., Palmquist, M., & Zubrow, D. (1991). Patterns of social interaction and learning to write: Some effects of network technologies. *Written Communication, 8*(1), 79–113.

Hawisher, G.E., & Fortune, R. (1989). Word processing and the basic writer. *Collegiate Microcomputer, 7*(3), 275–284,287.

Hawisher, G.E., & Selfe, C.L. (1992). Voices in college classrooms: The dynamics of electronic discussion. *Quarterly of the National Writing Project and the Center for the Study of Writing and Literacy, 14*(3), 24–28,32.

Kiefer, K., & Palmquist, M. (1996). Adapting to the classroom setting: Research on teachers moving between traditional and computer classrooms. In G. Rijlaarsdam & M. Couzijn (Eds.), *Current trends in writing research: Effective learning and teaching of writing.* Amsterdam: University of Amsterdam Press.

Kiefer, K., & Palmquist, M. (1996). How does access to a computer network shape writing students' interactions with peers and teachers? In G. Rijlaarsdam & M. Couzijn (Eds.), *Current trends in writing research: Effective learning and teaching of writing.* Amsterdam: University of Amsterdam Press.

Klem, E., & Moran, C. (1992). Teachers in a strange LANd: Learning to teach in a networked writing classroom. *Computers and Composition, 9*(3), 5–22.

Logan, S. (1988). A study of four undergraduate computer-writers. *Collegiate Microcomputer, 6*(2), 135–146.

Mcginnis, J. (1989). Computers in composition at the University of Arizona (Doctoral dissertation, The University Of Arizona, 1989). *Dissertation Abstracts International, 50,* 1228.

Palmquist, M. (1993). Network-supported interaction in two writing classrooms. *Computers and Composition 10*(4), 25–57.

Posey, E., & Ward, D. (1991). Ideas in practice. Computer-supported writing instruction: The student-centered classroom. *Journal of Developmental Education, 15*(2), 26–28,30.

Reynolds, T., & Bonk, C.J. (1996). Facilitating college writers' revisions within a generative-evaluative computerized prompting framework. *Computers and Composition 13*(1), 93–108.

Rubin, A., & Bruce, B. (1990). Alternate realizations of purpose in computer-supported writing. *Theory into Practice, 29*(4), 256–263.

SELECTED TITLES ON TEACHING AND LEARNING STRATEGIES IN COMPUTER-SUPPORTED WRITING CLASSROOMS

Carbone, N. (1993). Trying to create a community: A first day lesson plan. *Computers and Composition, 10*(4), 81.

Gooden, A.R., & Silverman, F. (1996). *Computers in the classroom: How teachers and students are using technology to transform learning.* San Francisco: Jossey-Bass.

Gruber, S. (1995). Re: Ways we contribute: Students, instructors, and pedagogies in the computer-mediated writing classroom. *Computers and Composition, 12*(1), 61.

Hawisher, G.E. (1988). Computers in the classroom: The computer daybook: A multifaceted tool. *English Journal, 77*(3), 71–73.

Howie, S.H. (1989). *Reading, writing, and computers: Planning for integration.* Boston: Allyn and Bacon.

Kemp, F. (1987). Getting smart with computers: Computer-aided heuristics for student writers. *Writing Center Journal, 8*(1), 3–10.

Klonoski, E. (1994). Using the eyes of the PC to teach revision. *Computers and Composition, 11*(1), 71.

Marcus, S., & Blau, S. (1983, April). Not seeing is relieving: Invisible writing with computers. *Educational Technology* pp.12–15.

Monroe, R.B. (1993). *Writing and thinking with computers: A practical and progressive approach.* Urbana, IL: National Council of Teachers of English.

Moran, C. (1991). Using what we have. *Computers and Composition, 9*(1), 39–46.

Neuwirth, C., Palmquist, M., & Gillespie, T. (1989). Role playing and peer review: The devil's advocate exercise. In D. Beil (Ed.), *Teacher's guide to using computer networks for written interaction* (pp.157–164). Washington, D.C.: Realtime Learning Systems.

Schwartz, H. (1984). Teaching writing with computer aids. *College English, 46*(3), 239–247.

Schwartz, H. (1988). The student as producer and consumer of text: Computer uses in English studies. *Journal of Teaching Writing, 7*(1), 57–66.

Schwartz, H. (1989). Literacy theory in the classroom: Computers in literature and writing. *Computers and Composition, 7*(1), 49–63.

Sharples, M. (1985). *Cognition, computers, and creative writing.* New York: Halsted Press.

Susser, B. (1993). Networks and project work: Alternative pedagogies for writing with computers. *Computers and Composition, 10*(3), 63–89.

Wresch, W. (1982). Computers in English class: Finally beyond grammar and spelling drills. *College English, 44*(5), 483–490.

Wresch, W. (1983). Computers and composition instruction: An update. *College English, 45*(8), 794–799.

Wresch, W. (1991). The computer in English class: Lessons learned. *English Journal, 80*(8), 93–96.

Zeni, J. (1990). *Writinglands: Composing with old and new writing tools.* Urbana, IL: National Council of Teachers of English.

SELECTED TITLES ON TEACHER TRAINING FOR COMPUTER CLASSROOMS

Burns, H. (1984). The challenge for computer-assisted rhetoric. *Computers and the Humanities, 18,* 173–180.

Burns, H. (1992). Teaching composition in tomorrow's multimedia, multinetworked classrooms. In G. E. Hawisher & P. LeBlanc (Eds.), *Re-imagining computers and composition: Teaching and research in the virtual age* (pp.115–130). Portsmouth, NH: Boynton-Cook.

Chappell, V.A. (1995). Theorizing in practice: Tutor training "Live from the VAX Lab." *Computers and Composition, 12*(2), 227.

Greenleaf, C. (1994). Technological indeterminacy: The role of classroom writing practices and pedagogy in shaping student use of the computer. *Written Communication, 11*(1), 85–130.

Johanek, C., & Rickly, R. (1995). Online tutor training: Synchronous conferencing in a professional community. *Computers and Composition, 12*(2), 237.

Jordan-Henley, J., & Maid, B. (1995). Tutoring in cyberspace: Student impact and college/university collaboration. *Computers and Composition, 12*(2), 211.

Kiefer, K. (1991). Computers and teacher education in the 1990s and beyond. In G.E. Hawisher & C. Selfe (Eds.), *Evolving perspectives on computers and composition studies: Questions for the 1990s* (pp.117–131). Urbana, IL: NCTE and Computers and Composition.

Klem, E., & Moran, C. (1991). Computers and instructional strategies in the teaching of writing. In G.E. Hawisher & C.L. Selfe (Eds.), *Evolving perspectives on computers and composition studies: Questions for the 1990s* (pp.132–149). Urbana, IL: NCTE.

Rodrigues, R., & Rodrigues, D. (1989). How word processing is changing our teaching: New technologies, new approaches, new challenges. *Computers and Composition, 7*(1), 13–25.

Schipke, R. (1995). A constructivist approach to computer technology. *The ACE Newsletter, IX, 3* (Summer), 1–2.

Schroeder, E.J., & Boe, J. (1990). Minimalism, populism, and attitude transformation: Approaches to teaching writing in computer classrooms. In C. Handa (Ed.), *Computers and community: Teaching composition in the twenty-first century* (pp.28–46). Portsmouth, NH: Boynton-Cook.

Selfe, C.L. (1992). Preparing English teachers for the virtual age: The case for technology critics. In G.E. Hawisher & P. LeBlanc (Eds.), *Reimagining computers and composition: Teaching and research in the virtual Age* (pp.24–42). Portsmouth, NH: Boynton-Cook.

Selfe, C., & Wahlstrom, B. (1988). Computers and writing: Casting a broader net with theory and research. *Computers and the Humanities, 22*, 57–66.

Wresch, W. (1983, March). Computer essay generation. *The Computing Teacher, 11*, pp.63–65.

Wresch, W. (1987). Preparing the next generation of English teachers to use computers. *Computing Teacher, 15*(3), 41–43.

SELECTED TITLES ON WORD PROCESSING

Boiarsky, C. (1991). Fluency, fluidity, and word processing. *Journal of Advanced Composition, 11*(1), 123–131.

Bridwell, L., Nancarrow, P.R., & Ross, D.(1983). The writing process and the writing machine: Current research on word processors relevant to the teaching of composition. In R. Beach & L. Bridwell (Eds.), *New directions in composition research.* New York: Guildford Press.

Collier, R. (1983). The word processor and revision strategies. *College Composition and Communication, 34*, 149–55.

Curtis, M. (1988). Windows on composing: Teaching revision on word processors. *College Composition and Communication, 39*(3), 337–344.

Dowling, C. (1994). Word processing and the ongoing difficulty of writing. *Computers and Composition, 11*(3), 227.

Hawisher, G.E. (1986). Studies in word processing. *Computers and Composition, 4* (1), 6–31.

Hawisher, G.E. (1988). Research update: Writing and word processing. *Computers and Composition, 5*(2), 7–28.

Hawisher, G.E. (1989). Computers and writing: Where's the research? *English Journal, 78*(1), 89–91.

Kaplan, N., & Moulthrop, S. (1990). Other ways of seeing. *Computers and Composition, 7*(3), 89–102.

Kiefer, K. (1987). Revising on a word processor: What's happened, what's ahead. *ADE Bulletin,* 24–27.

LeBlanc, P. (1988). How to get the words just right: A reappraisal of word processing and revision. *Computers and Composition, 5*(3), 29–42.

Markel, M. (1994). Behaviors, attitudes, and outcomes: A study of word processing and writing quality among experienced word-processing students. *Computers and Composition, 11*(1), 49–58.

McAllister, C.H. (1985). The effects of word processing on the quality of writing: Fact or illusion? *Computers and Composition, 2*(4), 36–44.

Moran, C. (1983). Word processing and the teaching of writing. *English Journal, 72*(3), 113–115.

Nydahl, J. (1990). Teaching word processors to be CAI programs. *College English, 52*(8), 904–915.

Nydahl, J. (1991). Ambiguity and confusion in word-processing research. *Computers and Composition, 8*(3), 21–37.

Owston, R., Murphy, S., & Wideman, H. (1991). On and off computer writing of eighth grade students experienced in word processing. *Computers in the Schools, 8*(4), 67–87.

Reed, W.M. (1990). The effects of computer-based writing instruction and mode of discourse on writing performance and writer anxieties. *Computers in Human Behavior, 6*(3), 211–221.

Rodrigues, D., & Rodrigues, R. (1986). *Teaching writing with a word processor, grades 7–13.* Urbana, Ill. ERIC Clearinghouse on Reading and Communication Skills; National Council of Teachers of English.

Rodrigues, D., & Rodrigues, R. (1989). How word processing is changing our teaching: New technologies, new approaches, new challenges. *Computers and Composition, 7*(1), 13–25.

Snyder, I. (1993). The impact of computers on students' writing: A comparative study of the effects of pens and word processors on writing context, process and product. *Australian Journal of Education, 37*(1), 5–25.

Snyder, I. (1993). Writing with word processors: A research overview. *Educational Research, 35*(1), 49–68.

Sommers, E. (1985). *The effects of word processing and writing instruction on the writing processes and products of college writers. ERIC DOCUMENT*

Yahner, W. (1991). Effective ideation in written texts: An empirical study of the rhetorical structures of first-year college writers' essays produced by word-processing and by handwriting (Doctoral dissertation, Indiana University Of Pennsylvania, 1990). *Dissertation Abstracts International, 51*, 3401.

SELECTED TITLES ON STYLE AND GRAMMAR CHECKERS

Day, J. (1988). Writers's Workbench: A useful aid, but not a cure-all. *Computers and Composition, 6*(1), 63–78.

Dobrin, D. (1986). Style analyzers once more. *Computers and Composition 3*(3), 22–32.

Garvey, J., & Lindstrom, D. (1989). Pros' prose meets "Writer's Workbench": Analysis of typical models for first-year writing courses. *Computers and Composition, 6*(2), 81–109.

Gingrich, P.S. (1983). The UNIX Writer's Workbench software: Results of a field study. *The Bell System Technical Journal, 62*(6), 1909–1921.

Kiefer, K. (1992). Should basic writers use text analysis software? *Collegiate Microcomputer, 10*(4), 204–208.

Kiefer, K., & Smith, C. (1983). Textual analysis with computers: Tests of Bell Laboratories' computer software. *Research in the Teaching of English, 17*(3), 201–214.

Kiefer, K., Reid, S., & Smith, C. (1989). Style analysis programs: Teachers using the tools. In C. Selfe, D. Rodrigues, & W. Oates (Eds.), *Computers in English and the language arts: The challenge of teacher education* (pp.213–226). Urbana, IL: National Council of Teachers of English.

Kinkead, J. (1986). Matching software and curriculum: A description of four text-analysis programs. *Computers and Composition, 3*(3), 33–55.

Pennington, M. (1993). Computer-assisted writing on a principled basis: The case against computer-assisted text analysis for non-proficient writers. *Language-and-Education, 7*(1), 43–59.

Wresch, W. (1988). Six directions for computer analysis of student writing. *Computing Teacher, 15*(7), 13–16,42.

Wresch, W. (1993). The imminence of grading essays by computer—25 years later. *Computers and Composition, 10*(2), 45–58.

SELECTED TITLES ON NETWORK TOOLS AND PEDAGOGIES

Barclay, D. (1995). Ire, envy, irony, and ENFI: Electronic conferences as unreliable. *Computers and Composition, 12*(1), 23.

Barker, T.T., & Kemp, F.O. (1990). Network theory: A postmodern pedagogy for the writing classroom. In C. Handa (Ed.), *Computers and community: Teaching composition in the twenty-first century* (pp.1–27). Portsmouth, NH: Boynton-Cook.

Batson, T. (1988). The ENFI Project: A networked classroom approach to writing instruction. *Academic Computing, 2*(5), 55–56.

Batson, T. (1989). Teaching in networked classrooms. In C. Selfe, D. Rodrigues, & W. Oates, (Eds.), *Computers in English and the language arts: The challenge of teacher education.* Urbana, IL: NCTE.

Batson, T. (1993). ENFI research. *Computers and Composition, 10*(3), 93–101.

Beil, D. (1989). *Teacher's guide to using computer networks for written interaction,* (pp.157–164). Washington, D.C.: Realtime Learning Systems.

Bruce, B., Peyton, J.K, & Batson, T. (Eds). (1993). *Network-based classrooms: Promises and realities.* New York: Cambridge University Press.

Bump, J. (1990). Radical changes in class discussion using networked computers. *Computers and the Humanities, 49*, 49–65.

Coogan, D. (1995). E-Mail tutoring, a new way to do new work. *Computers and Composition, 12*(2), 171–181.

Daisley, M. (1994). The game of literacy: The meaning of play in computer-mediated communication. *Computers and Composition, 11*(2), 107.

Eldred, J. (1991). Pedagogy in the computer-networked classroom. *Computers and Composition, 8*(2), 47–61.

Hawisher, G.E., & Moran, C. (1993). Electronic mail and the writing instructor. *College English, 55*(6), 627–643.

Hawisher, G.E. (1992). Electronic meetings of the minds: Research, electronic conferences, and composition studies. In G. E. Hawisher & P. LeBlanc (Eds.), *Re-imagining computers and composition: Teaching and research in the virtual age,* (pp. 81–101). Portsmouth, NH: Boynton/Cook-Heinemann.

Holdstein, D.H. (1996). Power, genre, and technology. *College Composition and Communication, 47*(2), 279–284.

Mabrito, M. (1991). Electronic mail as a vehicle for peer response: Conversations of high- and low-apprehensive writers. *Written Communication, 8*(4), 509–532.

Mason, L.D., Duin, A.H., & Lammers, E. (1994). Linking learners: Structuring a mentoring via telecommunications course. *Computers and Composition, 11*(2), 123.

Miller, C. (1996). This is not an essay. *College Composition and Communication, 47*(2), 284–288.

Minock, M., & Shor, F. (1995). Crisscrossing *Grand Canyon*: Bridging the gaps with computer conferencing. *Computers and Composition, 12*(3), 355–365.

Moran, C. (1991). We write, but do we read? *Computers and Composition, 8*(3), 51–61.

Moran, C. (1995). Notes toward a rhetoric of e-mail. *Computers and Composition, 12*(1), 15–22.

Neuwirth, C.M., Palmquist, M., Cochran, C., Gillespie, T., Hartman, K., & Hajduk, T. (1993). Why write-together-concurrently on a computer network? In Bruce, B., Peyton, J., & Batson, T. (Eds.), *Network-based classrooms: Promises and realities* (pp.181–209). Cambridge, MA: Cambridge University Press.

Palmquist, M. (1993). Network-supported interaction in two writing classrooms. *Computer and Composition, 10*(4), 25–57.

Peyton, J.K. (1989). Computer networks for real-time written interaction in the writing classroom: An annotated bibliography. *Computers and Composition, 6*(3), 105–22.

Peyton, J.K. (1990). Technological innovation meets institution: Birth of creativity or murder of a great idea. *Computers and Composition, 7*(S.I.), 15–32.

Rodrigues, D., & Kiefer, K. (1993). Moving toward an Electronic Writing Center at Colorado State University. In J.A. Kinkead & J.G. Harris (Eds.), *Writing centers in context: Twelve case studies,* (pp.216–226). Urbana, IL: National Council of Teachers of English.

Selfe, C.L., & Eilola, J.D. (1988). The tie that binds: Building discourse communities and group cohesion through computer-based conferences. *Collegiate Microcomputer, 6*(4), 339–348.

Selfe, C.L. & Meyer, P. (1991). Testing claims for on-line conferences. *Written Communication, 8*(2), 163–192.

Sirc, G. (1995). The twin worlds of electronic conferencing. *Computers and Composition, 12*(3), 265–277.

Sirc, G. & Reynolds, T. (1990). The face of collaboration in the networked writing classroom. *Computers and Composition, 7*, 53–70.

Sosnoski, J.J. (1996). Notes on postmodern double agency and the arts of lurking. *College Composition and Communication, 47*(2), 288–292.

Spooner, M., & Yancey, K. (1996). Postings on a genre of Email. *College Composition and Communication, 47*(2), 252–278.

Sullivan, P. (1993). Research design issues for the study of electronic discussions. *Bulletin of the Association for Business Communication, 56*(2), 43–45.

Susser, B. (1993). Networks and project work: Alternative pedagogies for writing with computers. *Computers and Composition, 10*, 63–77.

Takoyoshi, P. (1994). Building new networks from the old: Women's experiences with electronic communications. *Computers and Composition, 11*(1), 21.

Tuman, M. (1993). Campus word processing: Seven design principles for a new academic writing environment. *Computers and Composition, 10*(3), 49–62.

Van der Geest, T., & Remmers, T. (1994). The computer as means of communication for peer-review groups. *Computers and Composition, 11*(3), 237–250.

SELECTED TITLES ON CONTROL OR AUTHORITY ISSUES IN THE CLASSROOM

Balester, V., Halasek, K., & Peterson, N. (1992). Sharing authority: Collaborative teaching in a computer-based writing course. *Computers and Composition, 9* (3), 25–40.

Cooper, M., & Selfe, C. (1990). Computer conferences and learning: Authority, resistance, and internally persuasive discourse. *College English, 52*, 847–869.

George, L. (1990). Taking women professors seriously: Female authority in the computerized classroom. *Computers and Composition, 7*(SI), 45–52.

Janangelo, J. (1991). Technopower and technoppression: Some abuses of power and control in computer-assisted writing environments. *Computers and Composition, 9*(1), 46–64.

Kremers, M. (1990). Sharing authority on a synchronous network: The case for riding the beast. *Computers and Composition, 7*(SI), 33–44.

Moran, C. (1990). The computer-writing room: Authority and control. *Computers and Composition, 7*(2), 61–69.

Ray, R., & Barton, E. (1990). Technology and authority. In G.E. Hawisher & C.L. Selfe, (Eds.), *Evolving perspectives on computers and composition studies: Questions for the 1990s.* Urbana, IL: NCTE and Computers and Composition.

Selfe, C.L. (1988). Technology in the English classroom: Computers through the lens of feminist theory. *ADE Bulletin, 90*, 63–67.

Selfe, C.L., & Selfe, R. (1994). The politics of the interface: Power and its exercise in electronic contact zones. *College Composition and Communication, 45*(4), 480–504.

Sudol, R. (1985). Applied word processing: Notes on authority, responsibility, and revision in a workshop model. *College Composition and Communication, 36*(3), 331–335.

SELECTED TITLES ON COMPUTERS AND COMPOSING PROCESSES

Bean, J. (1983). Computerized word-processing as an aid to revision. *College Composition and Communication, 34*, 146–48.

Bridwell Bowles, L. (1988). A computer tool for analyzing the composing process. *Collegiate Microcomputer, 6*(2), 155–160.

Bridwell-Bowles, L. (1989). Designing research on computer-assisted writing. *Computers and Composition, 7*(1), 79–91.

Esperet, E. (1991). Improving writing skills: Which approaches and what target skills? *European Journal of Psychology of Education, 6*(2), 215–224.

Haas, C. (1990). Composing in technological contexts: A study of note-making. *Written Communication, 7*(4), 512–547.

Harris, E. (1992). The relationship of attitudes and writing abilities to computer writing and peer critique of writing (Doctoral dissertation, Memphis State University, 1992). *Dissertation Abstracts International, 53*, 1828.

Hartley, J. (1991). Psychology, writing and computers: A review of research. *Visible Language, 25*(4), 339–375.

Hartley, J. (1993). Writing, Thinking and computers. *British Journal of Educational Technology, 24*(1), 22–31.

Hawisher, G.E. (1987). The effects of word processing on the revision strategies of college freshmen. *Research in the Teaching of English, 21*(2), 145–159.

Hawisher, G.E. (1989). Computers and writing: Where's the research? *English Journal, 78*(1), 89–91.

Iklundh, K.S. (1994). Linear and nonlinear strategies in computer-based writing. *Computers and Composition, 11*(3), 203.

Kozma, R. (1991). Computer-based writing tools and the cognitive needs of novice writers. *Computers and Composition, 8*(2), 31–45.

Kozma, R.B. (1991). The impact of computer-based tools and embedded prompts on writing processes and products of novice and advanced college writers. *Cognition and Instruction, 8*(1), 1–27.

Montague, M. (1990). *Computers, cognition, and writing instruction.* Albany, NY: State University of New York Press.

Pearce, R. (1990). The effect of word-processing experience on editing while composing (Masters thesis, The University of British Columbia, 1992). *Masters Abstracts International, 30*, 1016.

Pennington, M. (1993). Modeling the student writer's acquisition of word processing skills: the interaction of computer, writing, and language media. *Computers and Composition, 10*(4), 59–79.

Zellermayer, M., Salomon, G., Globerson, G., & Givon, H. (1991). Enhancing writing-related metacognitions through a computerized writing partner. *American Educational Research Journal, 28*(2), 373–391.

SELECTED TITLES ON COMPUTERS AND COLLABORATION

Forman, J. (1990). Leadership dynamics of computer-supported writing groups. *Computers and Composition, 7*(2), 35–46.

Jorn, L., & Duin, A. (1992). Information technology and the collaborative writing process in the classroom. *Bulletin of the Association for Business Communication, 55*(4), 13–20.

Kumpulainen, K. (1994). Collaborative writing with computers and children's talk: Cross-cultural study. *Computers and Composition, 11*(3), 263.

Sharples, M. (1993). *Computer supported collaborative writing.* New York: Springer-Verlag.

SELECTED TITLES ON HUMAN FACTORS ISSUES

Haas, C. (1989). "Seeing it on the screen isn't really seeing it": Computer writers' reading problems. In G. Hawisher & C. Selfe (Eds.), *Critical perspectives on computers and composition instruction* (pp.16–29). New York: Teachers College Press.

Haas, C., & Hayes, J.R. (1986). What did i just say? Reading problems in writing with the machine. *Research in the Teaching of English, 20*(1), 22–35.

Muter, P. & Muarutto, P. (1991). Reading and skimming from computer screens and books: The paperless office revisited?. *Behaviour and Information Technology, 10*(4), 257–266.

Sullivan, P. (1989). Human-computer interaction perspectives on word-processing issues. *Computers and Composition, 6*(3), 11–33.

SELECTED TITLES ON COMPUTER CLASSROOM DESIGN

Anonymous (1989). *Computers and college writing. Selected college profiles.* City University of New York: National Project on Computers and College Writing.

Boiarsky, C. (1990). Computers in the classroom: The instruction, the mess, the noise, the writing. In C. Handa (Ed.), *Computers and community: Teaching composition in the twenty-first century* (pp.47–67). Portsmouth, NH: Boynton-Cook.

Harralson, D. (1992). We've barely started—and we've already done it wrong: How not to start a computer-assisted writing classroom. *Computers and Composition, 9*(3), 71–77.

Moran, C. (1992). Computers and the writing classroom: A look to the future. In G. E. Hawisher & P. LeBlanc (Eds.), *Re-imagining computers and composition: teaching and research in the virtual age* (pp.7–23). Portsmouth, NH: Boynton-Cook.

Rodrigues, D., & Kiefer, K. (1993). Moving toward an electronic writing center at Colorado State University. In *Writing centers in context: Twelve case studies.* Urbana, IL: National Council of Teachers of English.

Schwartz, H. (1987). Planning and running a computer lab for writing: A survival manual. *ADE Bulletin, 86*, 43–47.

Selfe, C.L. (1987). Creating a computer lab that composition teachers can live with. *Collegiate-Microcomputer, 5*(2), 149–158.

Selfe, C.L. (1987). Creating a computer-supported writing lab: Sharing stories and creating vision. *Computers and Composition, 4*(2), 44–65.

Selfe, C.L. (1989). *Creating a computer-supported writing facility: A blueprint for action.* Houghton, MI: Computers and Composition.

SELECTED TITLES ON SOFTWARE SELECTION, EVALUATION, AND DEVELOPMENT

Condon, W. (1992). Selecting computer software for writing instruction: Some considerations. *Computers and Composition, 10*(1), 53–56.

Kemp, F. (1987). The user-friendly fallacy. *College Composition and Communication, 38*(1), 32–39.

Kemp, F. (1992). Who programmed this? Examining the instructional attitudes of writing-support software. *Computers and Composition, 10*(1), 9–24.

LeBlanc, P. (1992). Ringing in the virtual age: Hypermedia authoring software and the revival of faculty-based software development in composition. In G.E. Hawisher & P. LeBlanc (Eds.), *Reimagining computers and composition: Teaching and research in the virtual age* (pp.191–206). Portsmouth, NH: Boynton-Cook.

LeBlanc, P. (1993). *Writing teachers writing software: Creating our place in the electronic age. (Advances in Computers and Composition Studies Series).* Urbana, IL: National Council of Teachers of English.

Selfe, C.L. (1986). *Computer-assisted instruction in composition: Create your own.* Urbana, IL: National Council of Teachers of English.

OTHER CITATIONS

Braddock, R., Lloyd-Jones, R., & Schoer, L. (1963). *Research in Written Composition.* Urbana, IL: National Council of Teachers of English.

Charney, D., Newman, J.H., & Palmquist, M. (1995). "I'm just no good at writing:" Epistemological style and attitudes toward writing. *Written Communication, 12*(3), 298–329.

Hairston, M. (1982). The winds of change: Thomas Kuhn and the revolution in the teaching of writing. *College Composition and Communication, 33*(1), 76–88.

Hillocks, G., Jr. (1986). *Research on written composition: New directions for teaching.* Urbana, IL: ERIC Clearinghouse on Reading and Communication Skills and National Council of Teachers of English.

Murray, D. (1979, September). The listening eye: Reflections on the writing conference. *College English.* Also reprinted in D. Murray (1982). *Learning by teaching: Selected articles on writing and teaching* (pp. 157–63). Montclair, NJ: Boynton/Cook. See also "Conference Guidelines" in the same collection.

Ong, W.J., S.J. (1977). *Interfaces of the word: Studies in the evolution of consciousness and culture.* Ithaca, NY: Cornell University Press.

Palmquist, M., & Young, R.E. (1992). The notion of giftedness and student expectations about writing. *Written Communication, 9*(1), 137–168.

Zoellner, R. (1969). Talk-write: A behavioral pedagogy for composition. *College English, 30*(40), 267–320.

ONLINE INFORMATION SOURCES

Note: Online resources so often change addresses and new sites appear with such frequency that we hesitate to provide a comprehensive list here. Instead, we ask you to consult a listing of online information sources for teachers at the Colorado State University Online Writing Center: http://www.colostate.edu/Depts/WritingCenter. Select "Other Online Resources" for an up-to-date list of online resources.

Author Index

Subject Index

www.ingramcontent.com/pod-product-compliance
Ingram Content Group UK Ltd.
Pitfield, Milton Keynes, MK11 3LW, UK
UKHW041639031026
15587UKWH00001B/392

9 781567 503524